The CRACK Book

D0596682

RONNIE
SELLERS
PRODUCTIONS
PORTLAND, MAINE

The CRACK Book

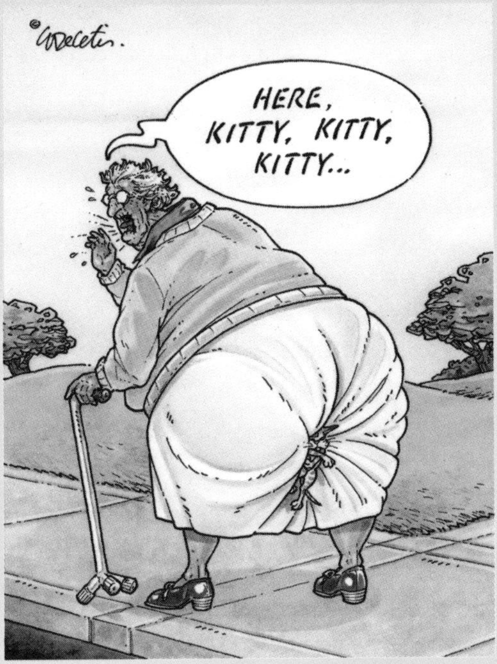

©Decetis.
HERE,
KITTY, KITTY,
KITTY...

by

Eric Decetis

DEDICATION

*Dedicated in loving memory to the last real
American hero, my father, Julius "Jay" Decetis.*
~Eric Decetis

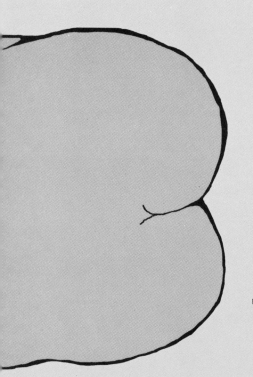

Published by Ronnie Sellers Productions, Inc.
Copyright © 2007 Eric Decetis
All rights reserved.

Edited by: Ari Meil and Robin Haywood
Managing Editor: Mary Baldwin
Assistant Production Editor: Charlotte Smith
Book Editorial Assistant: Nicole Cyr
Designer: George Corsillo, Design Monsters

81 West Commercial Street, Portland, Maine 04101
For ordering information:
(800) 625-3386 Toll Free
(207) 772-6814 Fax
Visit our Web site: www.makefun.com • E-mail: rsp@rsvp.com

ISBN: 13: 978-1-56906-975-2
ISBN 10: 1-56906-975-1

10 9 8 7 6 5 4 3 2 1

Printed and bound in India.

INTRODUCTION

Over the past three decades, Eric Decetis's fellow cartoonists have watched in awe as he grabbed the single panel cartoon by the scruff of its neck, hauled it into his studio, and showed us just how ingeniously the human body could be corrupted for a laugh. I know of no other cartoonist who possesses Eric's command of anatomy combined with a sense of humor that should probably be registered as a lethal weapon. I've yet to see a Decetis cartoon that didn't leave me laughing out loud, and if he doesn't already hold the patent on how to draw the human buttocks then the U.S. Congress should award it to him unconditionally.

A cartoonist is required to wear many hats, among them: artist, humorist, writer, philosopher, and journalist. Here is a collection of Eric's work which represents a unique and potent blend of these skills. After viewing them, I can promise that you'll never again walk through a crowd without seeing one of his characters in the flesh (fully clothed I hope.) You will never look at yourself in the mirror in quite the same way. You will never again be able to look at a fat lady with a Chihuahua without imagining the catastrophic possibilities. Mr. Decetis has brought us a powerful message . . . that even during our prettiest, coolest, and noblest moments we are, each and every one of us, just another ass in the crowd.

-Tom Cheney

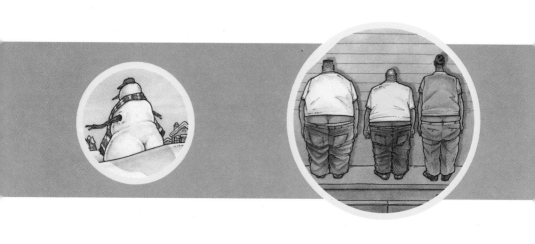

Chapter One:
Just Say No To Crack!

Crack [krâk]:
a slit or fissure where things may be hidden.

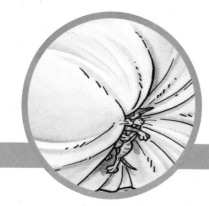

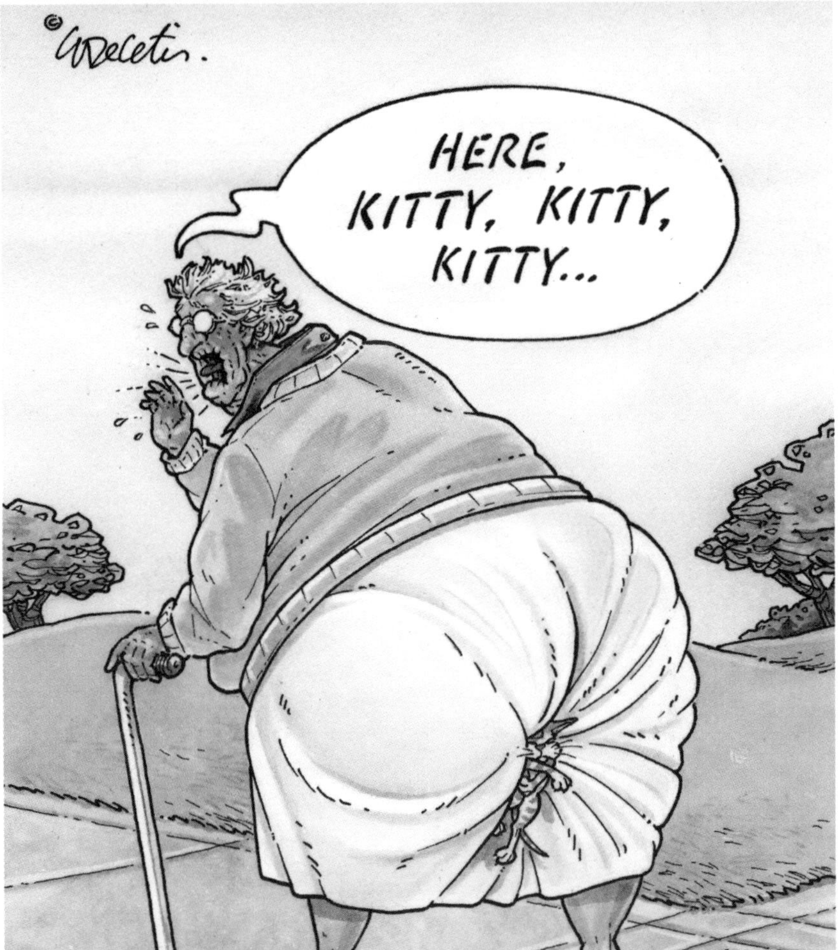
HERE, KITTY, KITTY, KITTY...

Crack [krâk]:
to break without complete separation of parts;
to split into fissures.

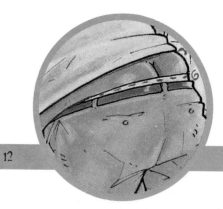

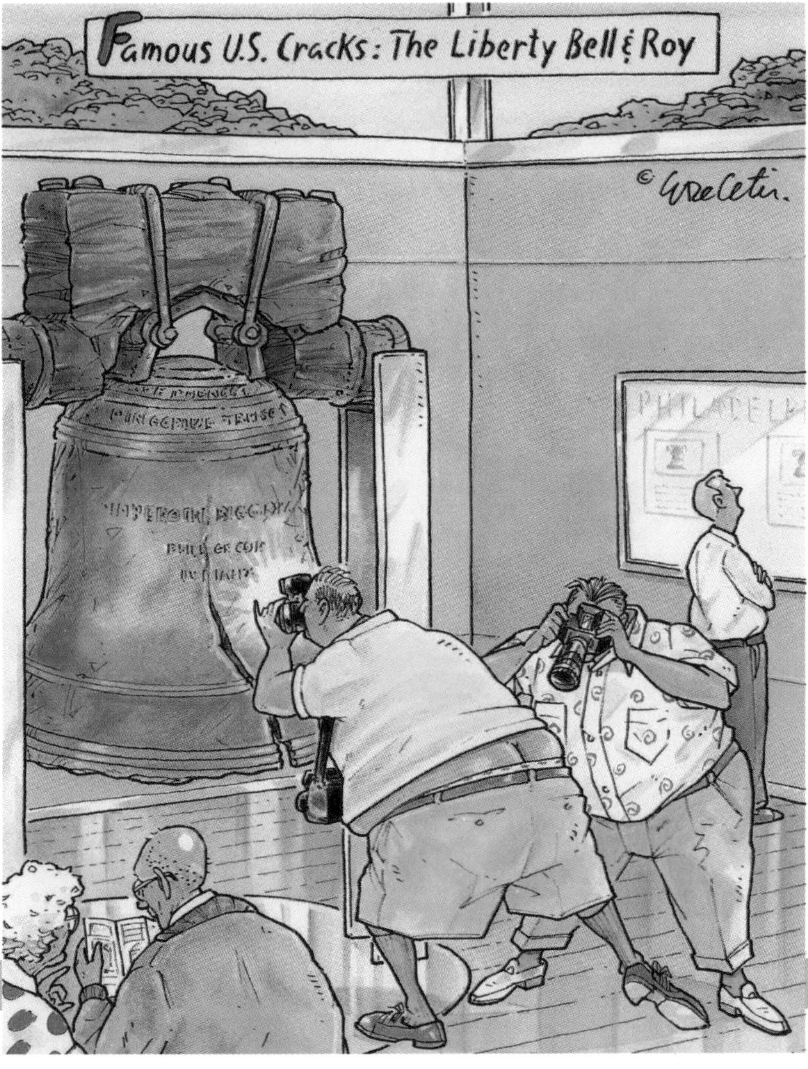
Famous U.S. Cracks: The Liberty Bell & Roy
© Gorrell

À rebours (attaquer l'ennemi) [Fr]:
from the rear; often where sound originates.

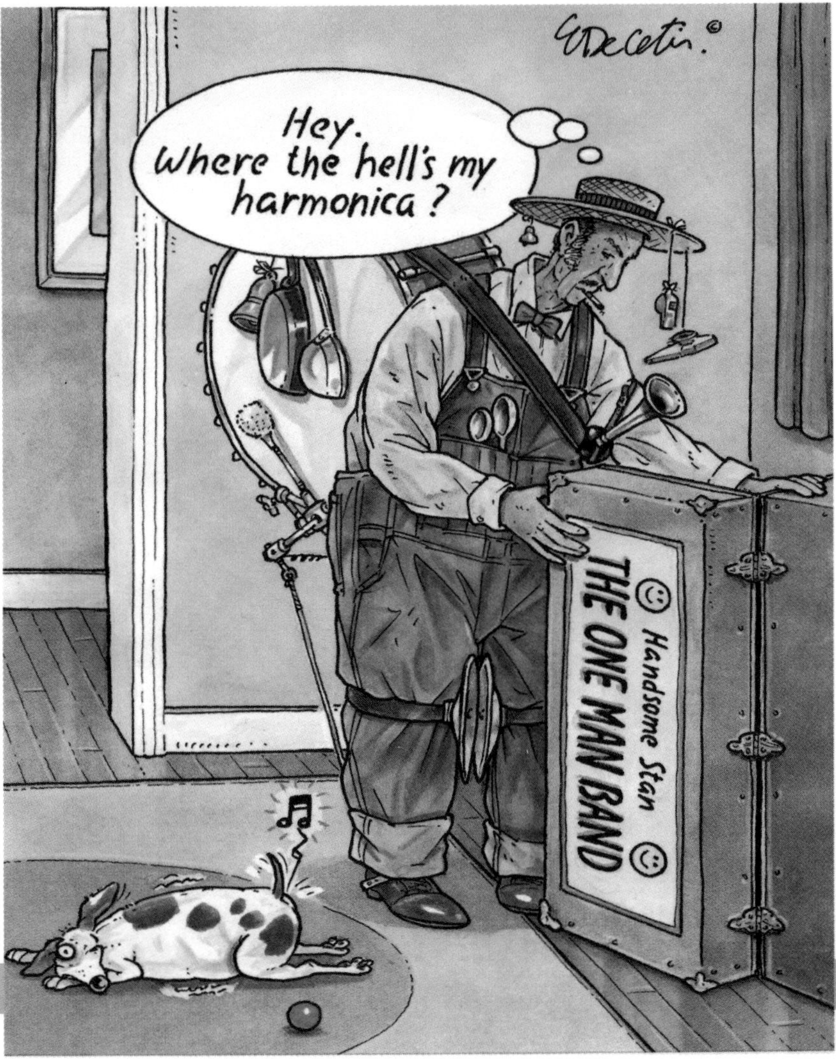
Hey.
Where the hell's my harmonica?
Handsome Stan
THE ONE MAN BAND

La fissure de fesses [Fr]:
butt crack, the split between two fleshy objects;
the buttocks.

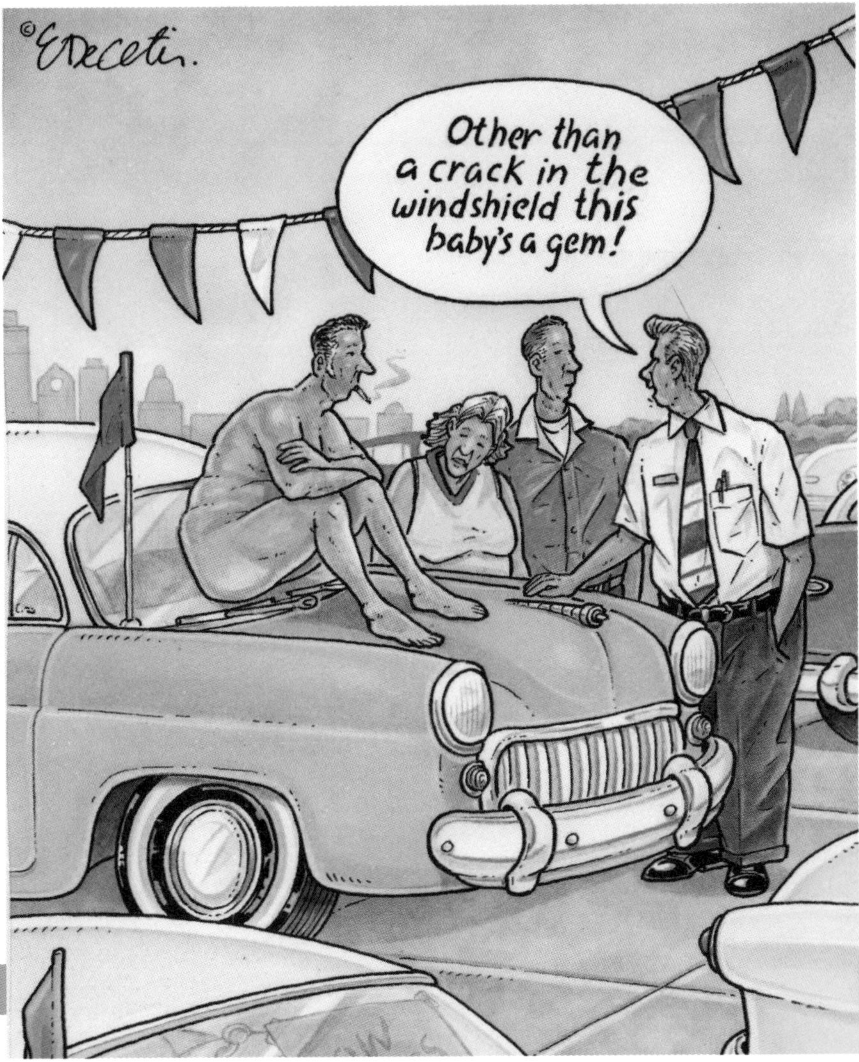
Other than a crack in the windshield this baby's a gem!

Rear end [reer-end]:
the back part of anything, even Santa.

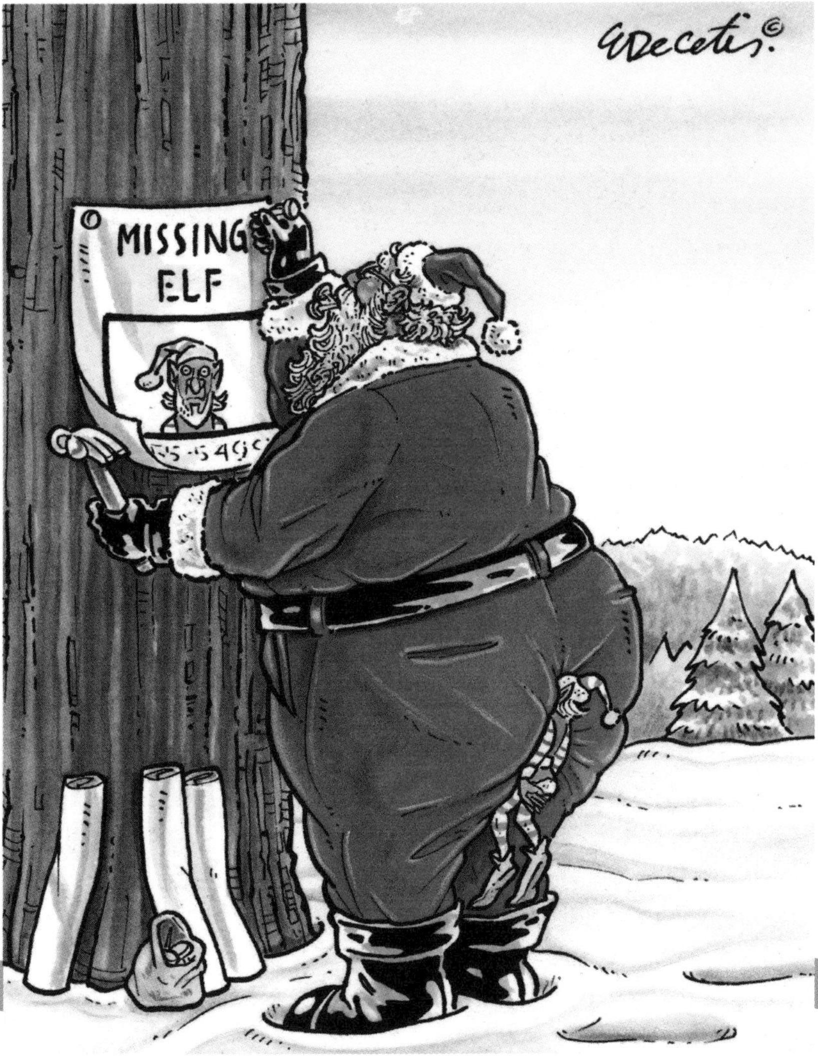
MISSING
ELF

Crack [krâk]:
opening between two large objects; the sight of which
can cause mental instability.

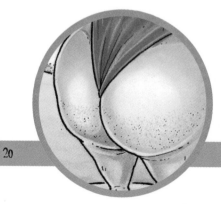

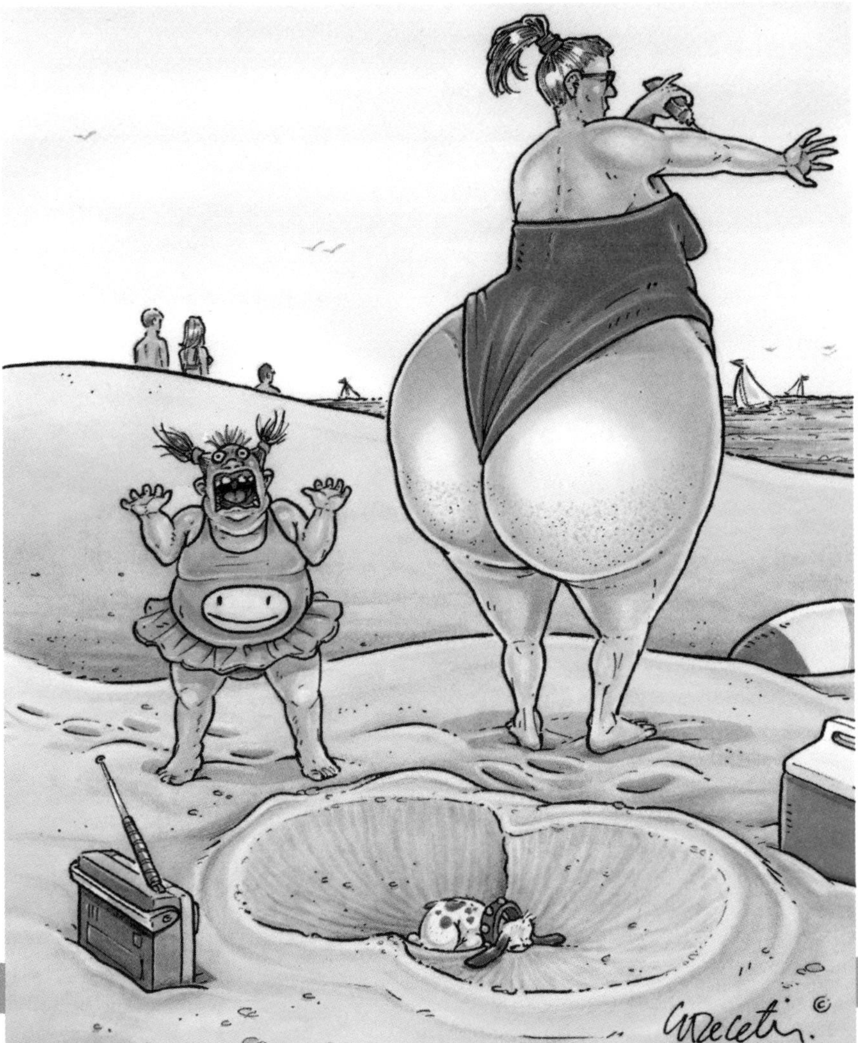

Gesäß [G]:
the behind; the showing of which often makes
a hell of a greeting at a party.

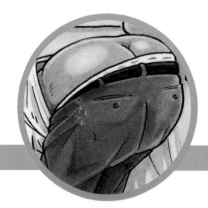

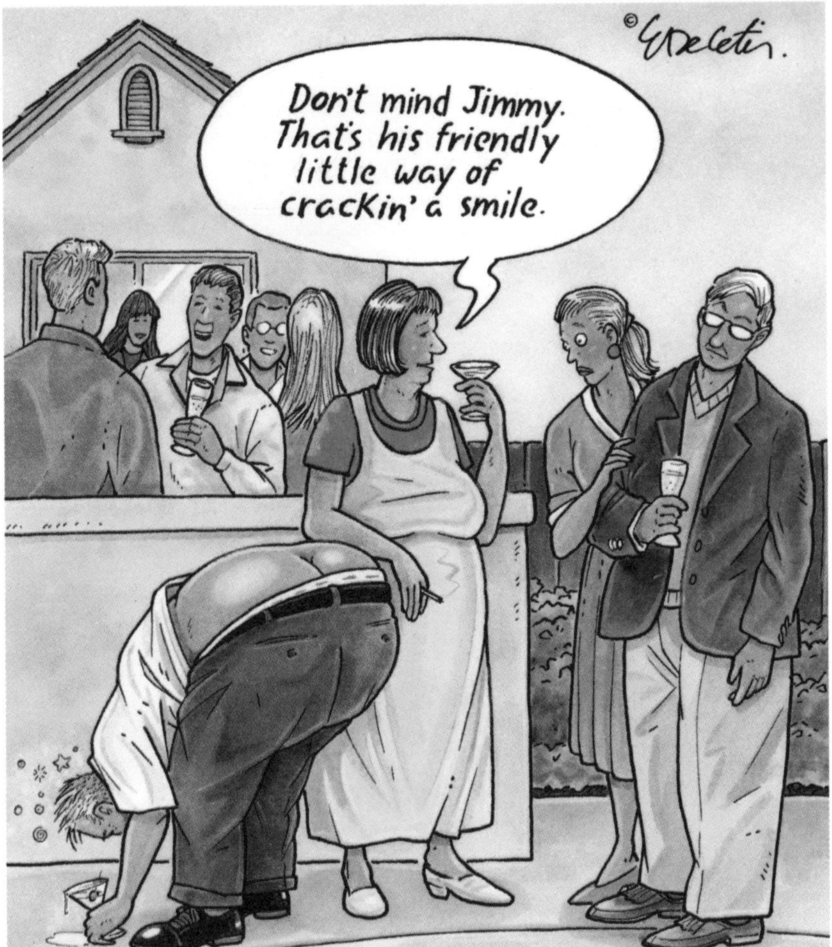
©Ed Seleter.
Don't mind Jimmy. That's his friendly little way of crackin' a smile.

keister [kees-ter]:
the buttocks; place where things are often misplaced.

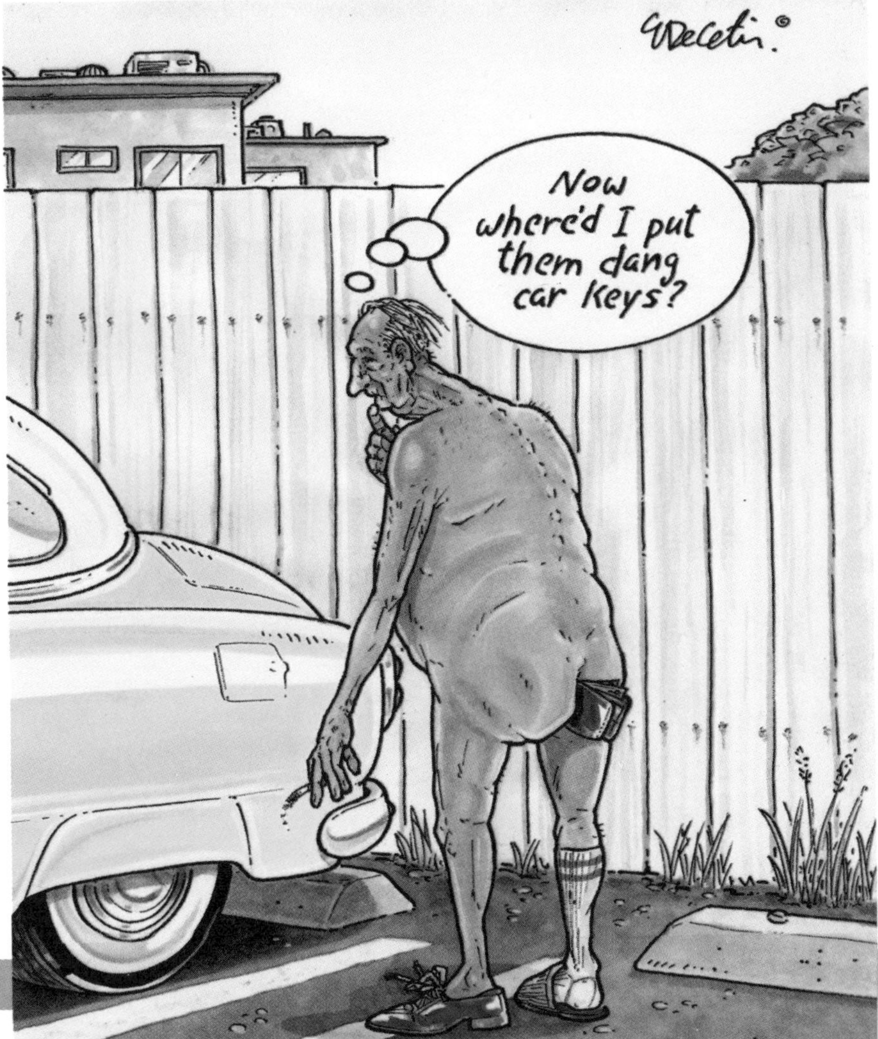
Now where'd I put them dang car keys?

Atrás [Sp]:
in the rear or where things become stuck.

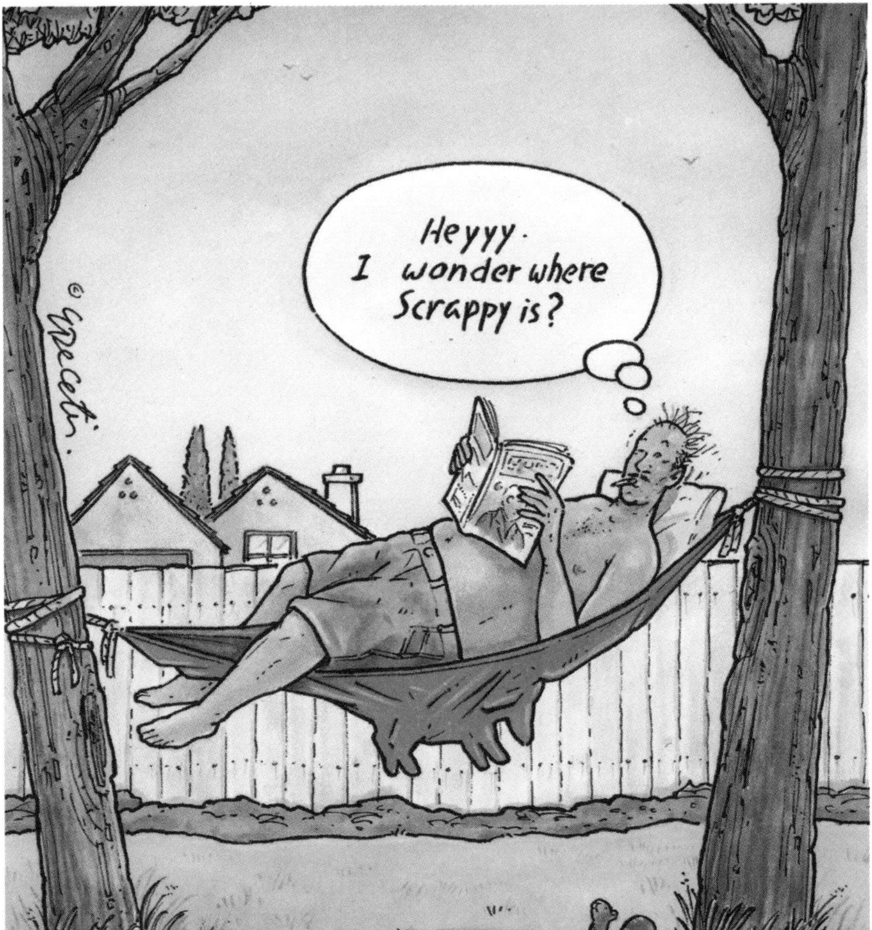
Heyyy.
I wonder where
Scrappy is?
© Speceti.

Crack [krâk]:
a slight opening, as between two large objects.

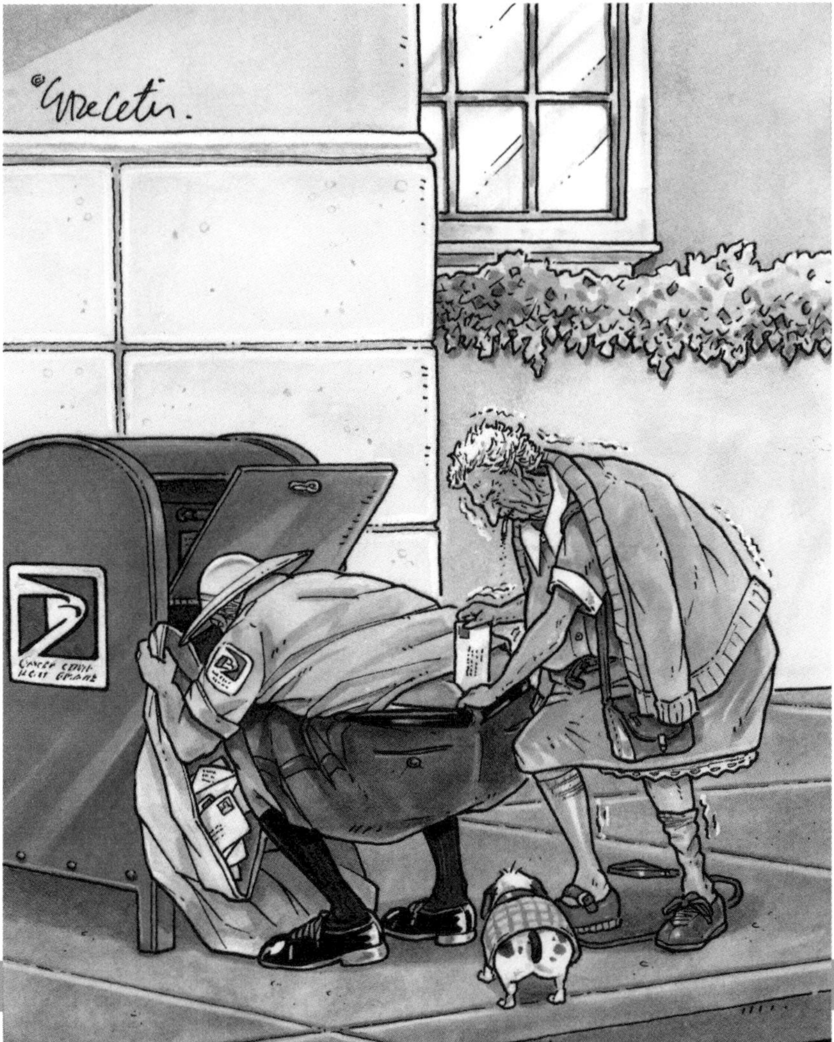

Crack [krâk]:
a great place to hide things.

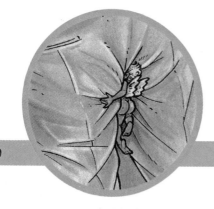

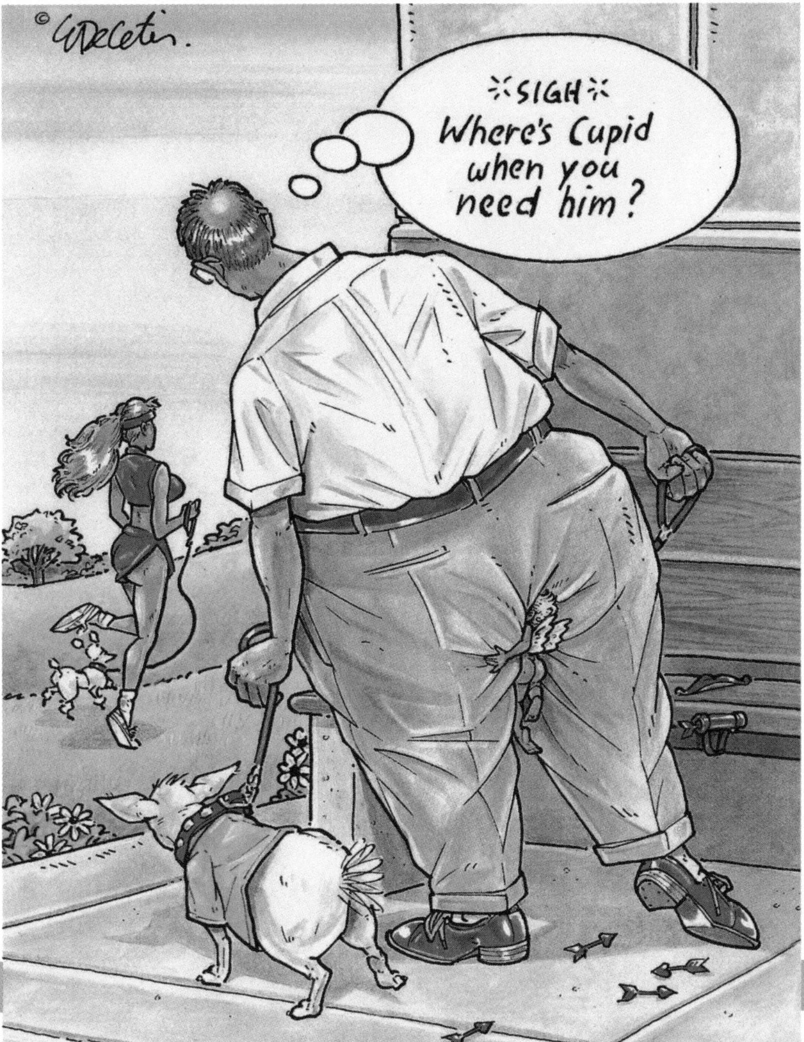
© GDeCeter.
SIGH Where's Cupid when you need him?

Crack [krâk]:
to utter or spill under pressure;
to crack jokes even if they're not funny.

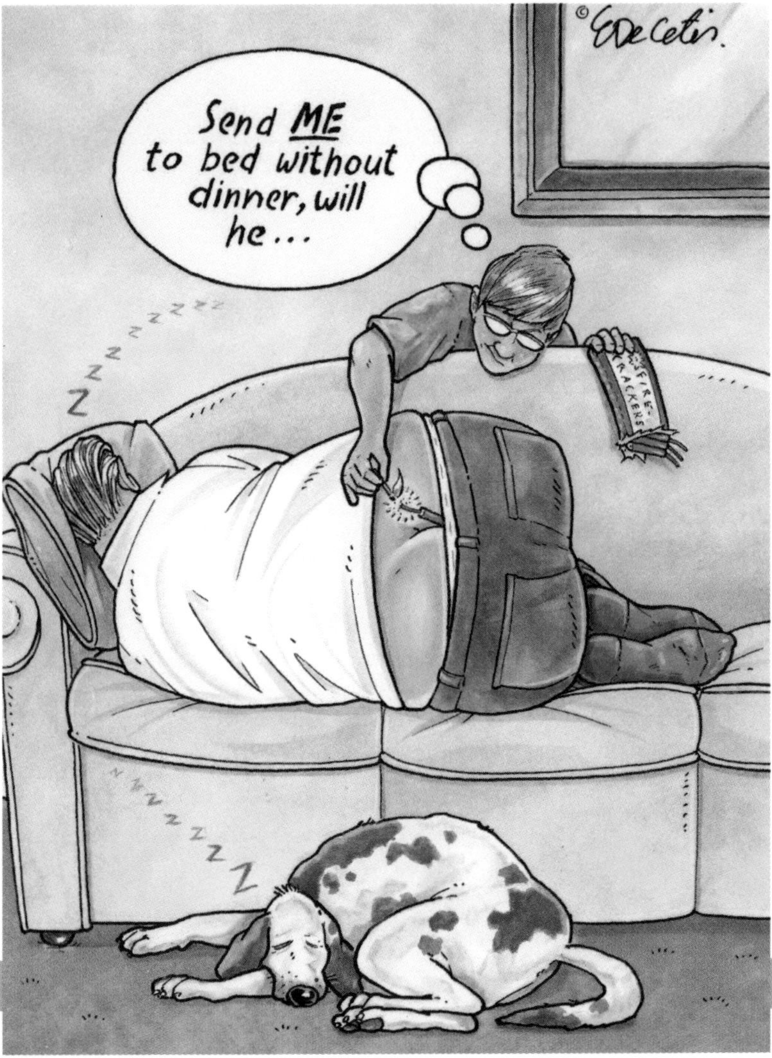

©EDeCetis.
Send ME to bed without dinner, will he...
Z Z Z Z Z Z Z Z Z
FIRE-CRACKERS
Z Z Z Z Z Z Z Z

Tuchis [tookh-uhs]:
the buttocks; often a place things are stuck.

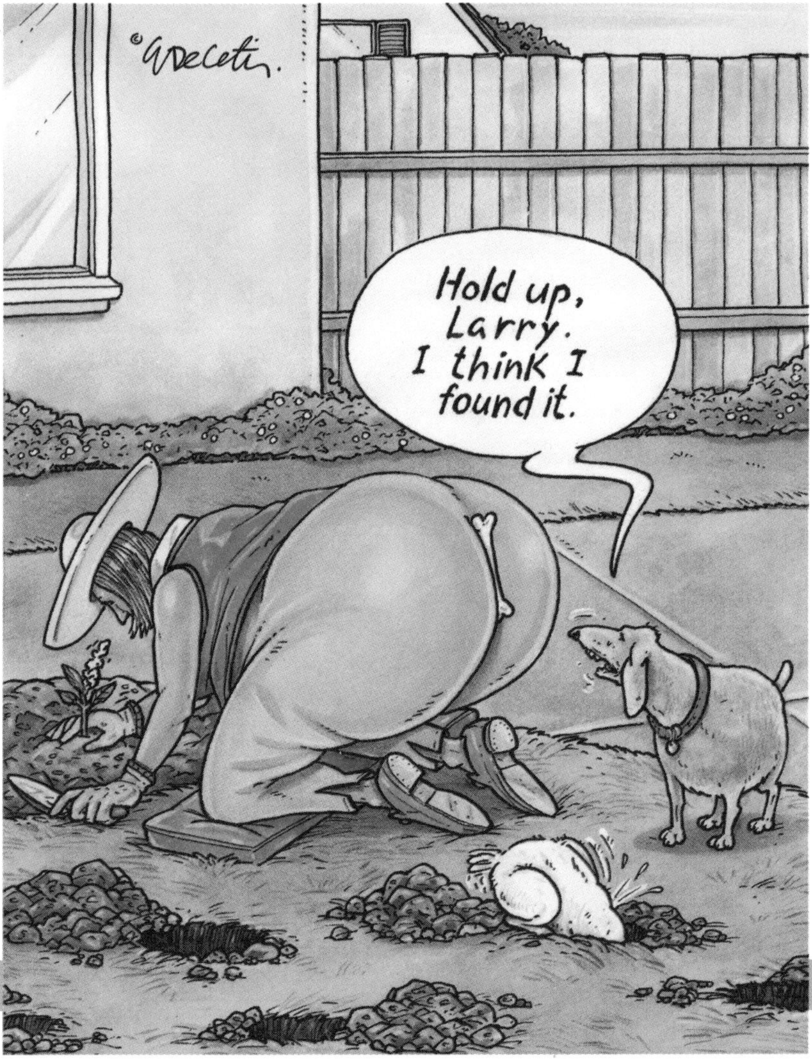
Hold up, Larry. I think I found it.

Derrière (dans le fonds)[Fr]:
at the rear; where lost puppies may turn up.

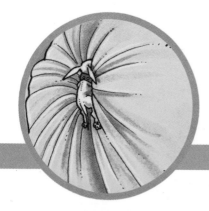

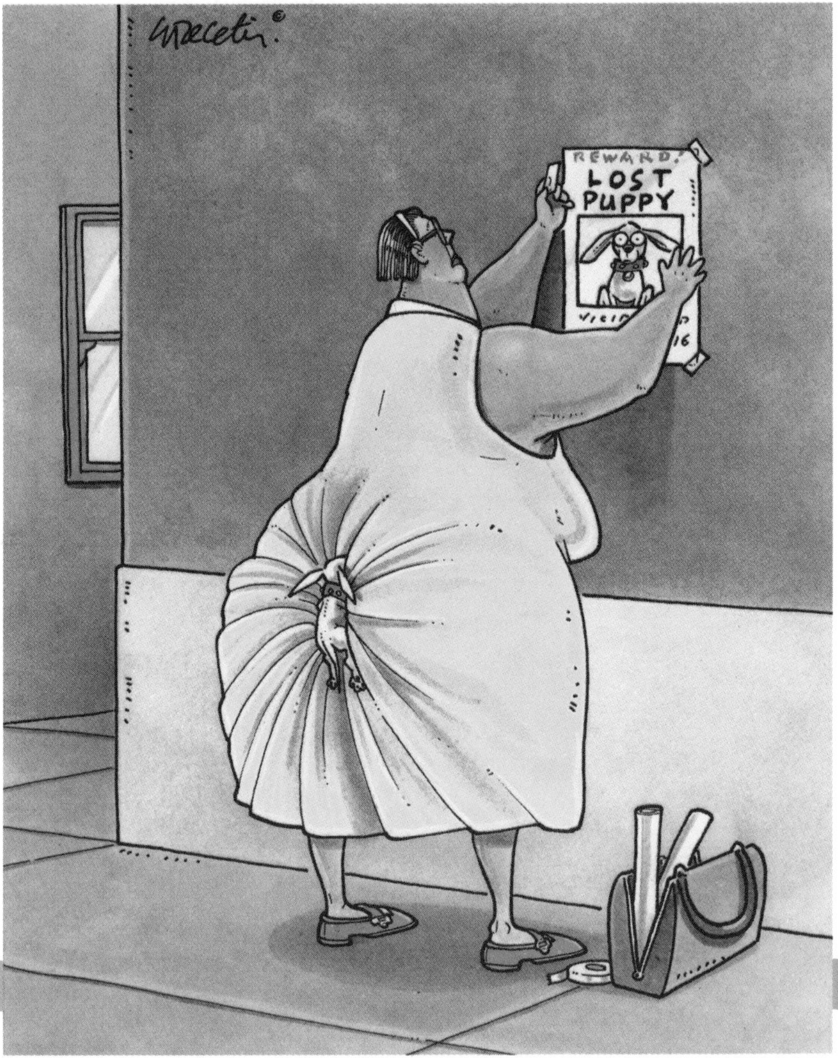
REWARD!
LOST
PUPPY

Crack [krâk]:
to fail; to give way when you have nothing else to give.

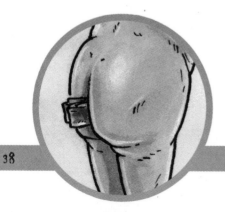

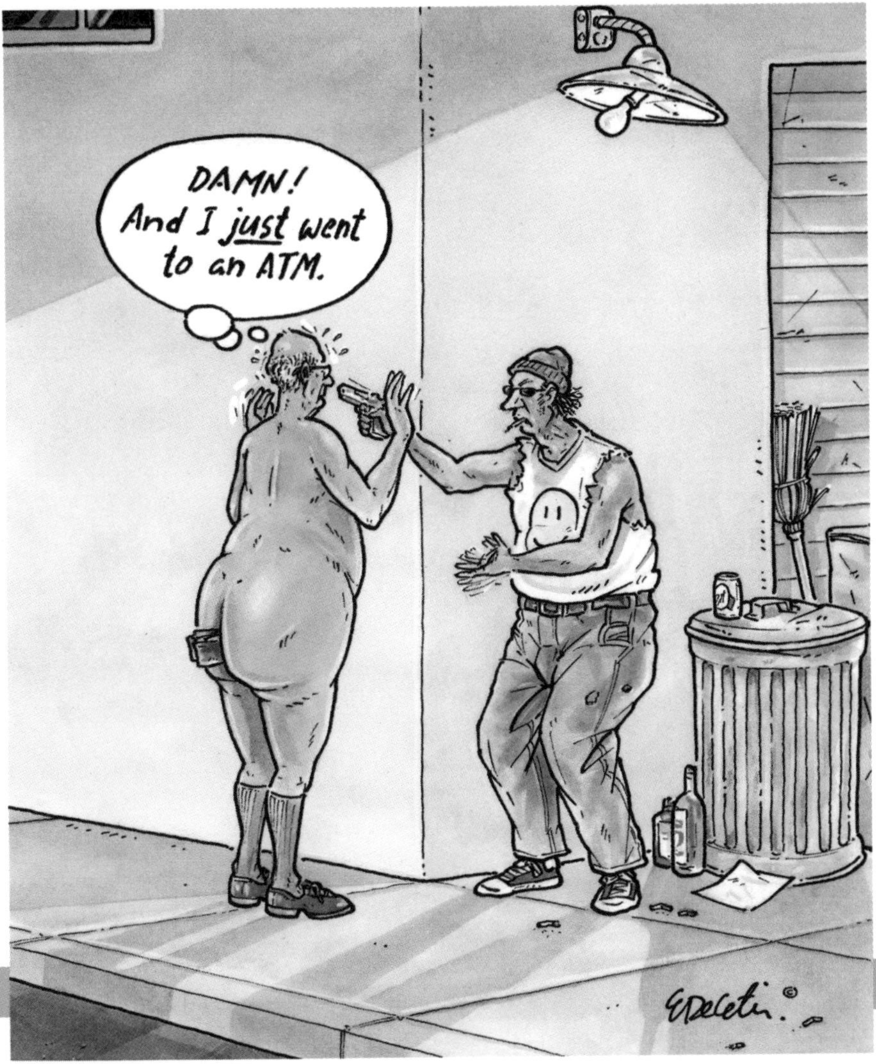
DAMN! And I just went to an ATM.
Edelstein©

Zadek [Cs]:
the backside; a place where certain things shouldn't be.

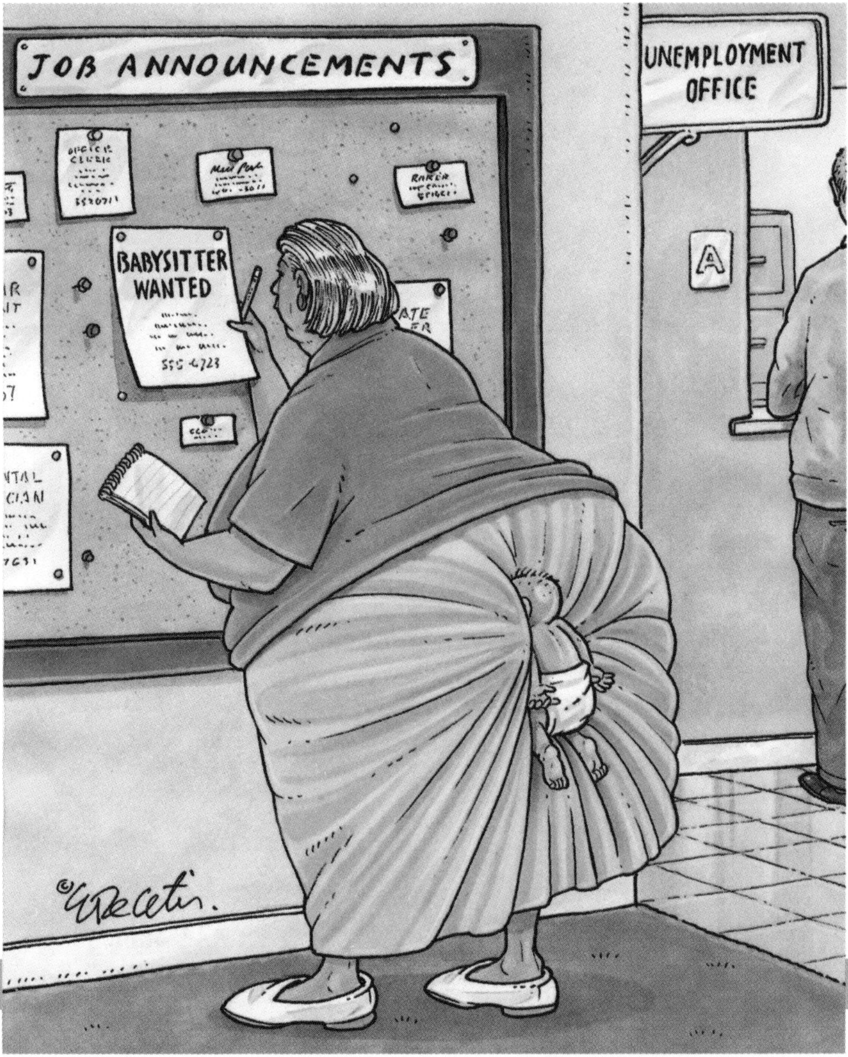
JOB ANNOUNCEMENTS
UNEMPLOYMENT OFFICE
BABYSITTER WANTED
555-4723
A

Crack up [krâk əp]:
break apart (literally).

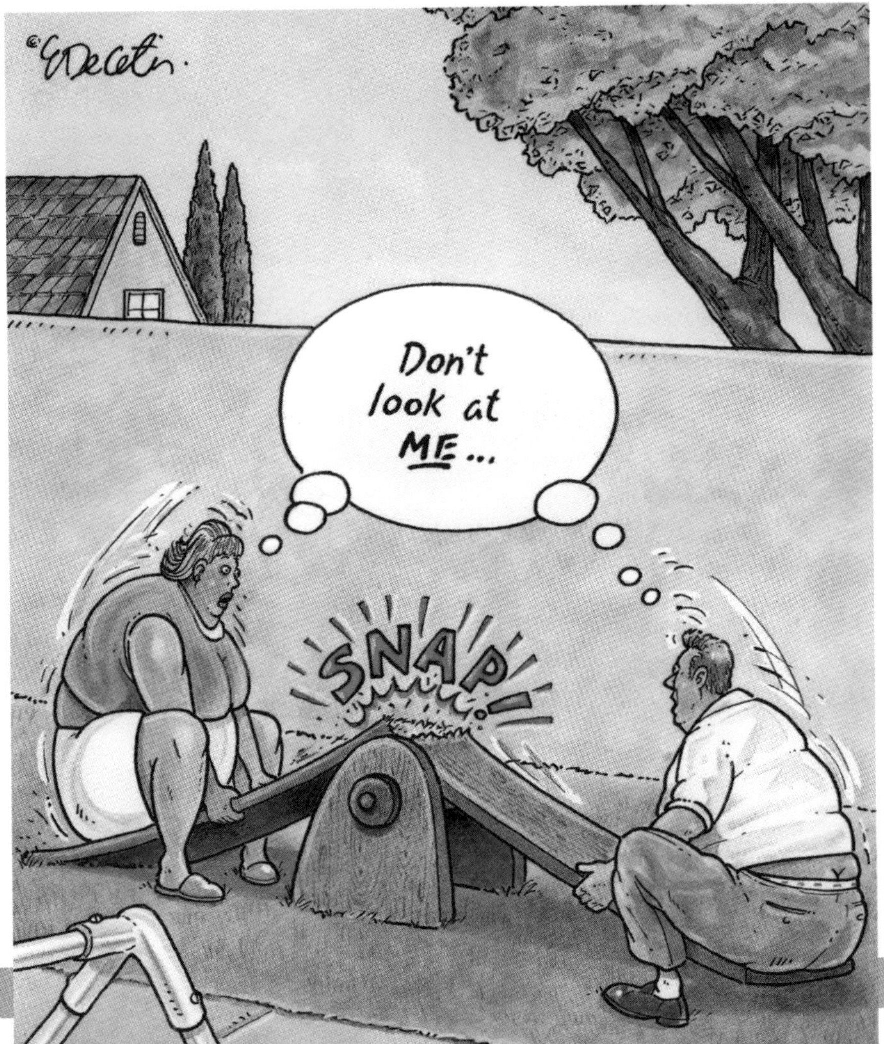
©EDeCeti.
Don't look at ME...
SNAP!

Achterste [Du]:
hindmost area that one is unable to see;
part that follows one everywhere.

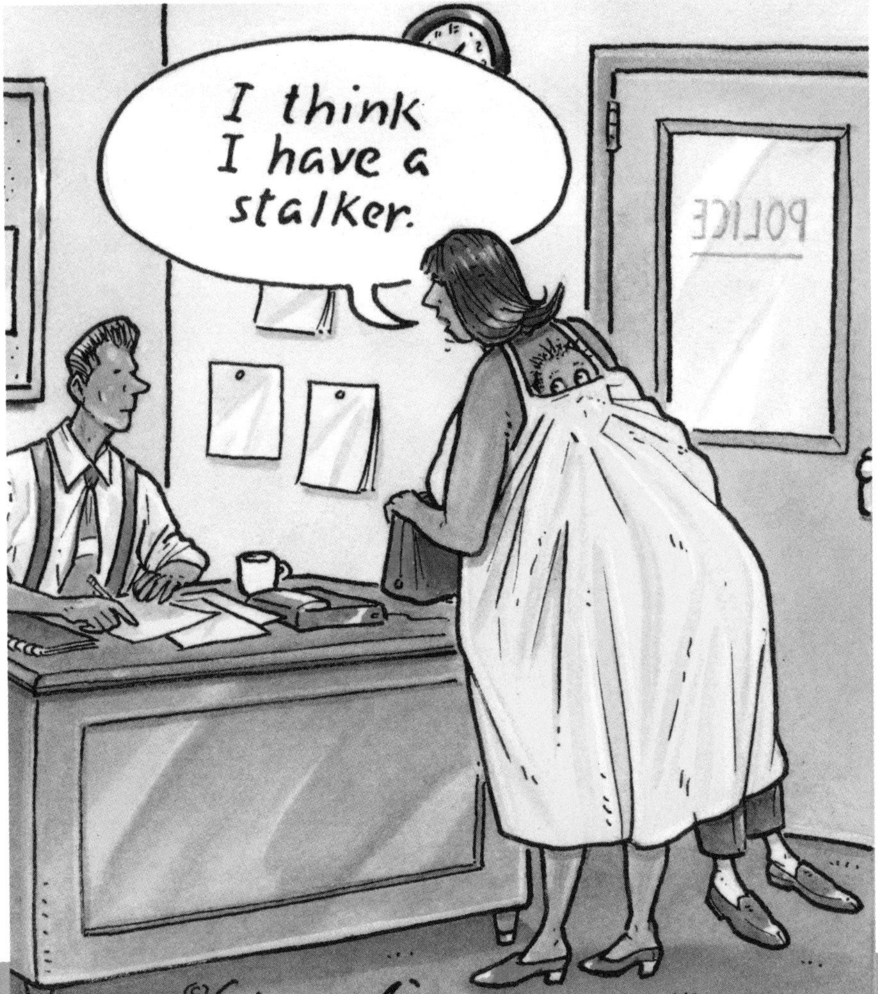
I think I have a stalker.
POLICE
©EDeCeti.

Crack [krâk]:
an opening or gateway from which liquids often flow.

A drunken night and a bad decision drastically alters the course of Mike's life.

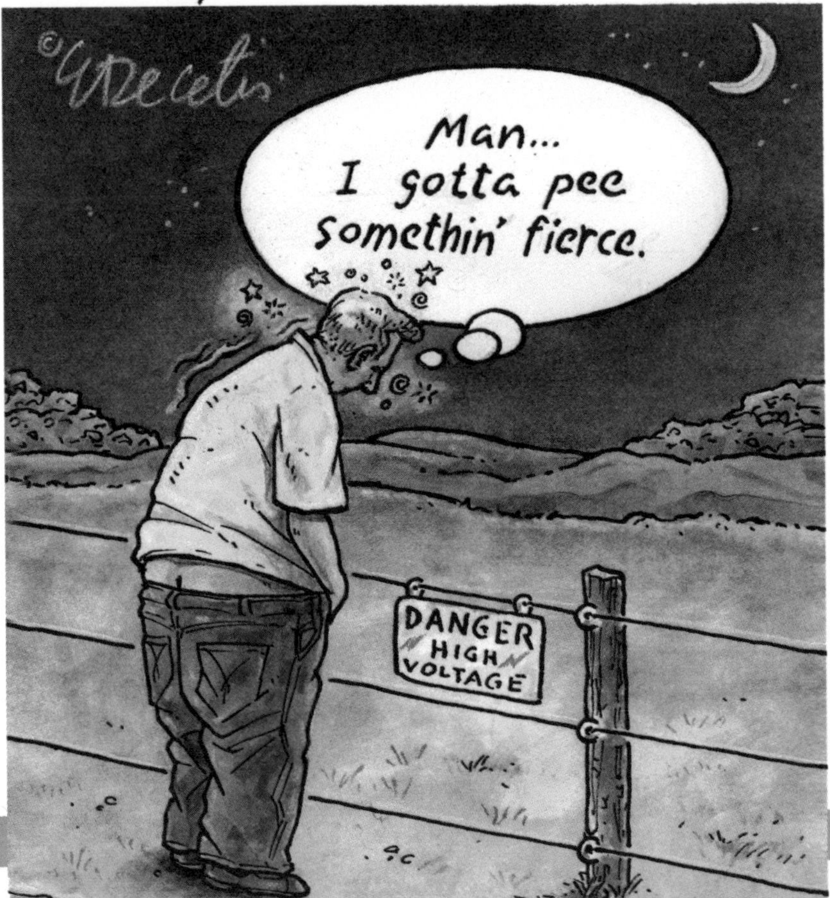
Man...
I gotta pee
somethin' fierce.
DANGER
HIGH
VOLTAGE

Grupa [Sp]:
hindquarters; spot where items often disappear.

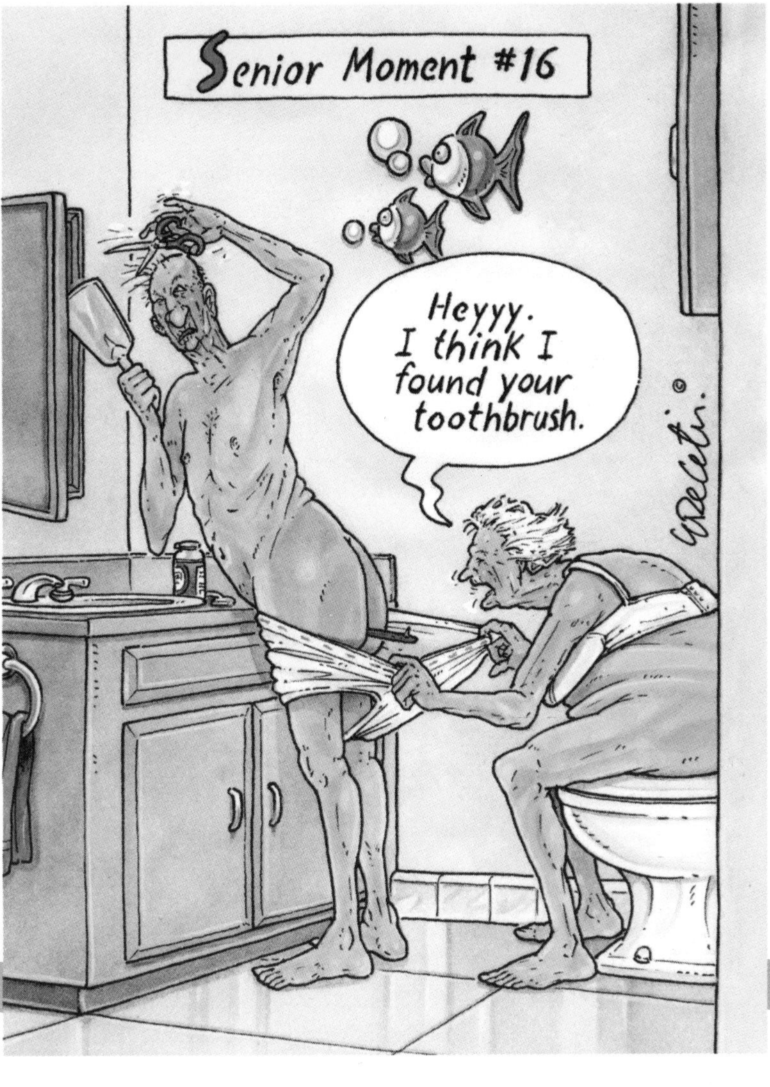
Senior Moment #16
Heyyy. I think I found your toothbrush.

Gat [Du]:
an aperture in which to put things; the spot.

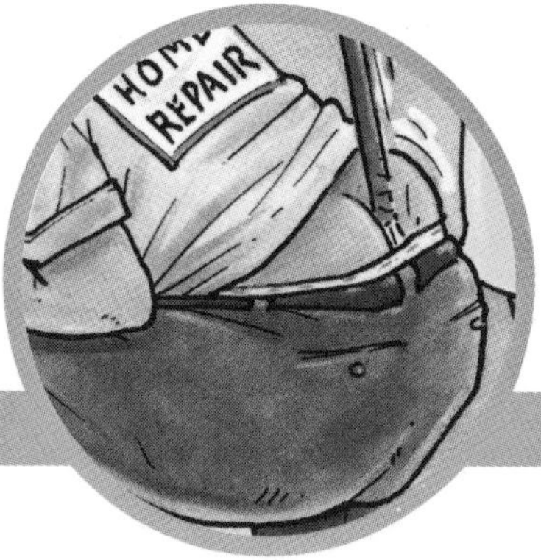
HOME
REPAIR

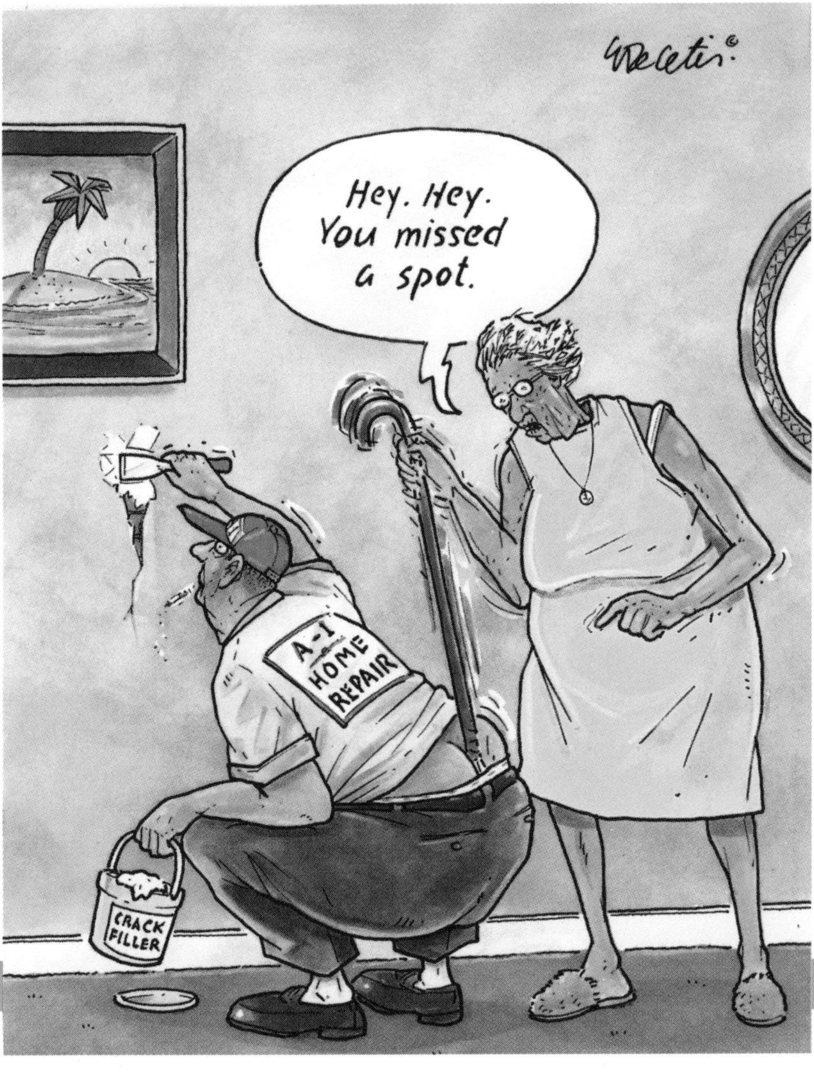
Hey. Hey.
You missed
a spot.
A-1
HOME
REPAIR
CRACK
FILLER

La craque de fesse [Fr]:
the separation between two large fleshy objects.

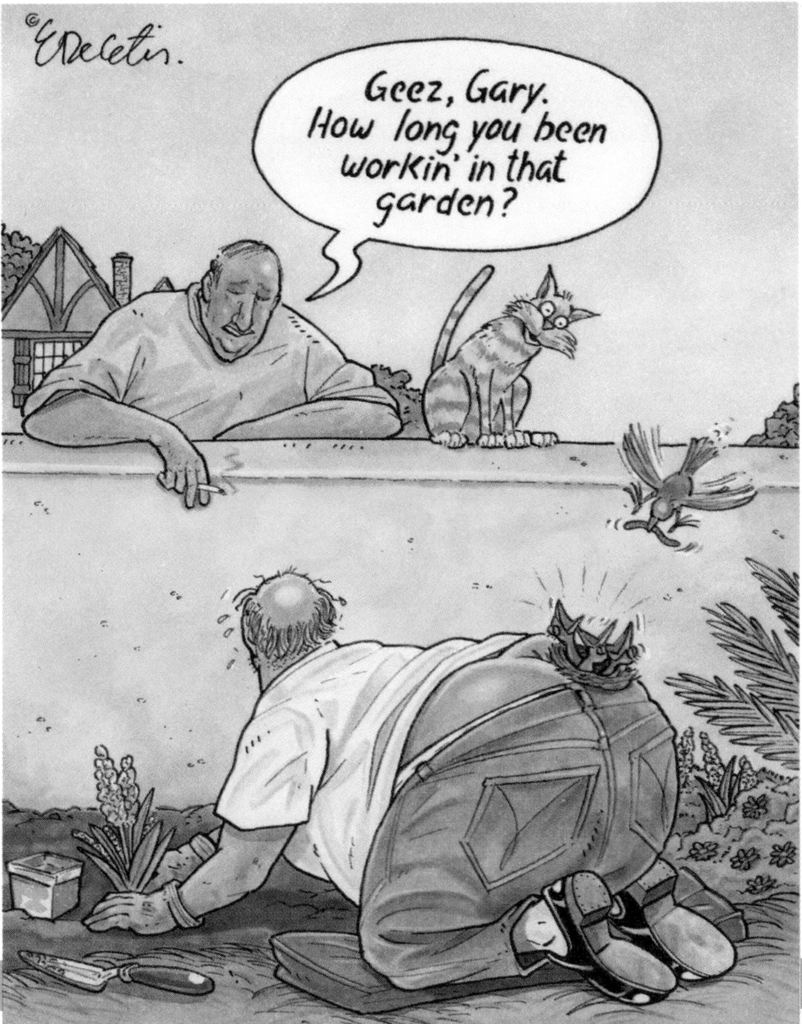
©EDeCetis.
Geez, Gary. How long you been workin' in that garden?

Posterior [po-steer-ee-er]:
situated behind or at the rear of the lap.

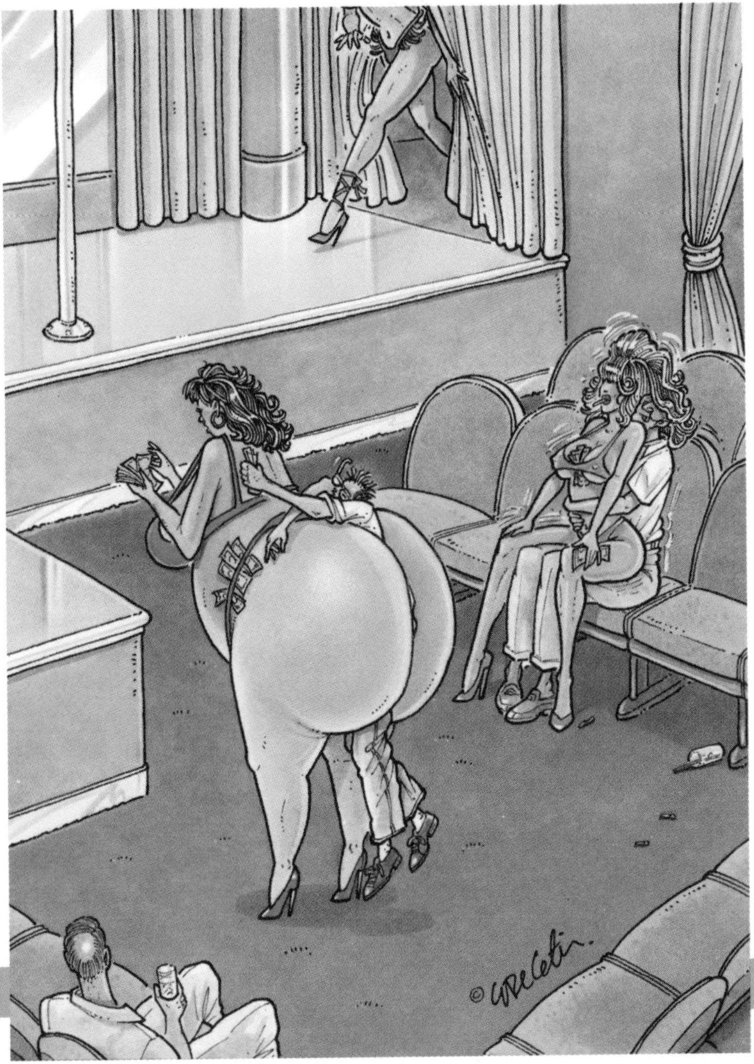

Crack [krâk]:

to make a sudden, sharp sound as in an explosion;
to break the tone of voice abruptly and discordantly, esp.
into an upper register; commonly heard when one is frightened.

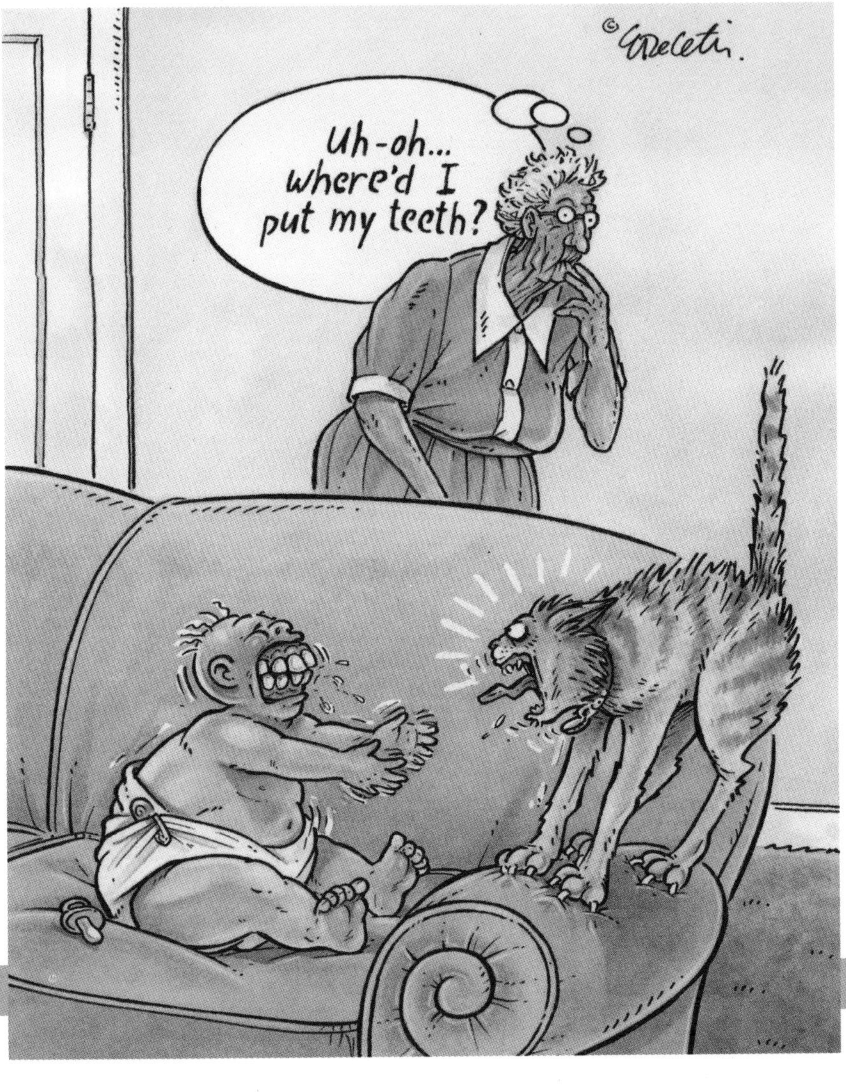
©Coreletti.
Uh-oh...
where'd I
put my teeth?

Behind [bee-hind]:
the part of the body a person sits on; the part
that squishes missing items.

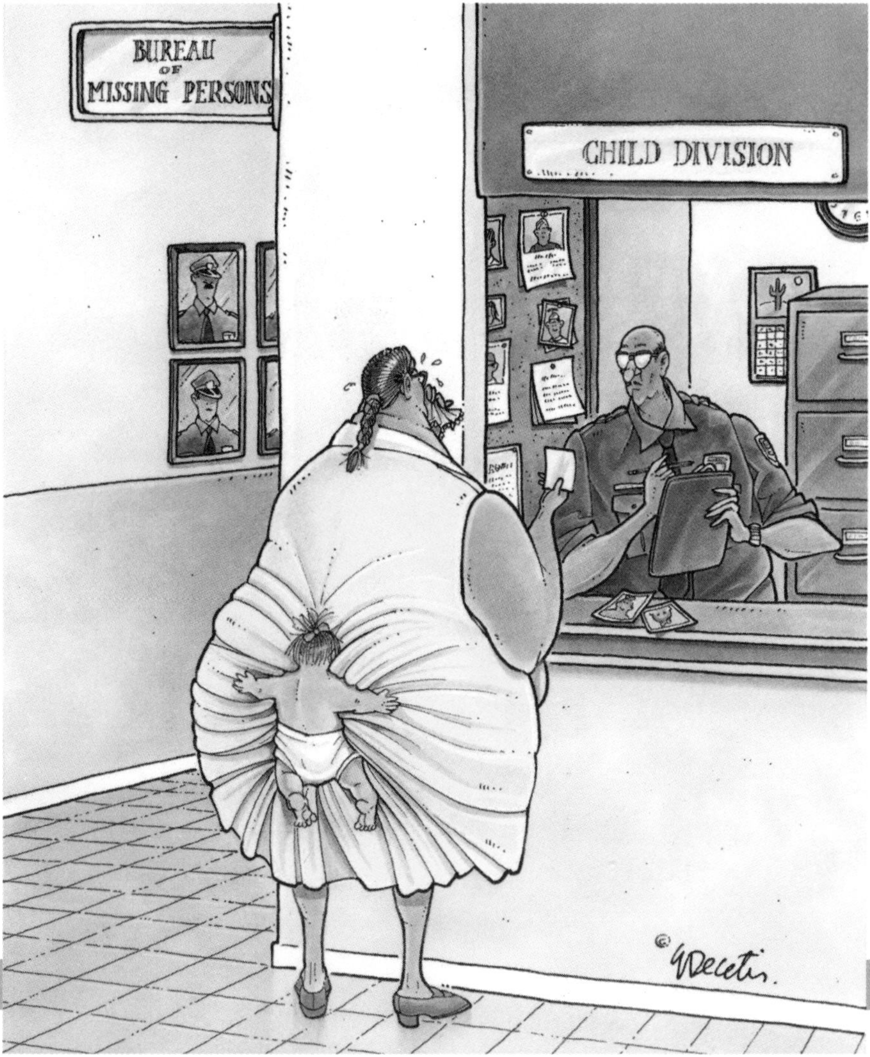
BUREAU OF MISSING PERSONS
CHILD DIVISION

Büyütmek [Turk]:
rear; an area that is familiar with the hand.

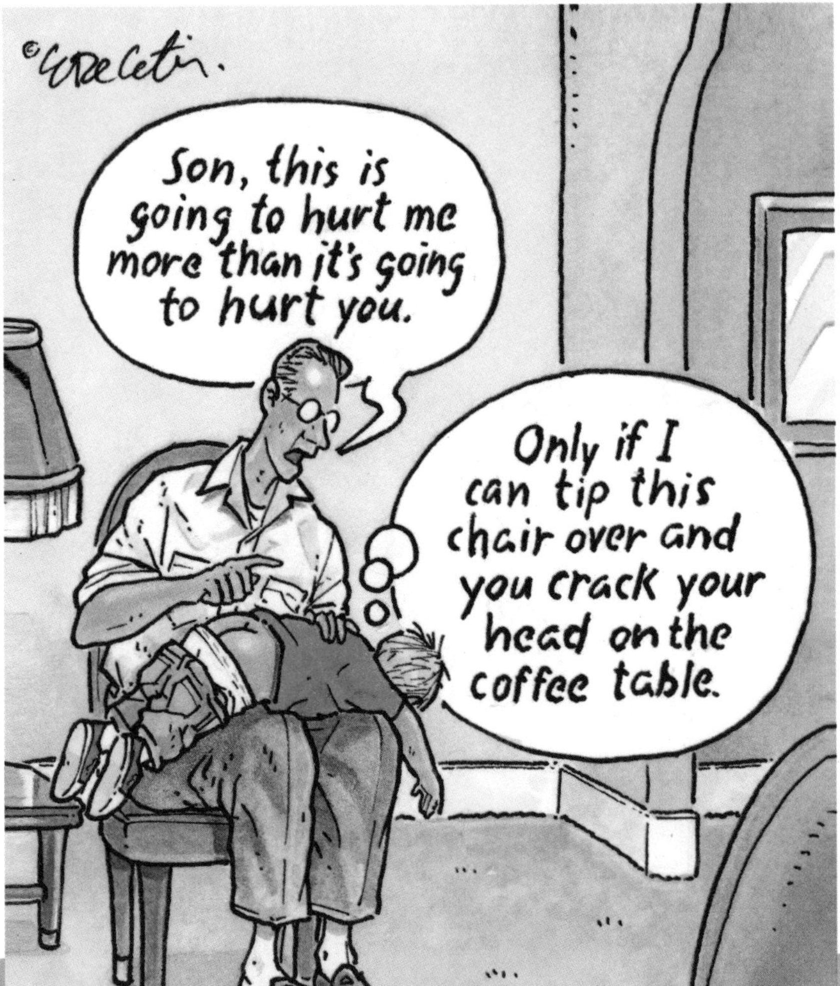
Son, this is going to hurt me more than it's going to hurt you.
Only if I can tip this chair over and you crack your head on the coffee table.

rear end [reer end]:
buttocks; spot where one sits.

This year Mike decides to make his own Valentine's cards.

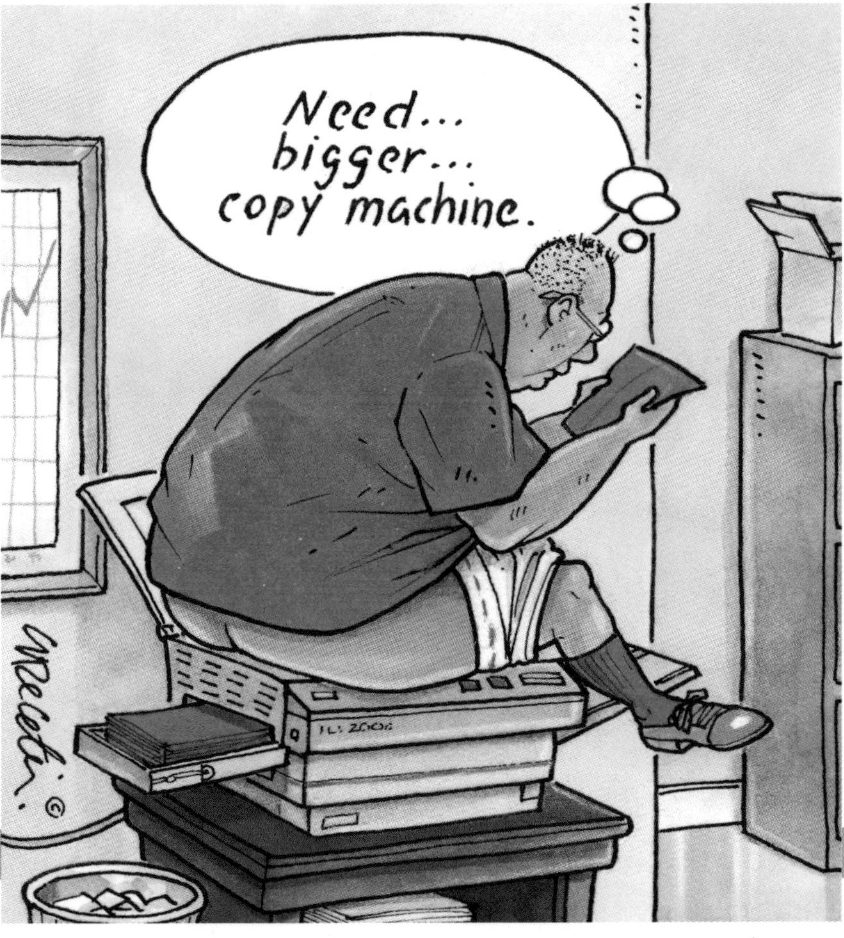
Need... bigger... copy machine.

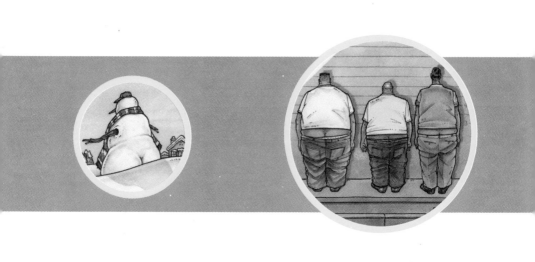

Chapter Two:
Hey, Good Lookin'

Crack [krâk]:
a witty comment about the size of someone's butt.

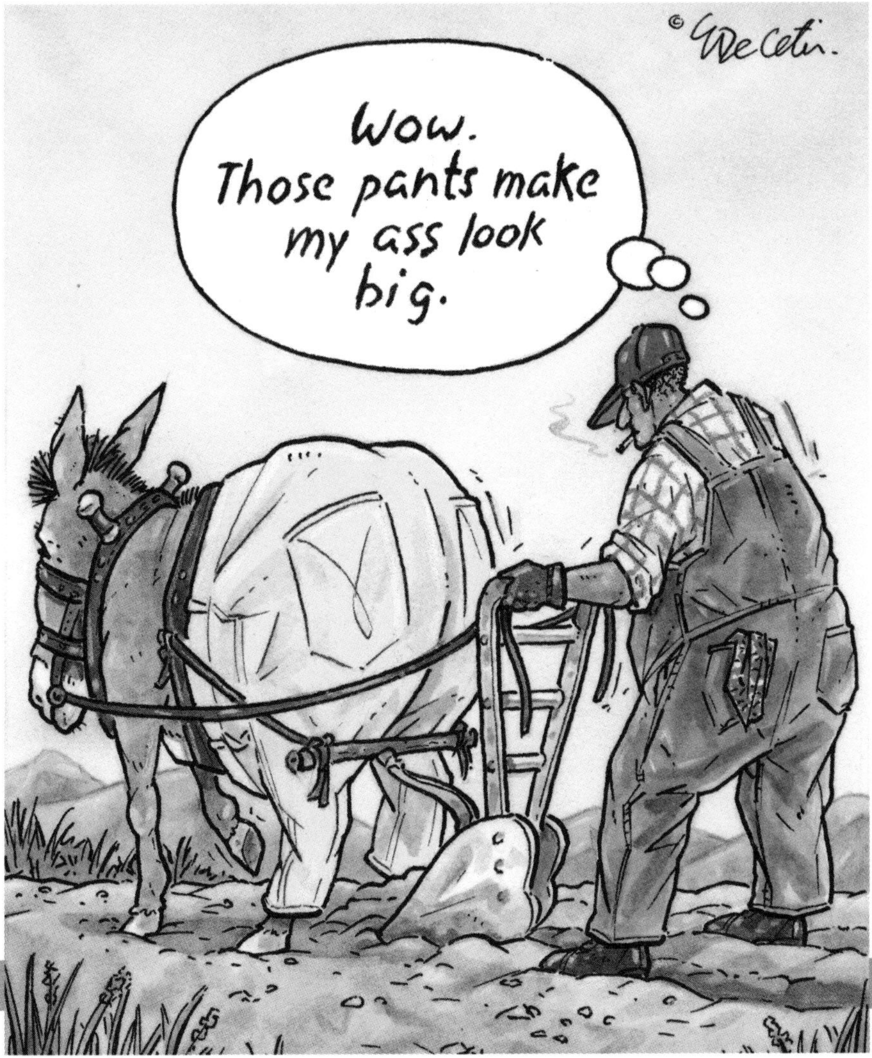
Wow.
Those pants make my ass look big.

Crack [krâk]:
to tell; to crack a joke.

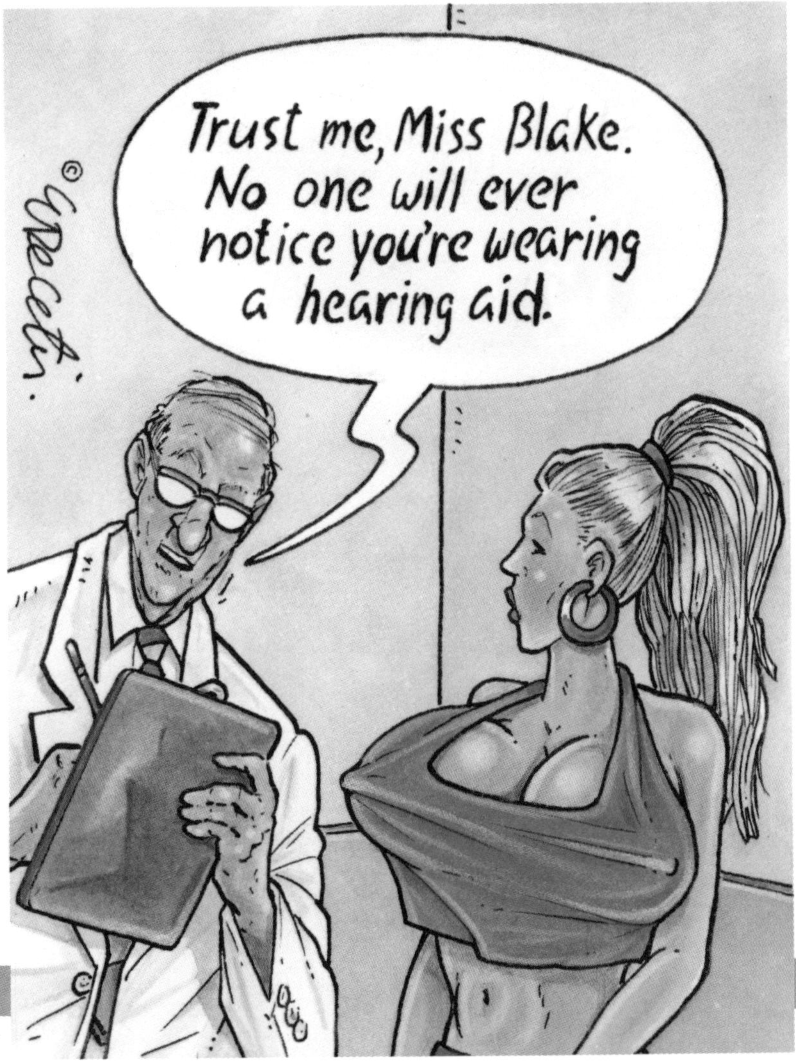
Trust me, Miss Blake. No one will ever notice you're wearing a hearing aid.

Crack [krâk]:
a wise remark that is often heard under the breath
or inside one's pants.

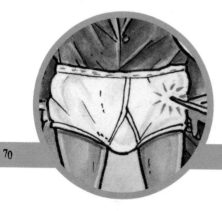

Legal Briefs

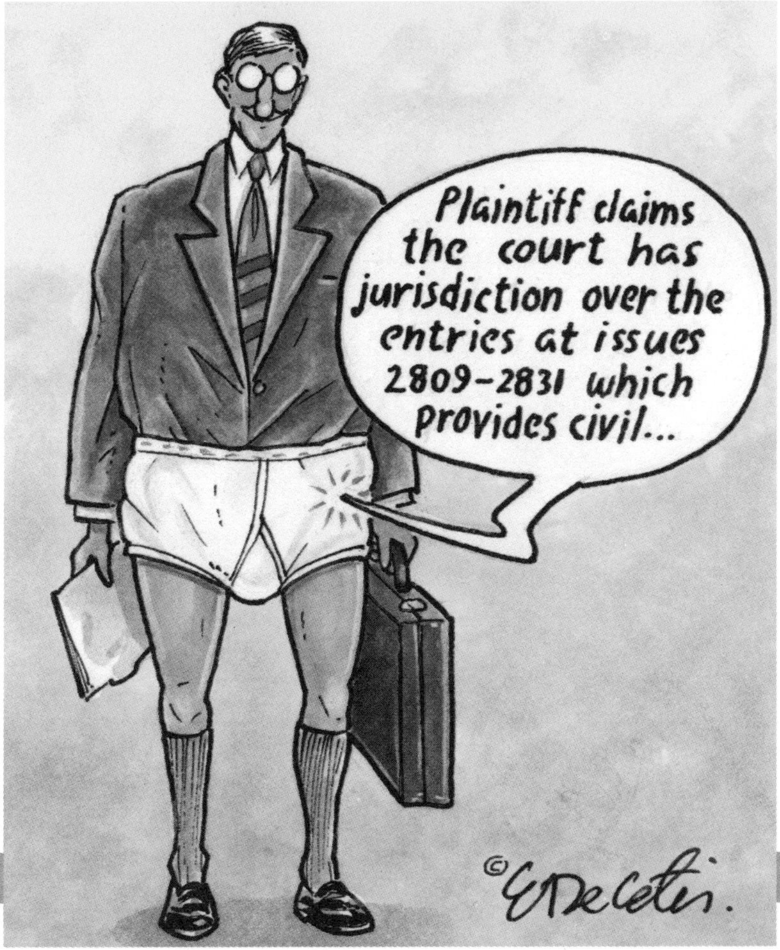
Plaintiff claims the court has jurisdiction over the entries at issues 2809-2831 which provides civil...
©EDeCeter.

Crack [krâk]:
to break, as in to break wind.

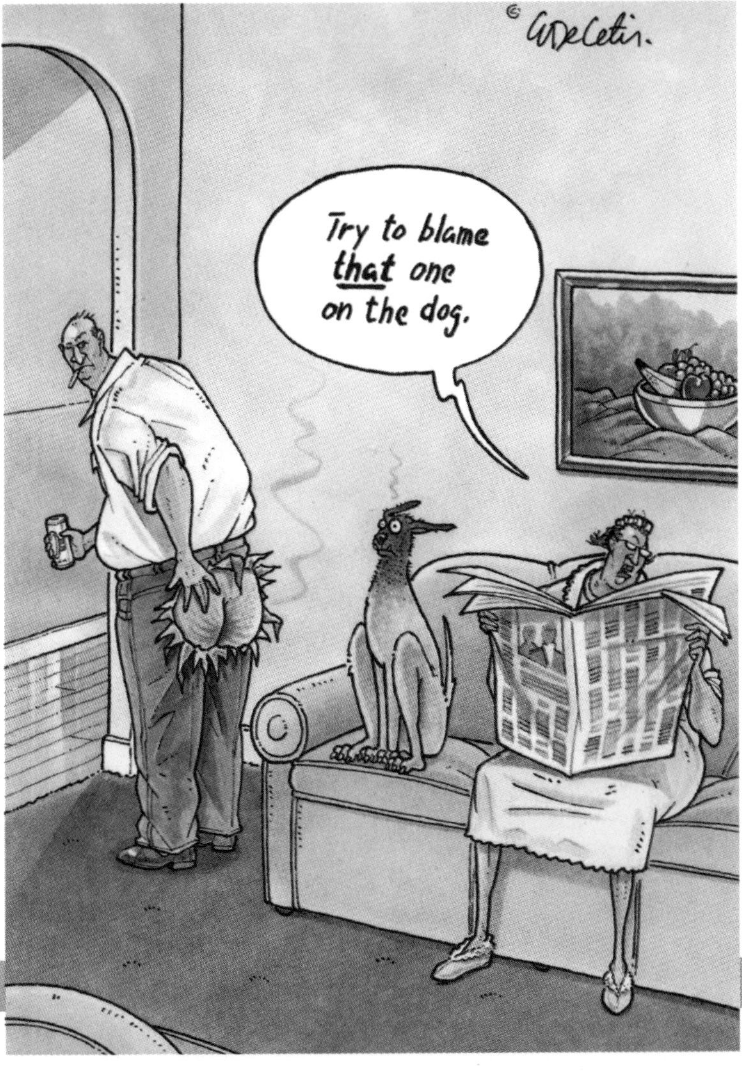
© WDeCetis.
Try to blame that one on the dog.

A la parte de atrás [Sp]:
at the rear, sometimes due to a deficiency.

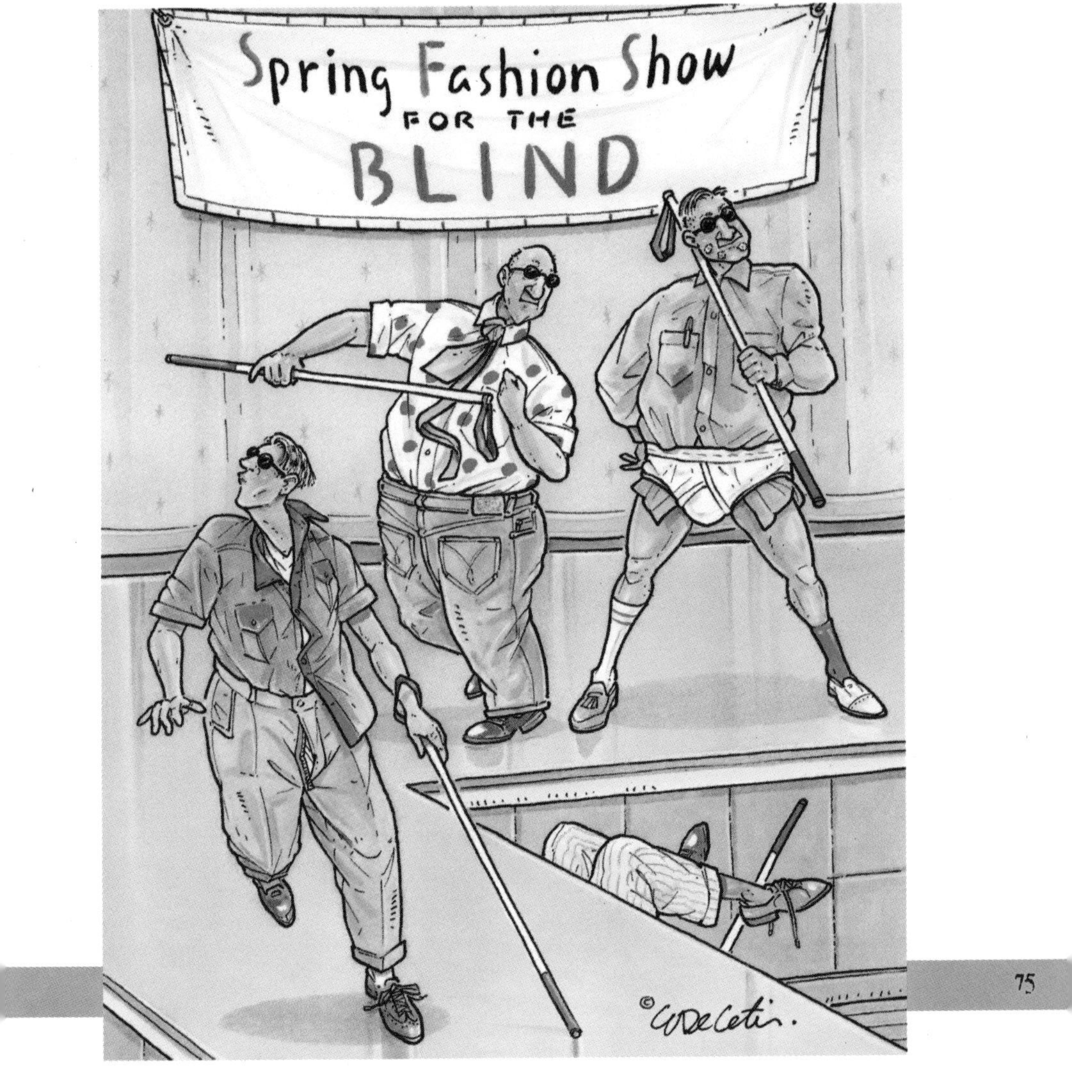
Spring Fashion Show
FOR THE
BLIND
©CDeCeti.

In fondo [It]:
in the rear or in your face.

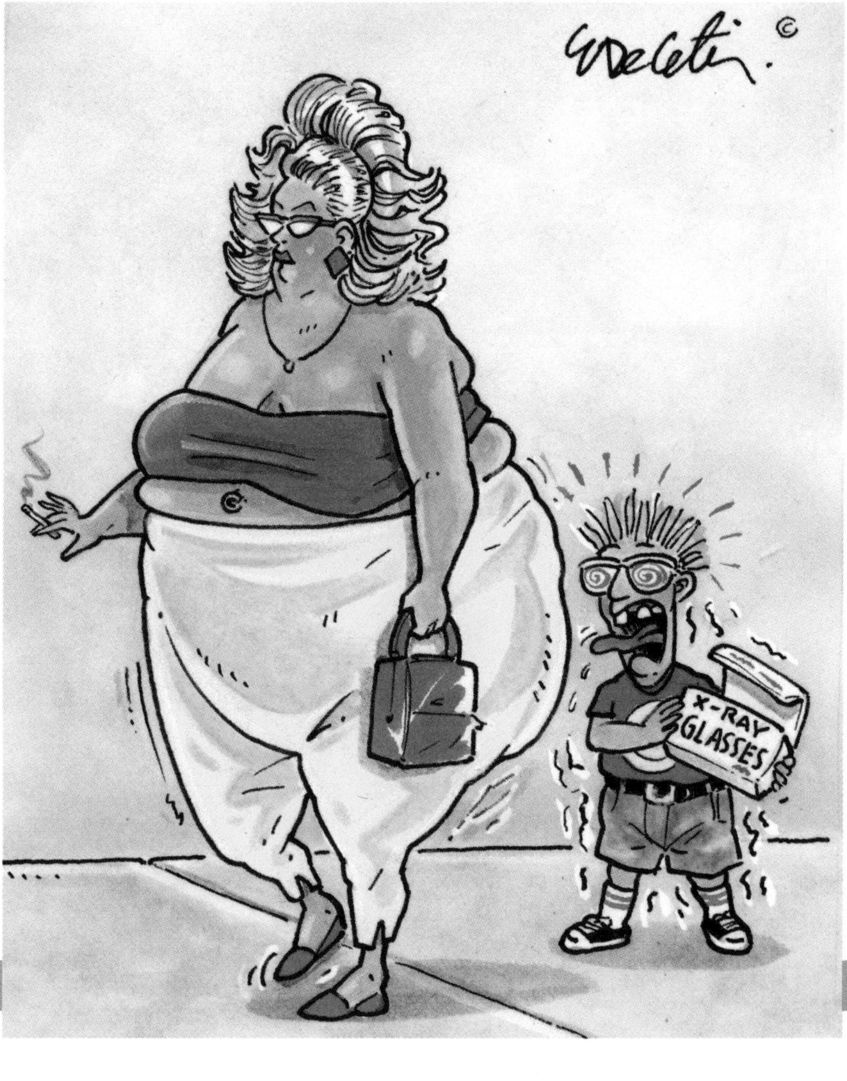
X-RAY
GLASSES

Butt [buht]:
the end or extremity; an unpleasant way to
start off one's day.

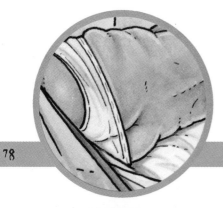

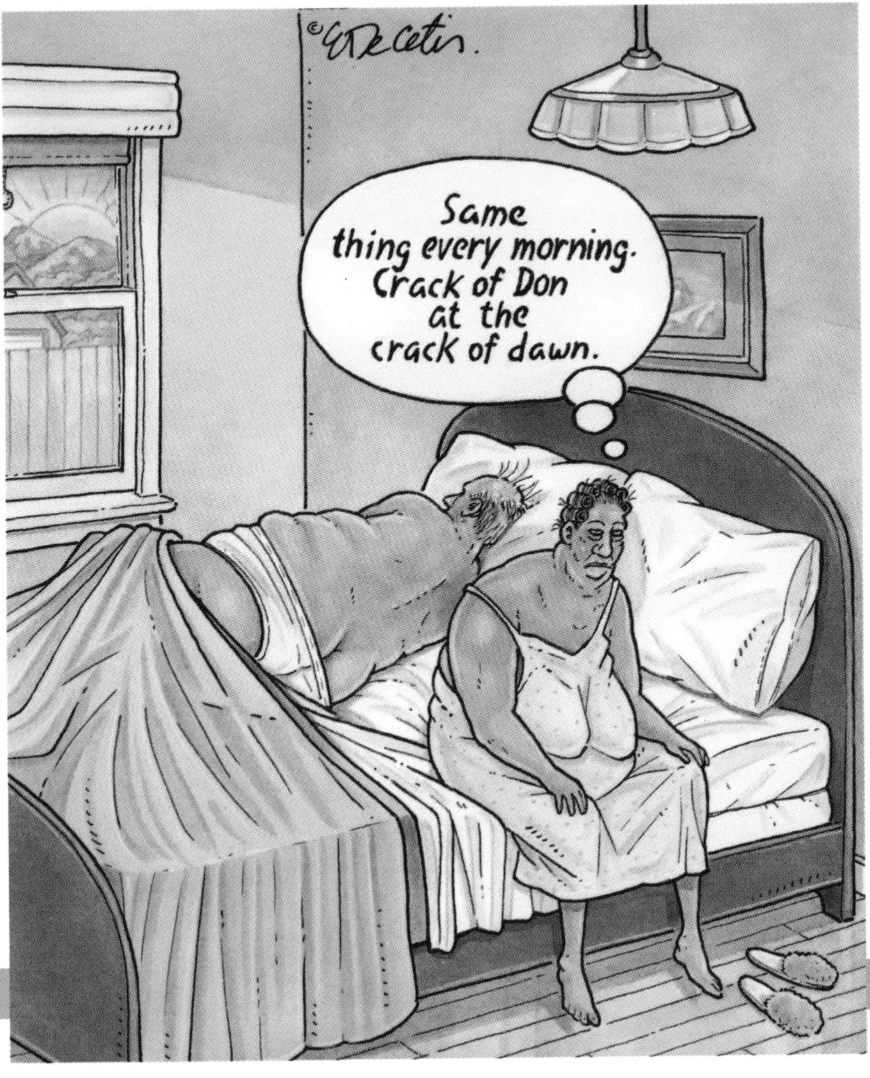
Same thing every morning. Crack of Don at the crack of dawn.

Crack [krâk]:
a flaw or defect which can affect the size of things.

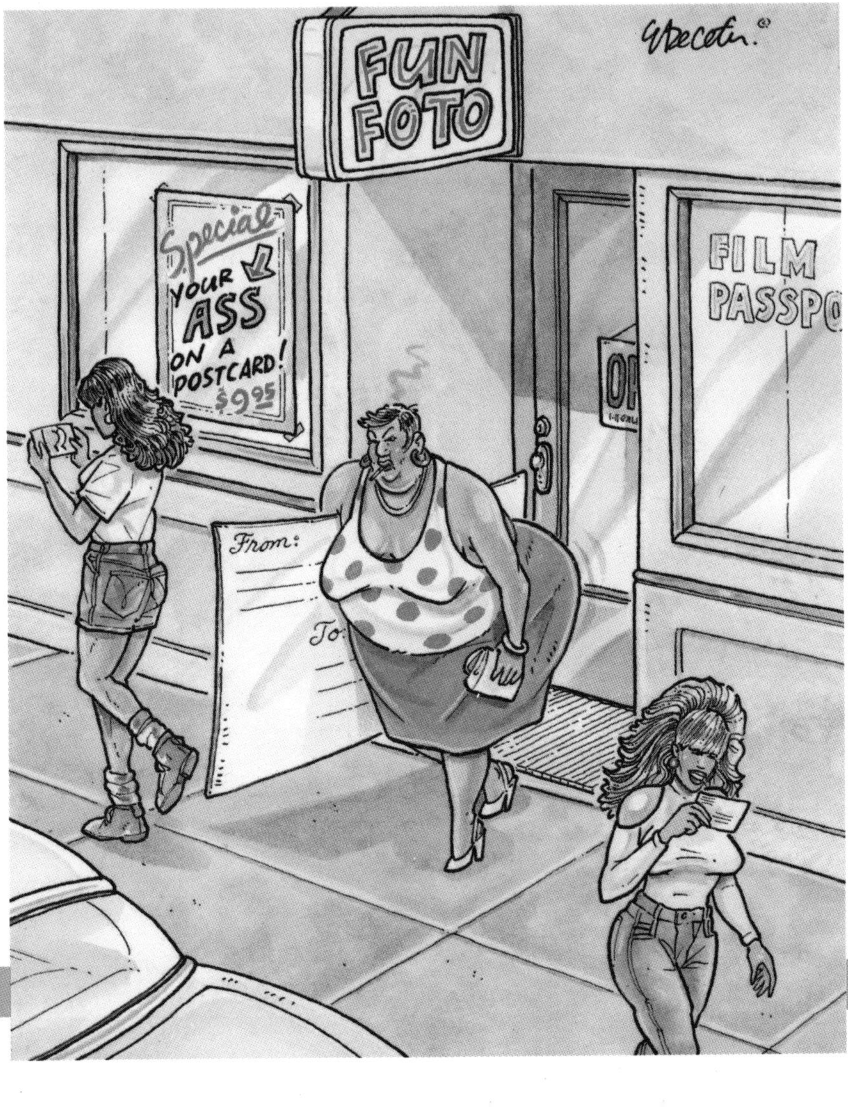
FUN FOTO
Special
YOUR ASS ON A POSTCARD!
$9.95
FILM
PASSPO
OP
From:
To:

Crack [krâk]:
to break or open; to break the ice with an opening line.

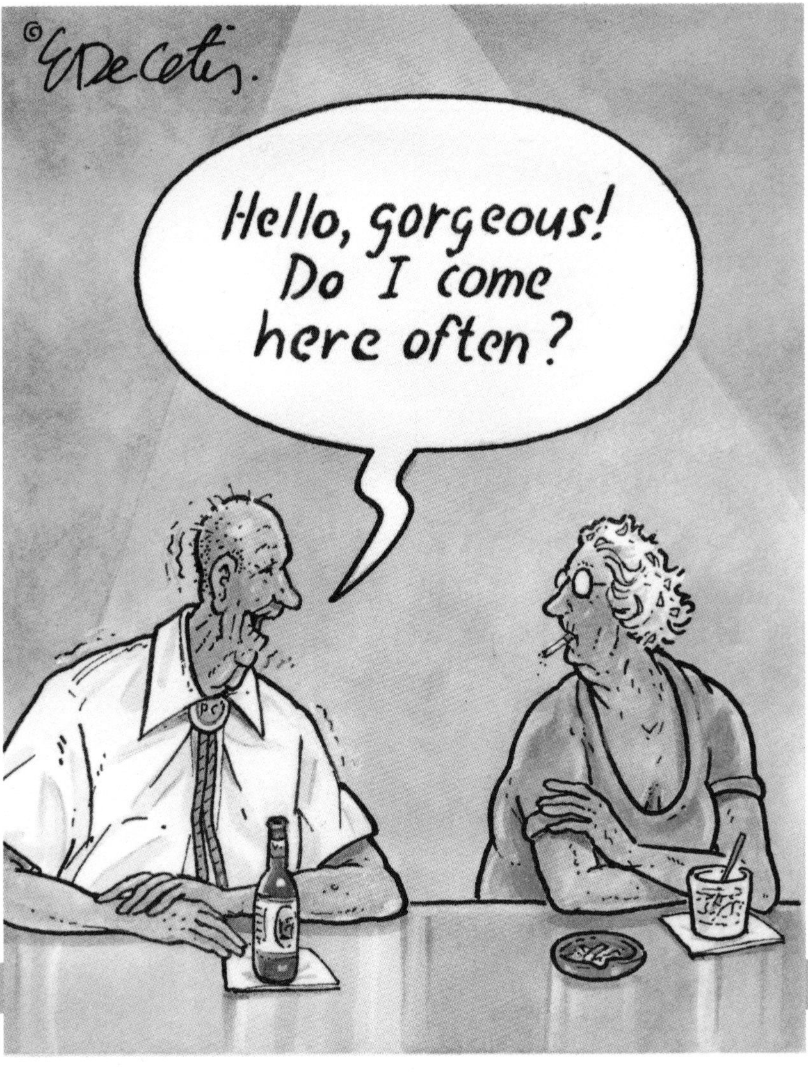
©EDeCeti.
Hello, gorgeous! Do I come here often?

Hinterteile [G]:
breeches; typically a hair-free zone.

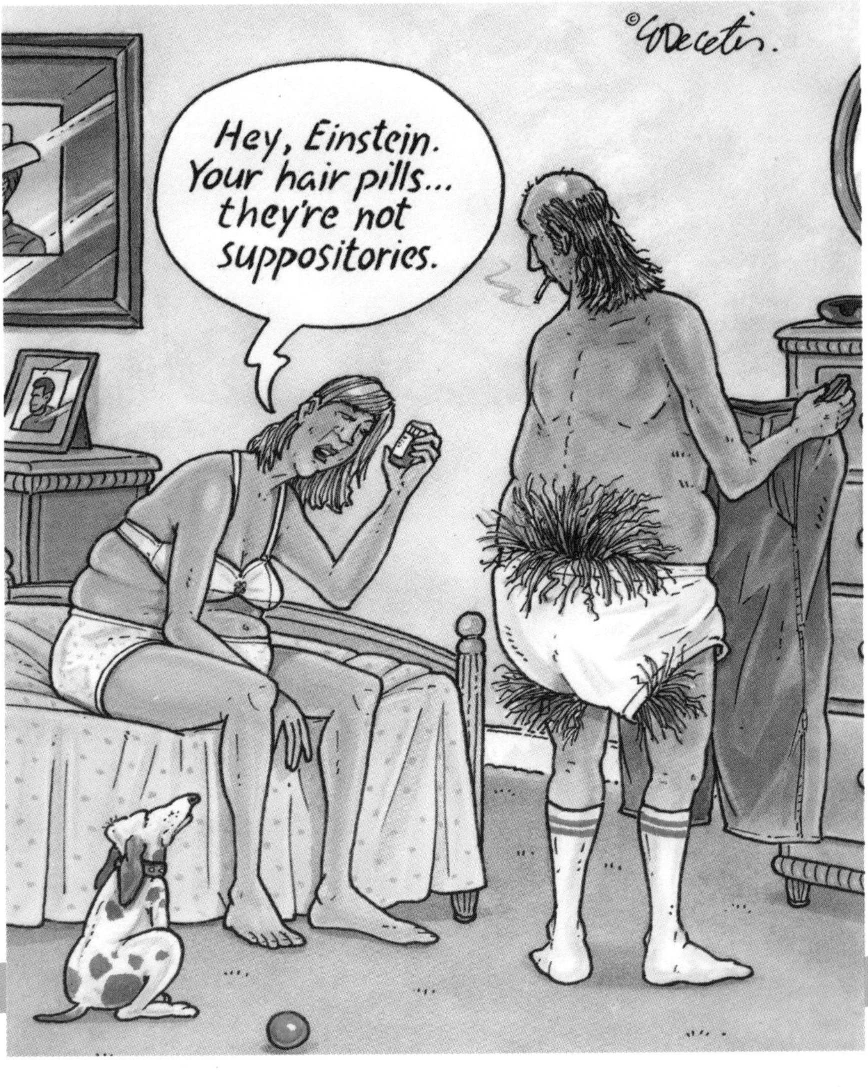
©Wecelis.
Hey, Einstein. Your hair pills... they're not suppositories.

Retaguardia [Sp]:
of the rear; rearguard: protected from exposure.

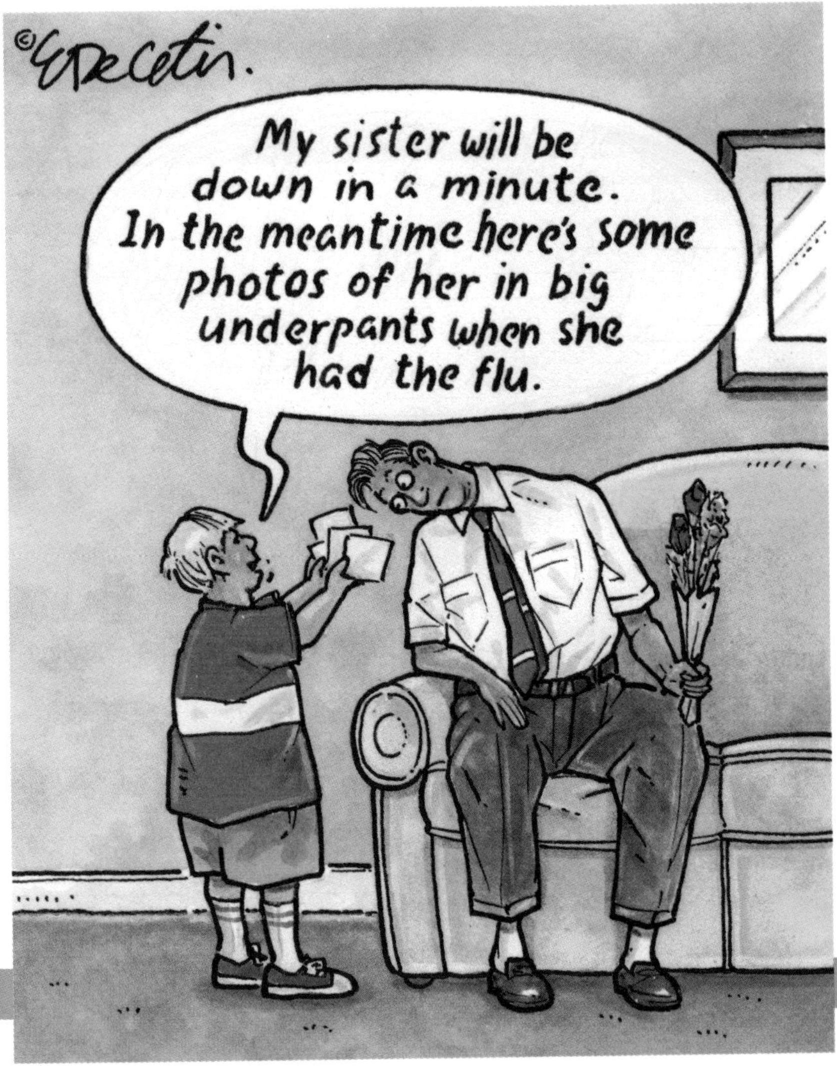
©EDeCetin.
My sister will be down in a minute. In the meantime here's some photos of her in big underpants when she had the flu.

Crack [krâk]:
first-rate, as in size.

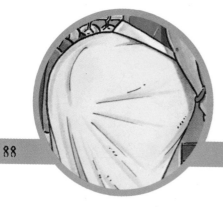

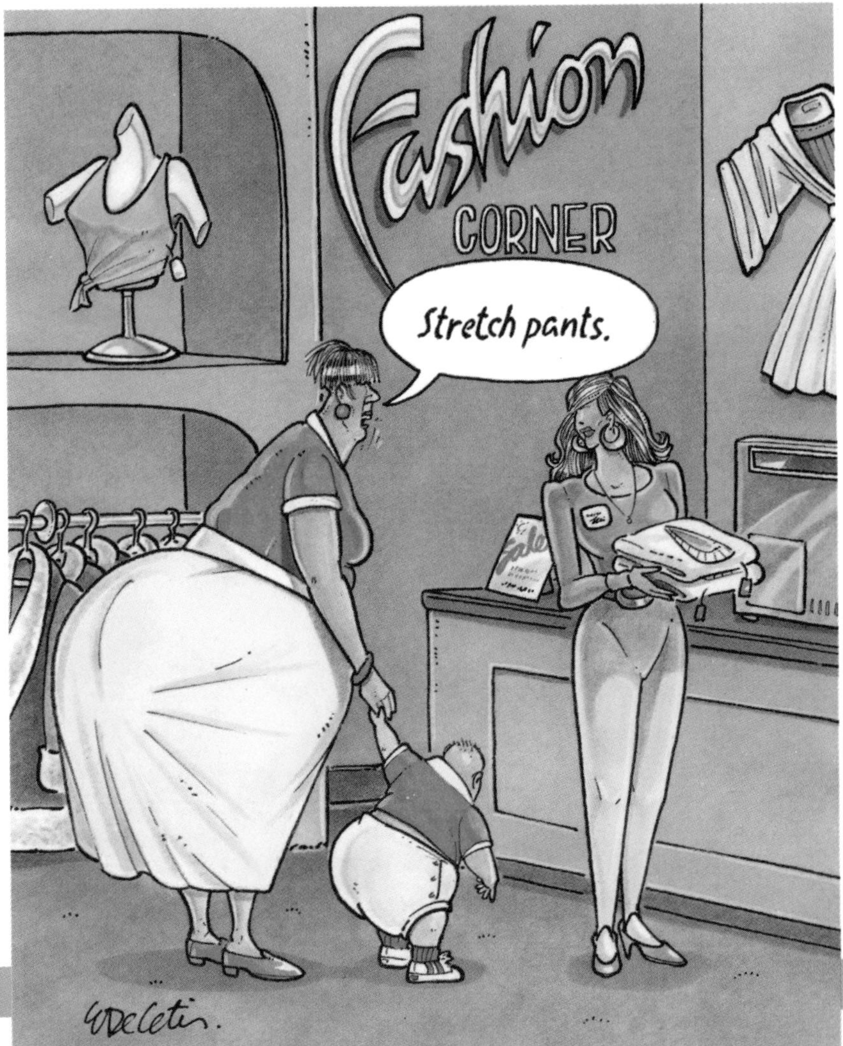
Fashion
CORNER
Stretch pants.
EDeCetis.

Croup [kroop] [Fr]:
bum; portion of the body that should not be
exposed in certain settings.

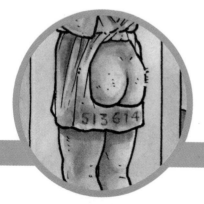

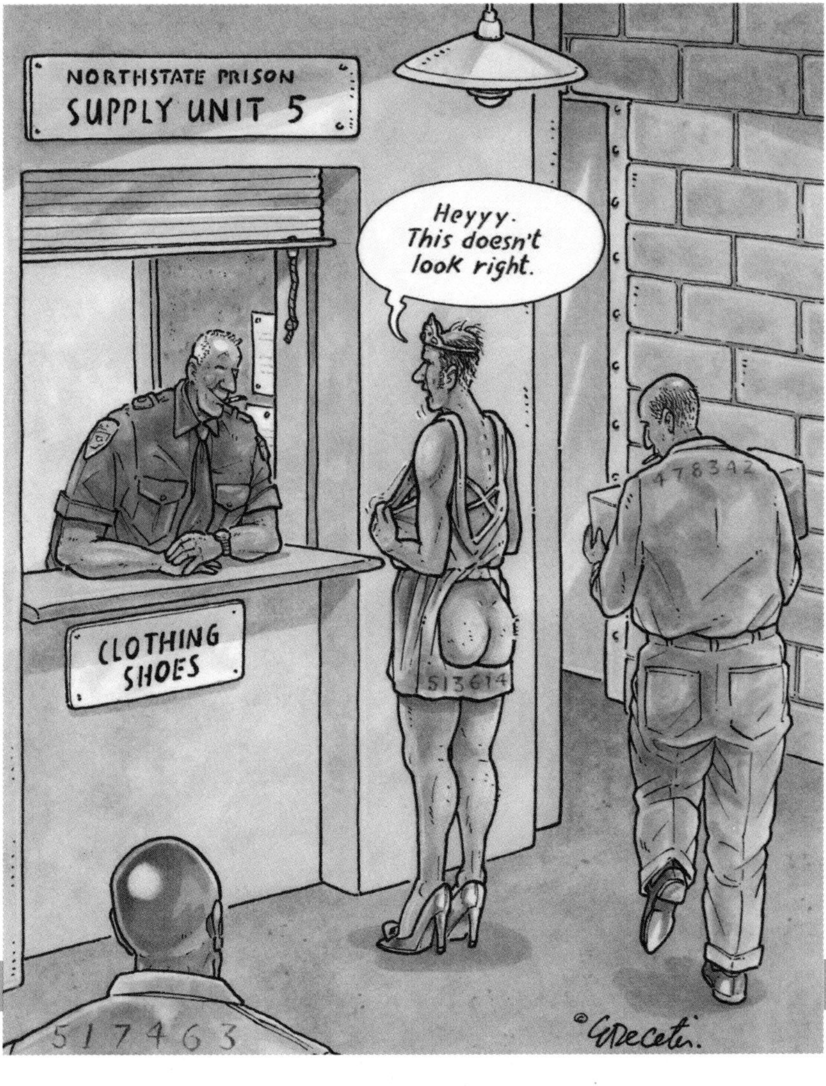
NORTHSTATE PRISON
SUPPLY UNIT 5
Heyyy.
This doesn't
look right.
CLOTHING
SHOES
478342
513614
517463
©GDecetí.

Crack [krâk]:
to split and reveal.

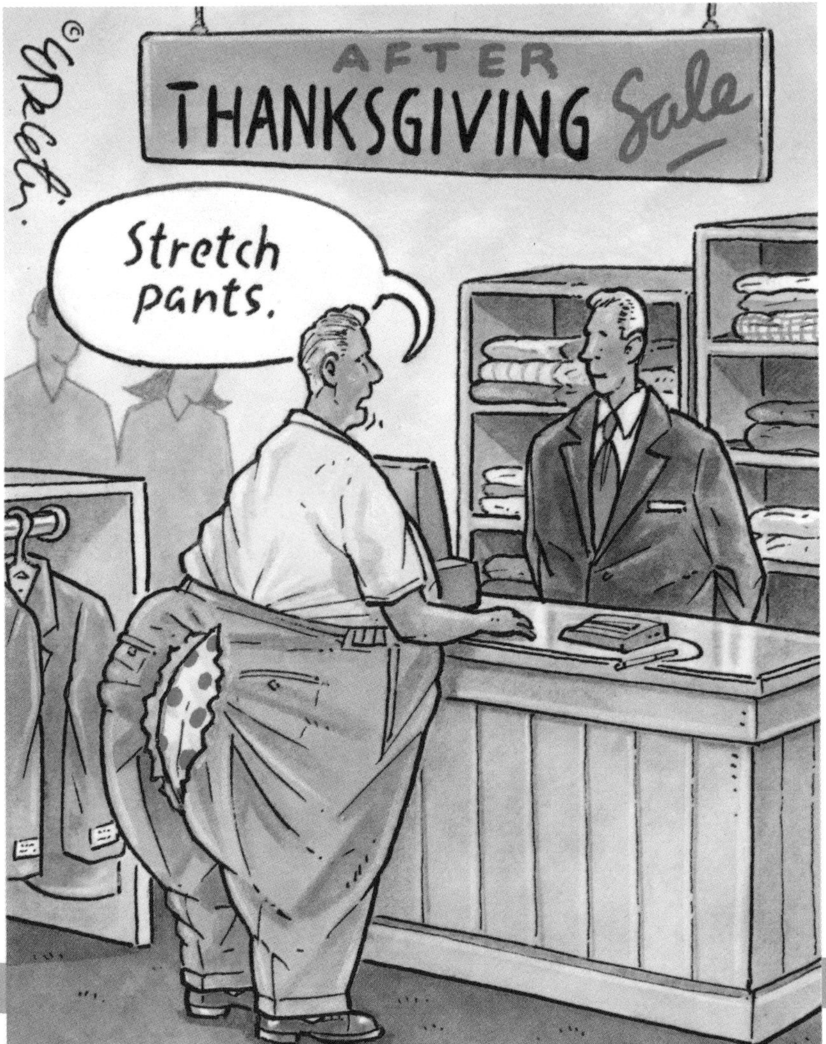
AFTER THANKSGIVING Sale
Stretch pants.

Crack [krâk]:
a discovery; a break in the facade.

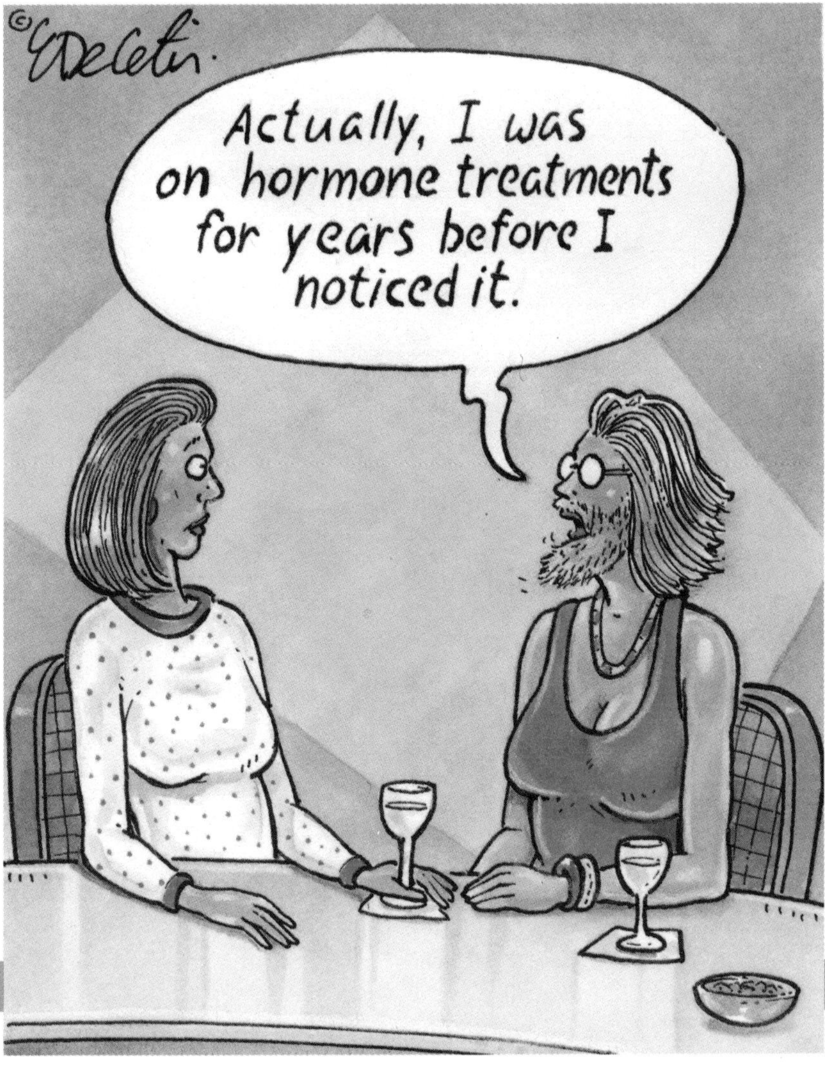
©EDeCeta
Actually, I was on hormone treatments for years before I noticed it.

Arse [ahrs]:
Someone who is held in great contempt.

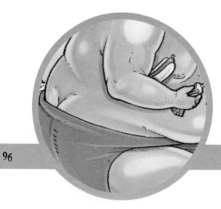

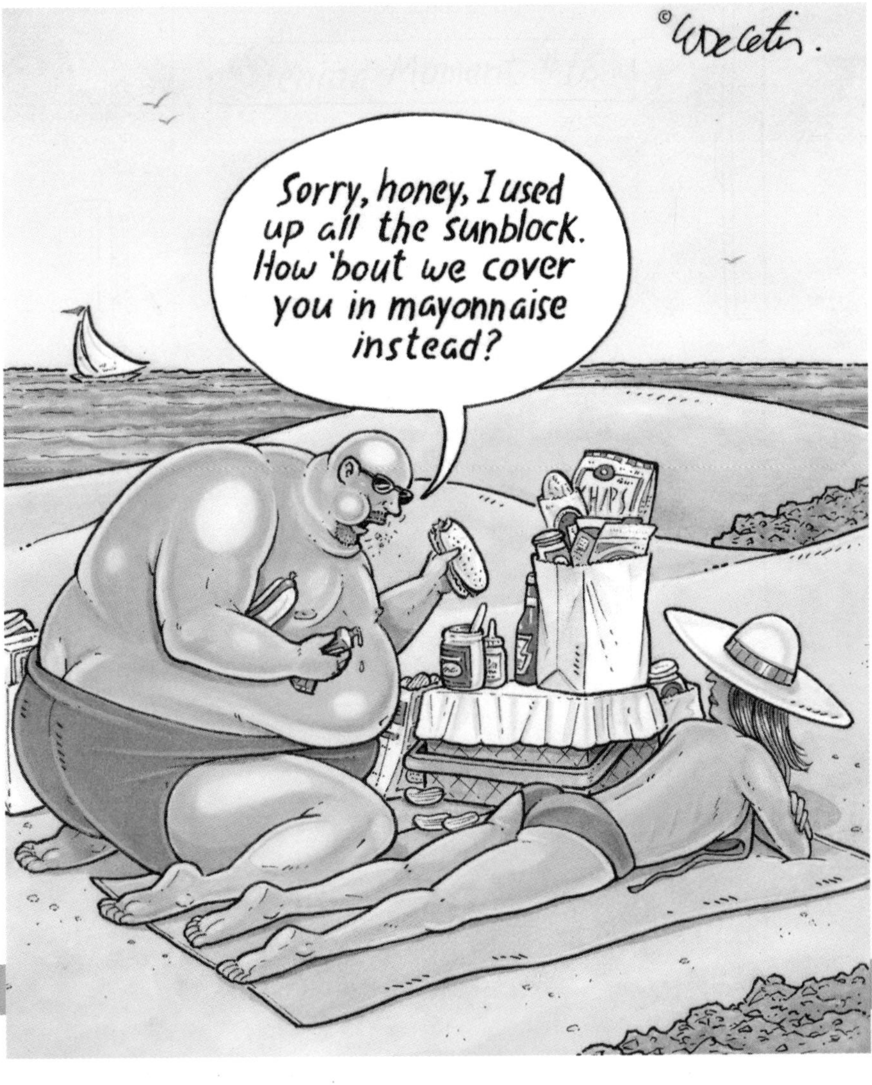
Sorry, honey, I used up all the sunblock. How 'bout we cover you in mayonnaise instead?
CHIPS

Glutus maximus [mak-suh-muhs]:
the largest of the buttock muscles.

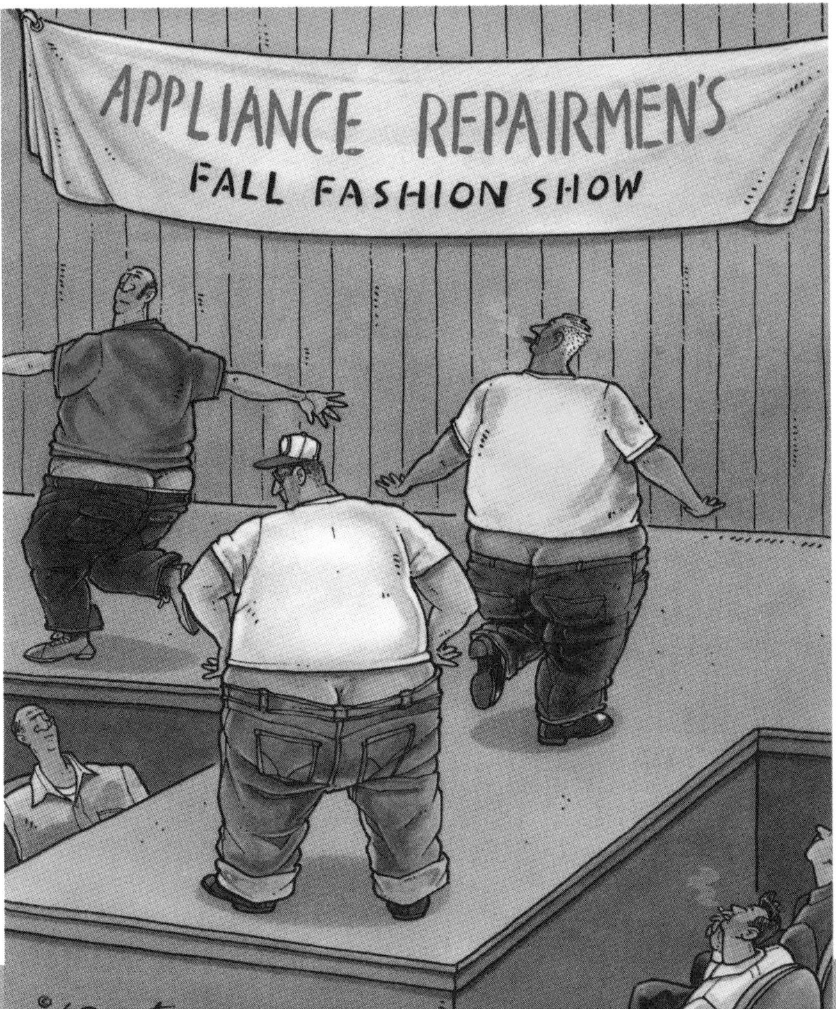
APPLIANCE REPAIRMEN'S
FALL FASHION SHOW
© Wdecetin.

Crack [krâk]:
something damaged or broken.

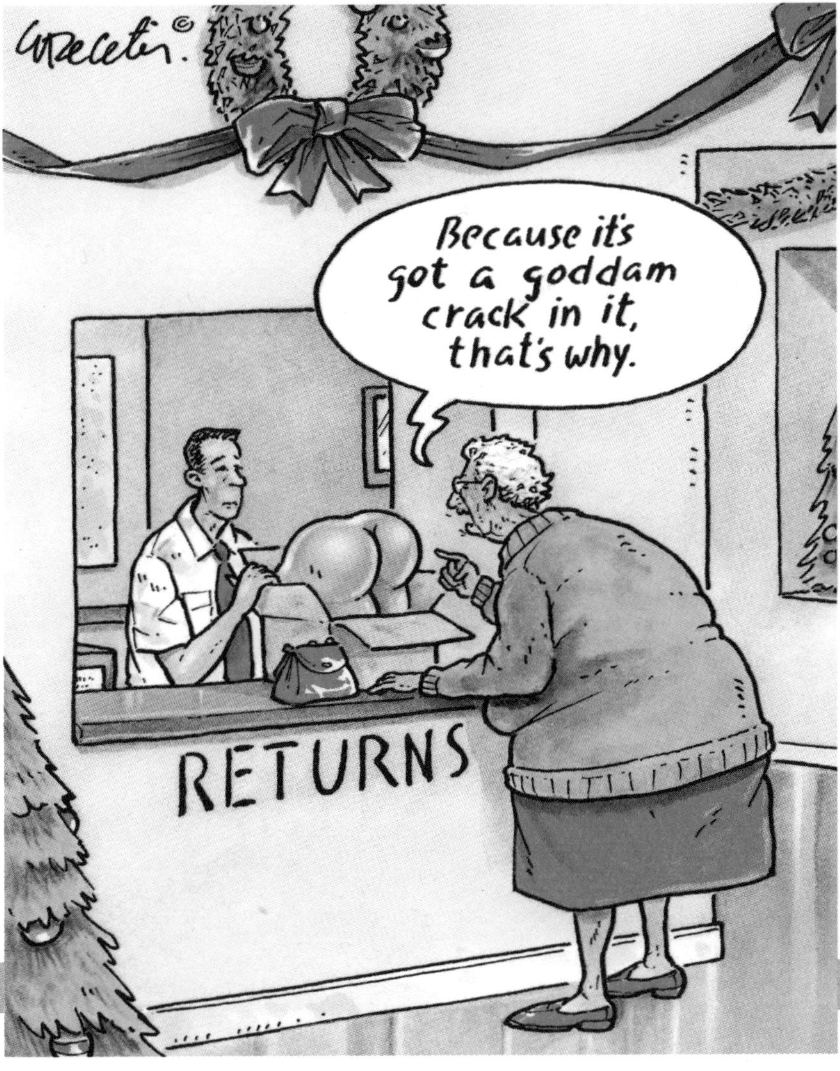
Because it's got a goddam crack in it, that's why.
RETURNS

Crack [krâk]:
a witty or scathing remark.

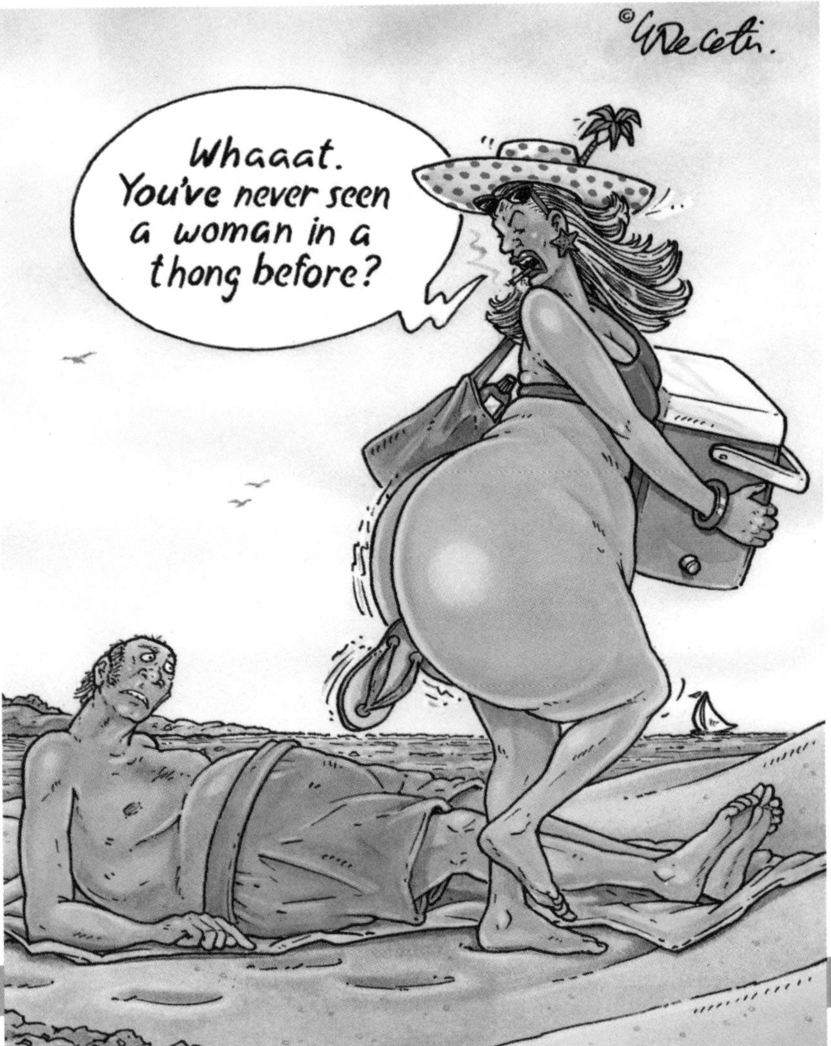
Whaaat. You've never seen a woman in a thong before?
©Werner Weckerle / Decetti

Crack [krâk]:

to attempt something, often to the point of no return.

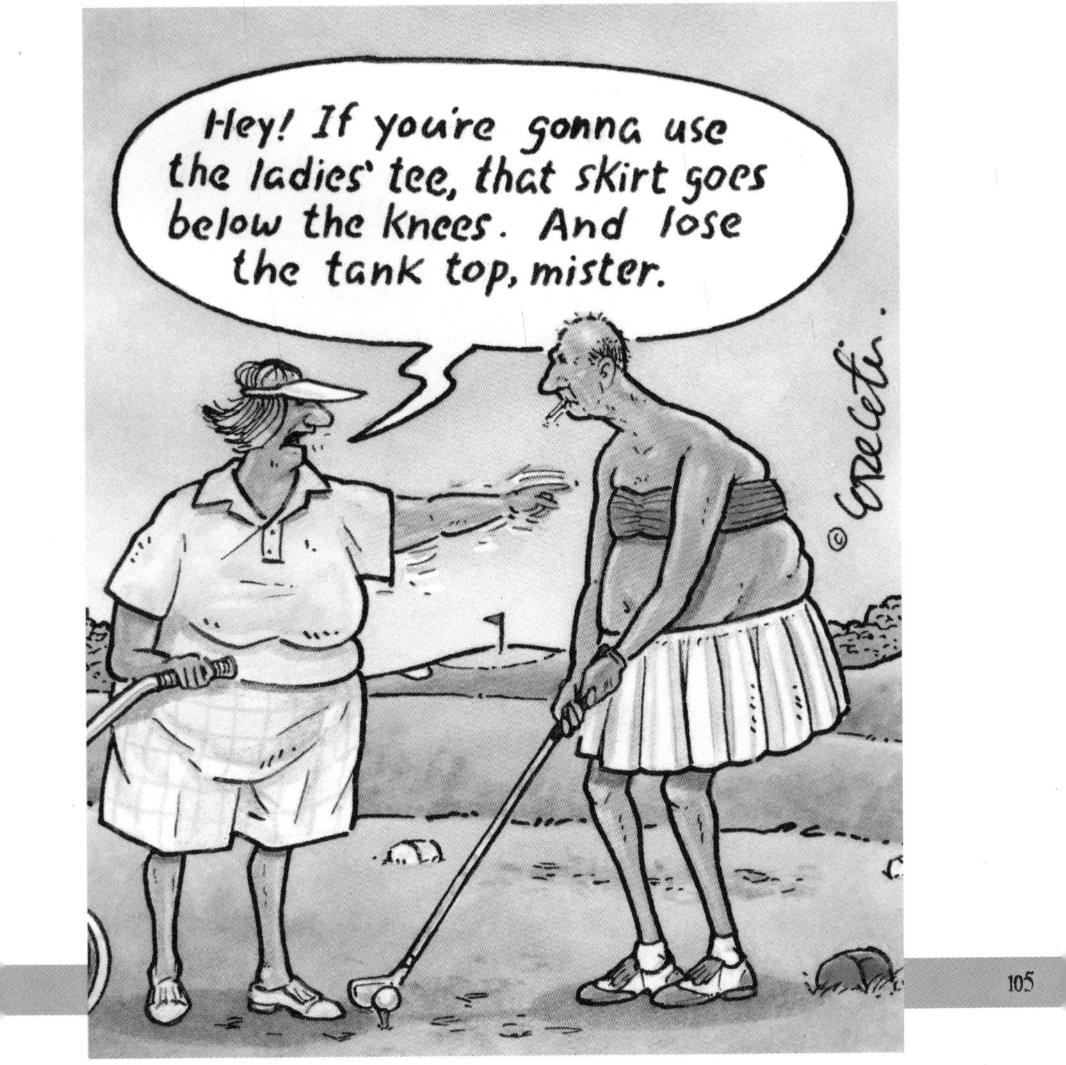
Hey! If you're gonna use the ladies' tee, that skirt goes below the knees. And lose the tank top, mister.

Nádegas [Pg]:
backside area that provides quite the mug shot view.

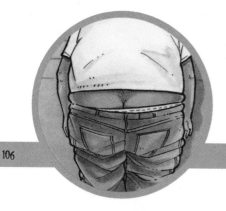

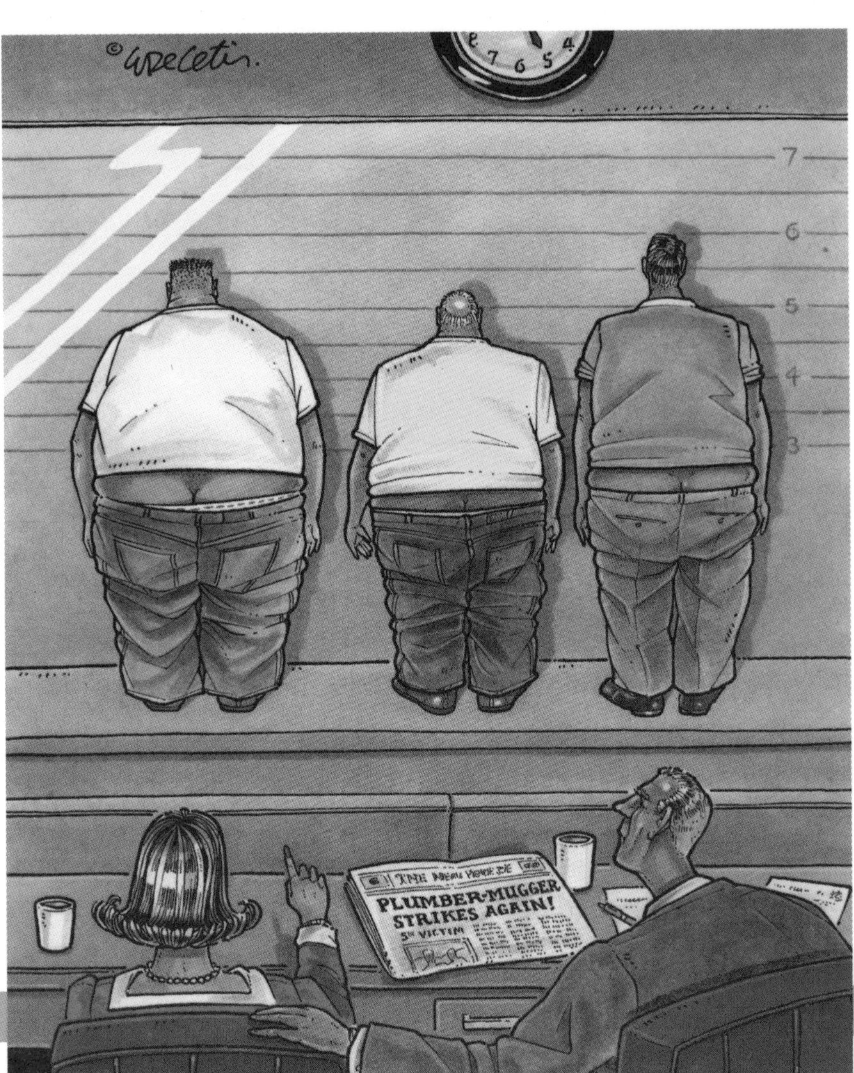
PLUMBER-MUGGER STRIKES AGAIN!
5th VICTIM

Trasero [Sp]:
behind; an area that should always be checked before
that big night out.

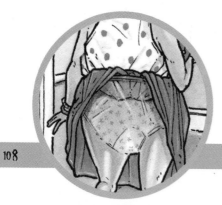

Lois rejoins her blind date, hoping he won't notice the makeup she has smudged on her blouse.

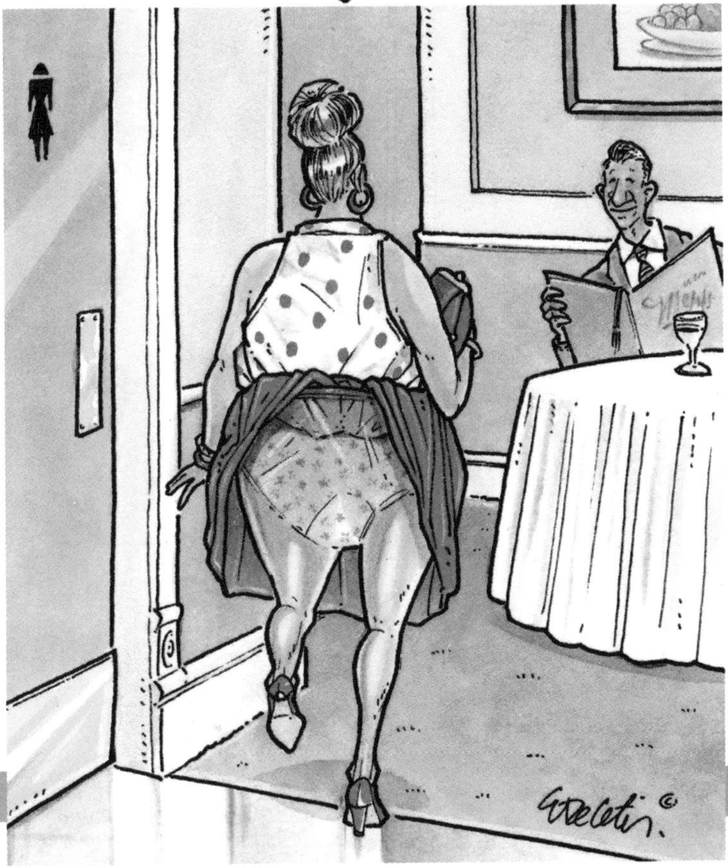

Istmik [Et]:
buttocks (exposed); birthday suit.

Dick was the kind of guy who wanted everyone to know it was his birthday.

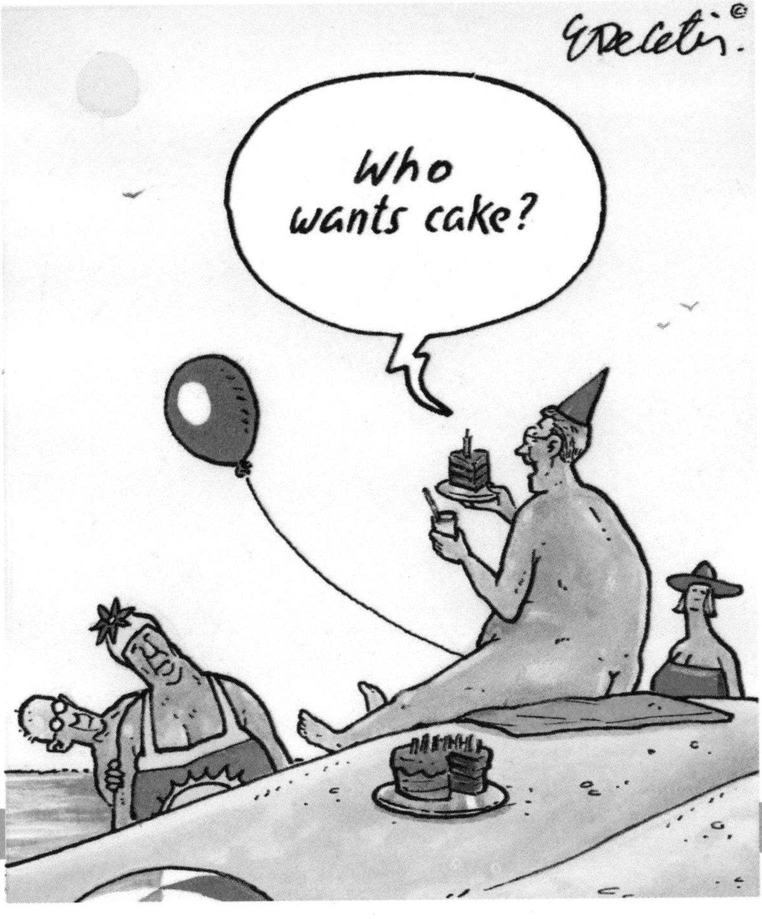
Who wants cake?

Crack [krâk]:
to get moving; to hurry up;
to move quickly past an unpleasant sight.

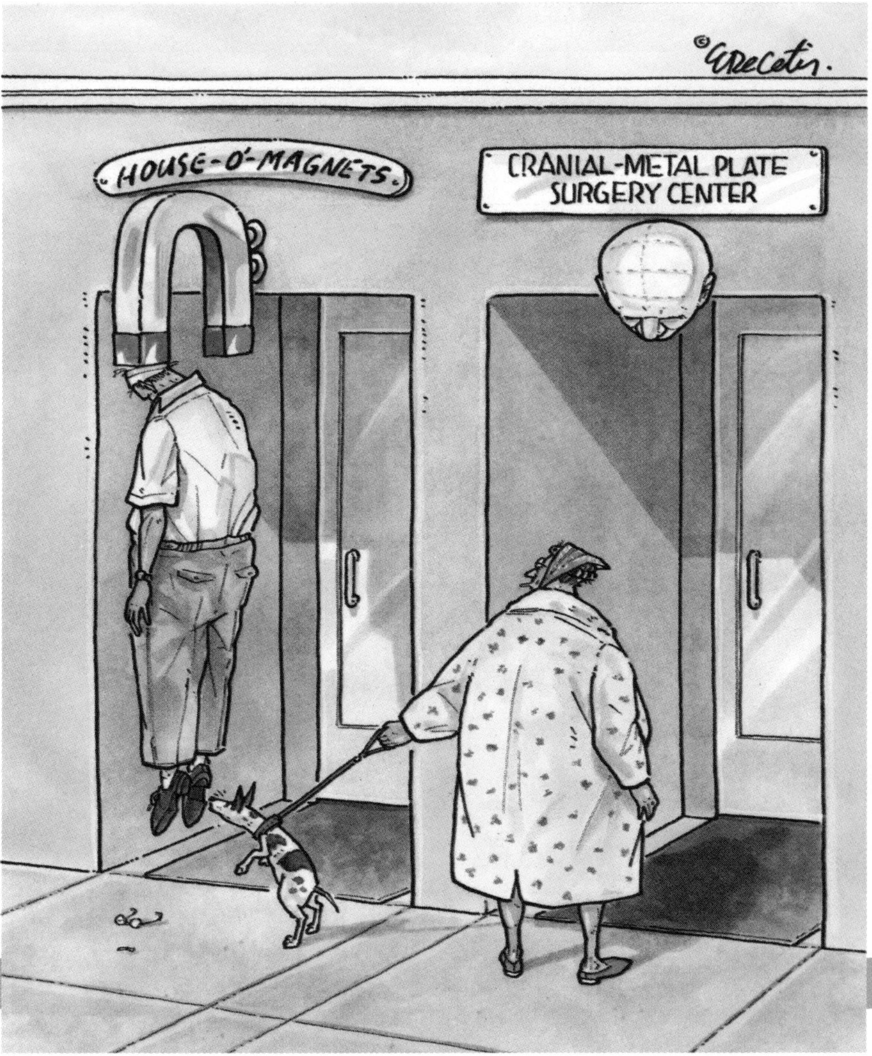
©Erecetin.
HOUSE-O'-MAGNETS
CRANIAL-METAL PLATE
SURGERY CENTER

Arsle [Sw]:
the rear; all its emanations.

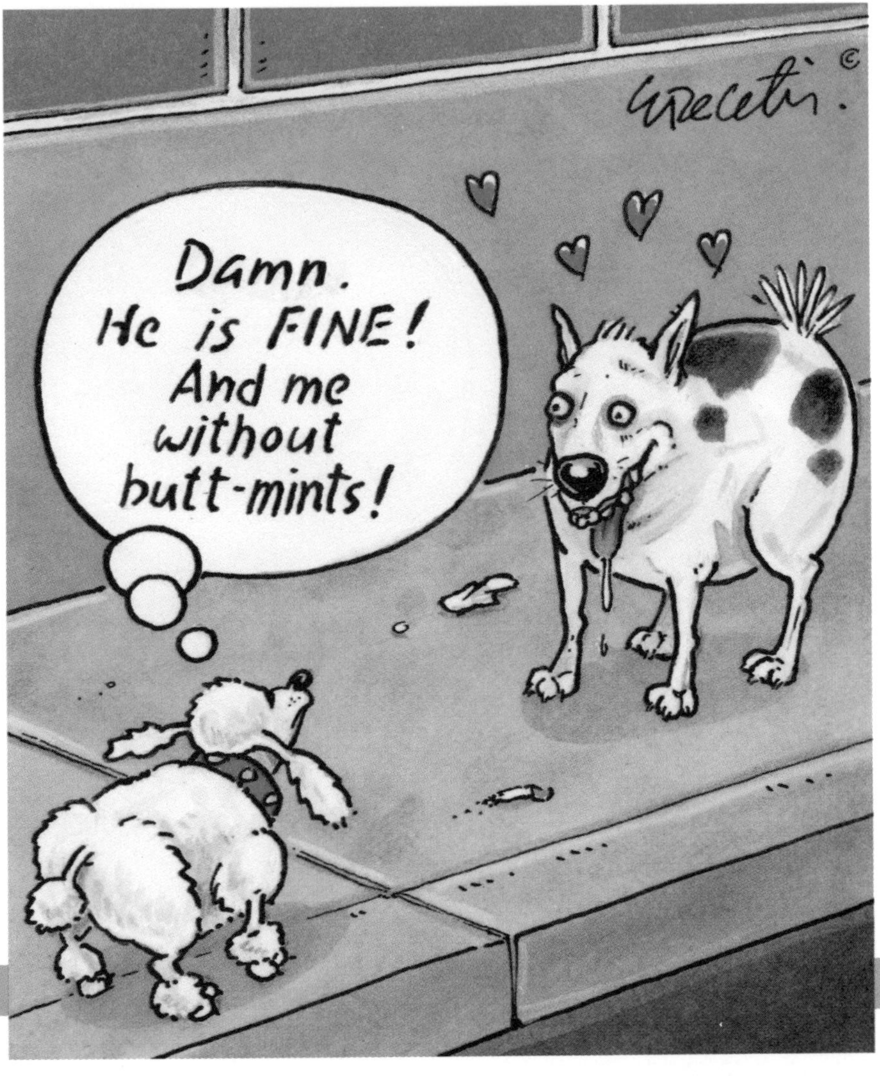
Damn. He is FINE! And me without butt-mints!

Crack [krâk]:
a witty comment.

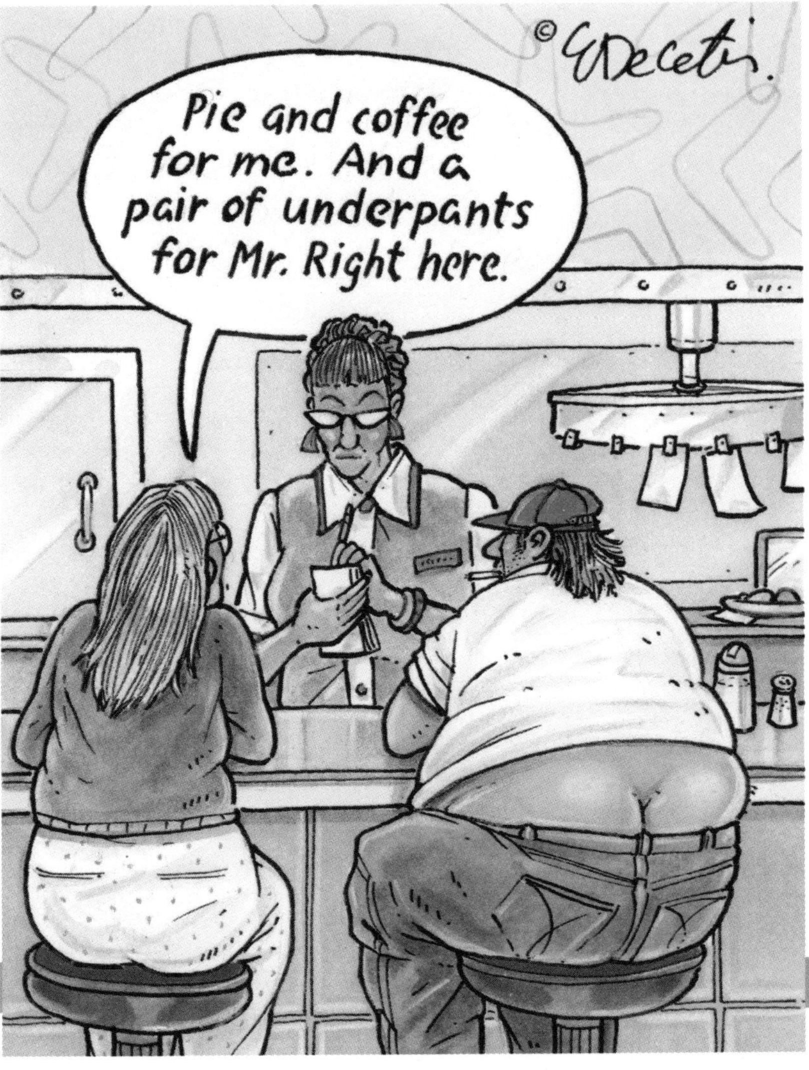
©EDecetis.
Pie and coffee for me. And a pair of underpants for Mr. Right here.

Ass [as]:

One deficient in judgment and common sense.

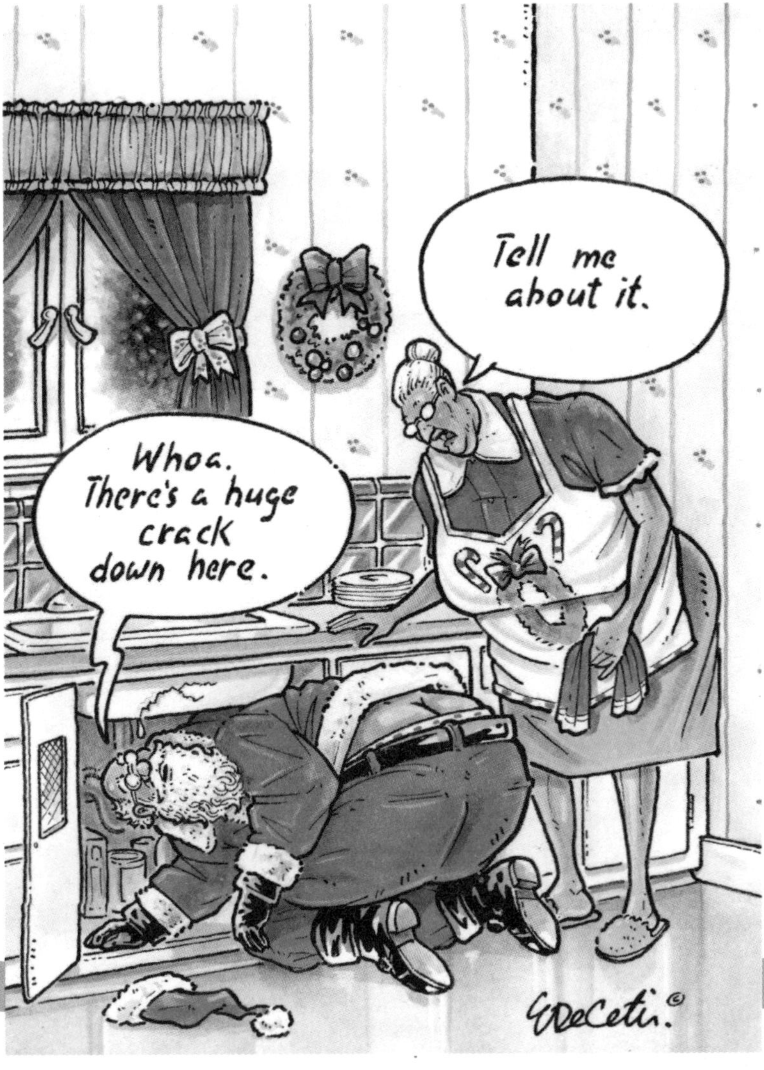
Tell me about it.
Whoa. There's a huge crack down here.
EDeCeti ©

Posteriore esposizione [It]:
the rear, behind; as in the buttocks; a rear exposure.

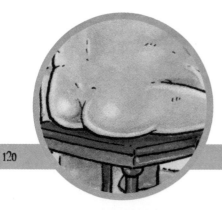

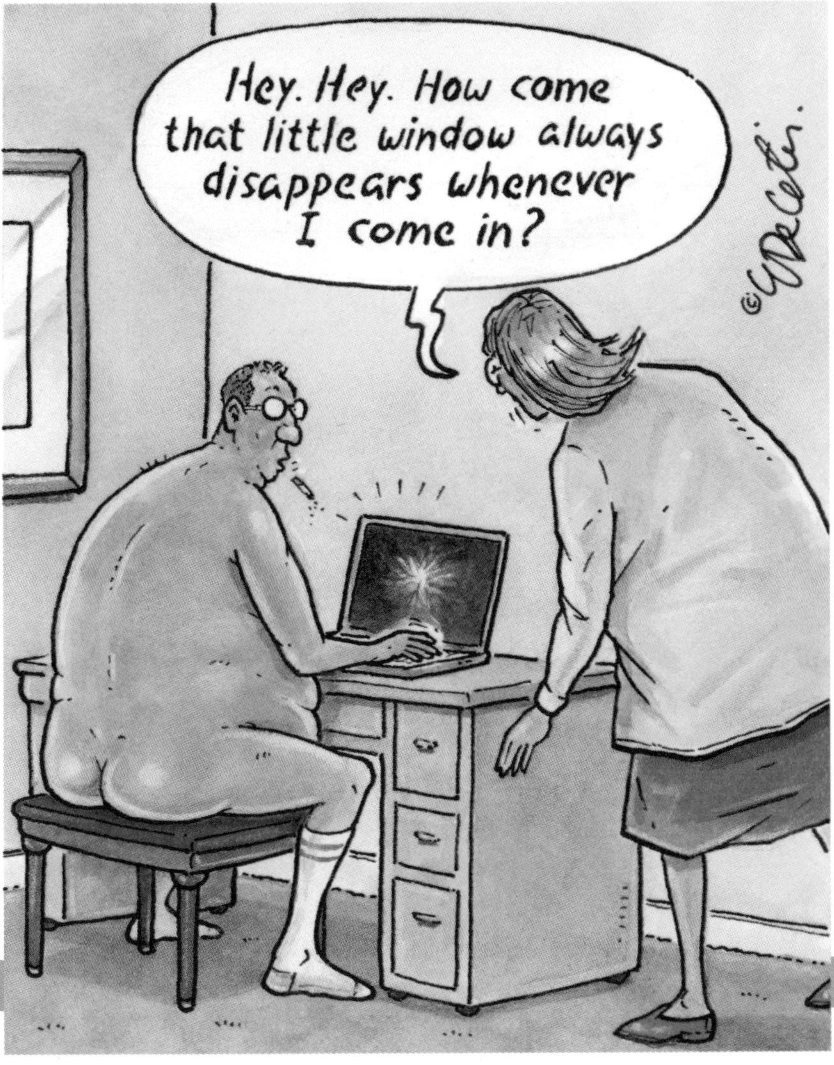
Hey. Hey. How come that little window always disappears whenever I come in?

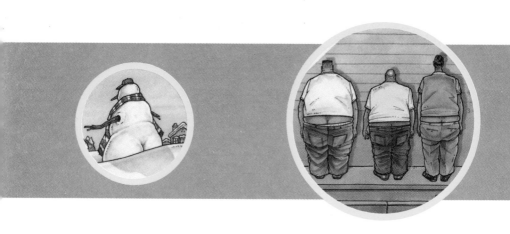

Chapter Three:
I'm with Stupid

Crack [krâk]:
an opportunity to get revenge.

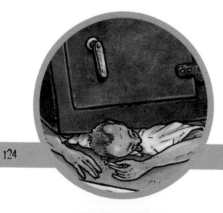

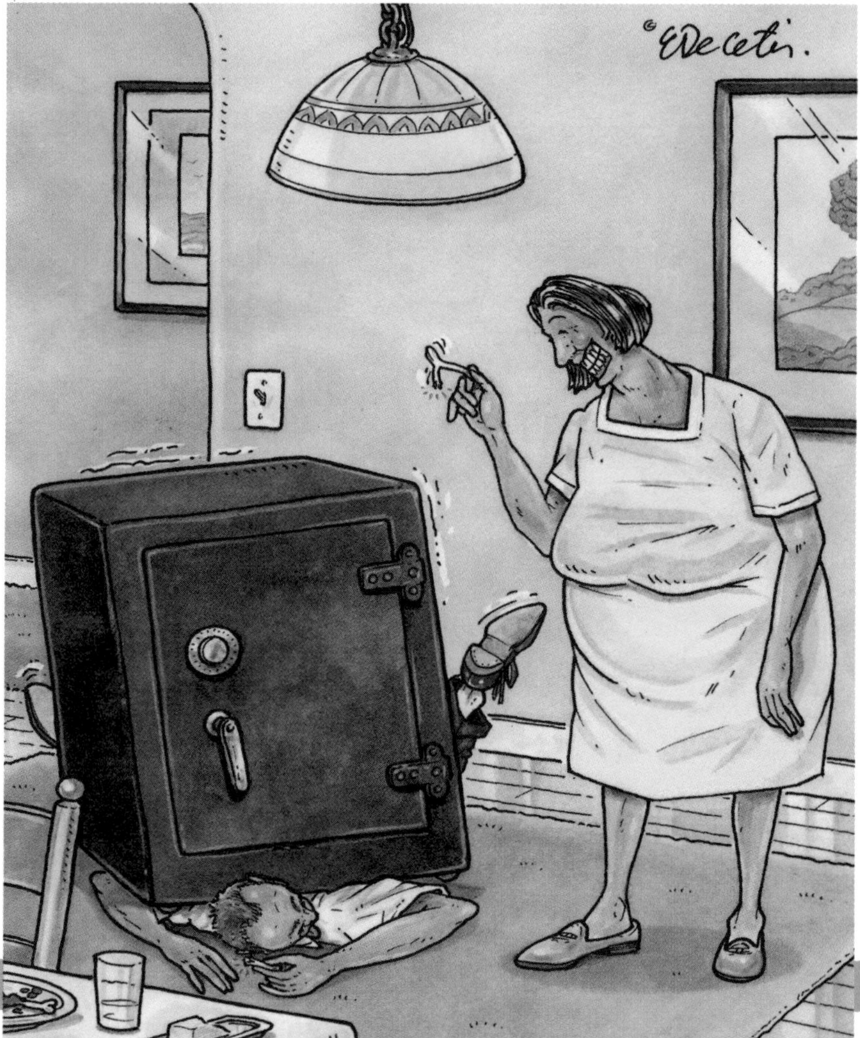
©EDeCeti.

Ass [as]:
a stupid, foolish, or stubborn person.

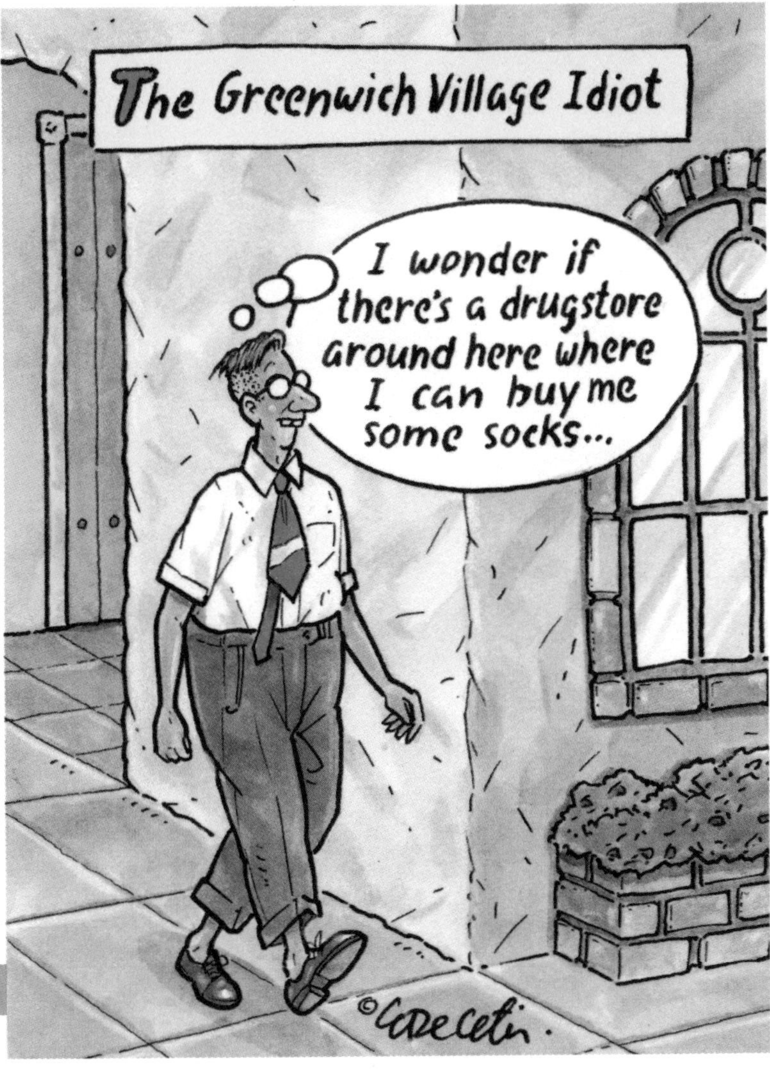
The Greenwich Village Idiot
I wonder if there's a drugstore around here where I can buy me some socks...
©Cotecetin

Crack [krâk]:
a usually brief attempt which does not always work out.

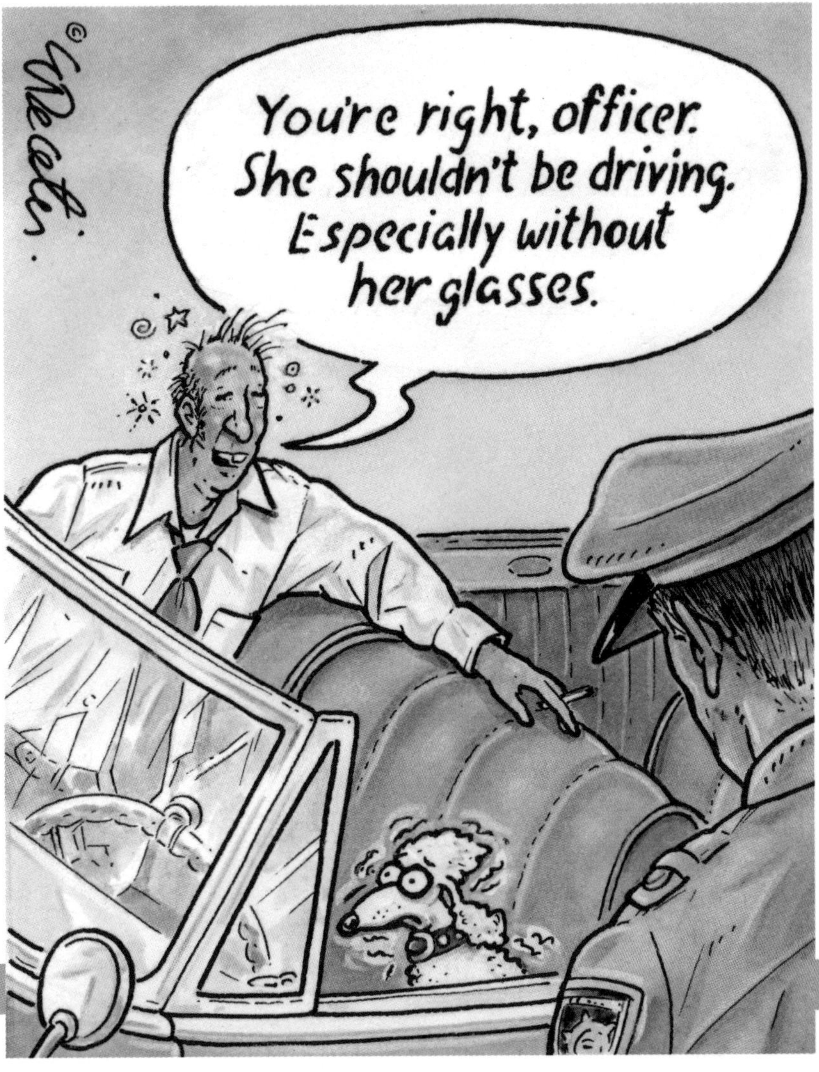
You're right, officer. She shouldn't be driving. Especially without her glasses.

Rückseite [G]:
backside; the region you should be cautious of
before making certain comments.

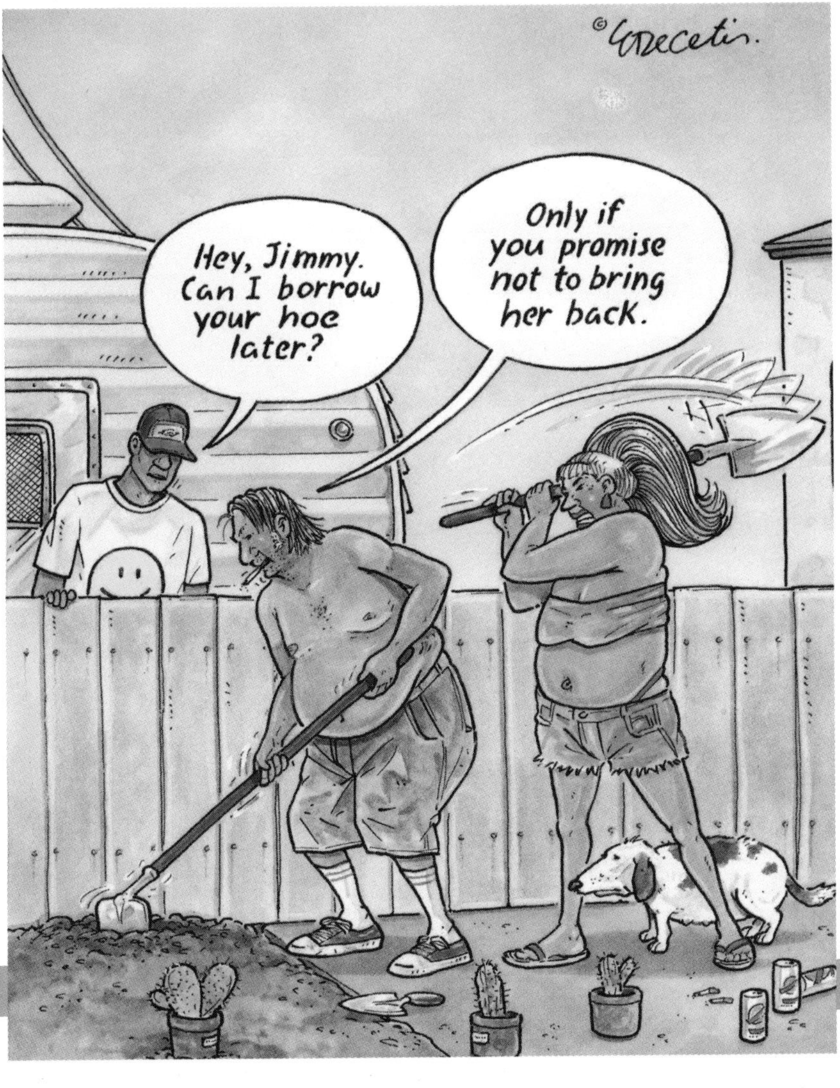
©Loreceti.
Hey, Jimmy. Can I borrow your hoe later?
Only if you promise not to bring her back.

Cracked [krâkd]:
crazy; mad.

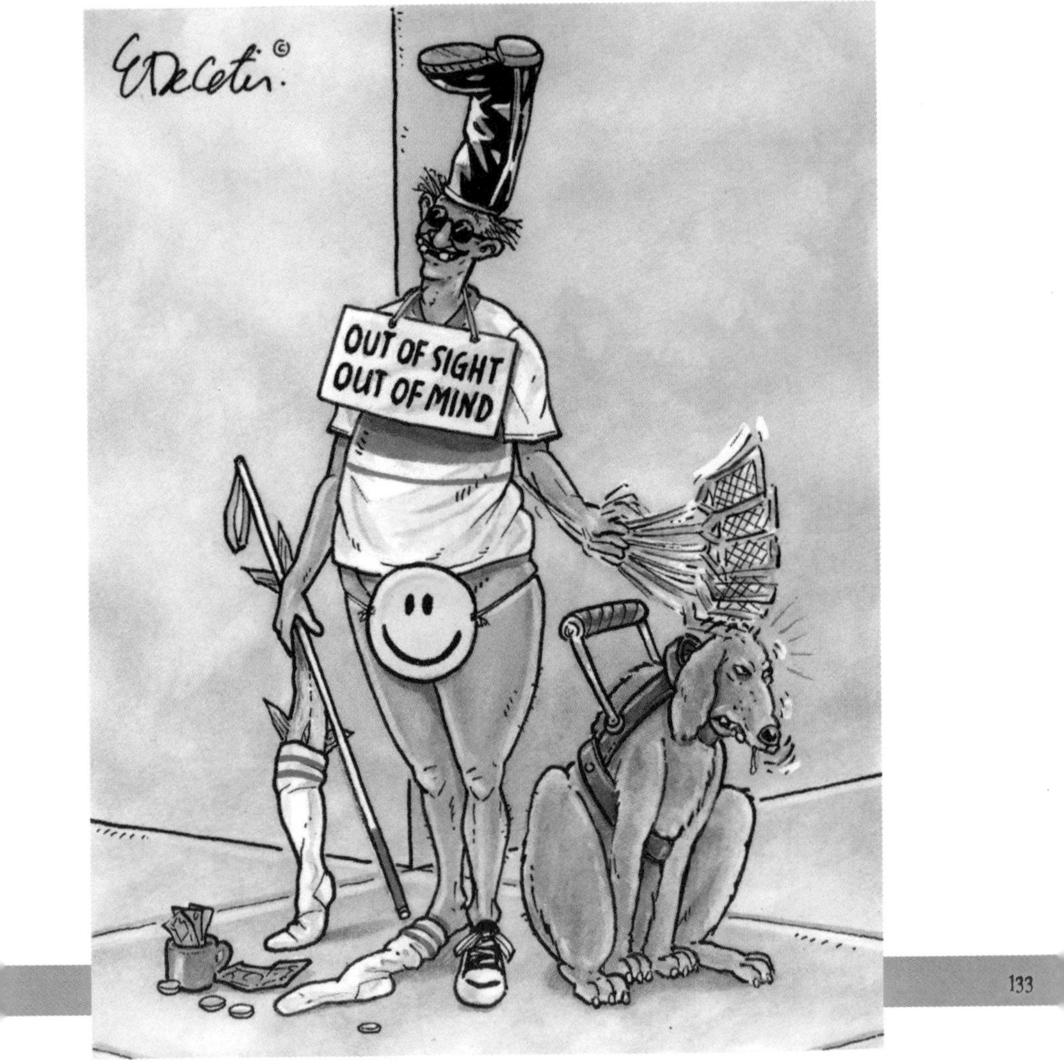
EDeCotis ©
OUT OF SIGHT
OUT OF MIND

Crack [krâk]:
to make a remark; to tell a joke.

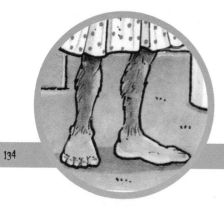

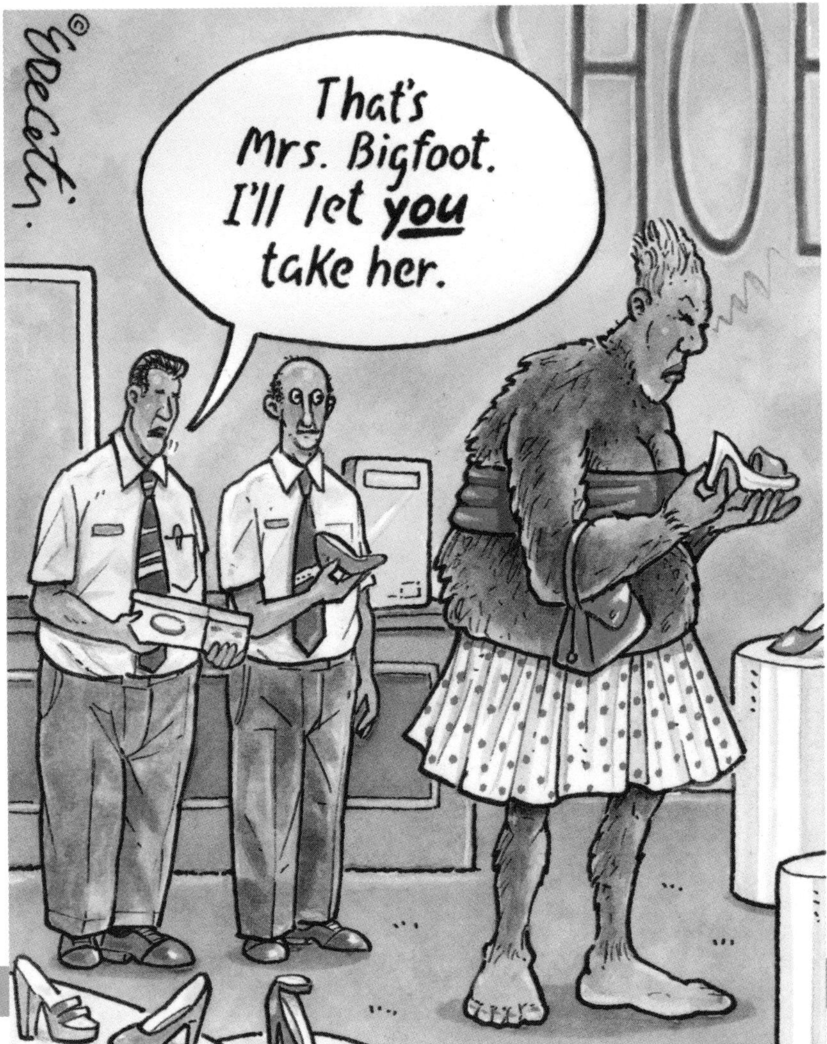
That's Mrs. Bigfoot. I'll let you take her.

Crack-up [krâk up]:
mentally unsound state; a breakdown.

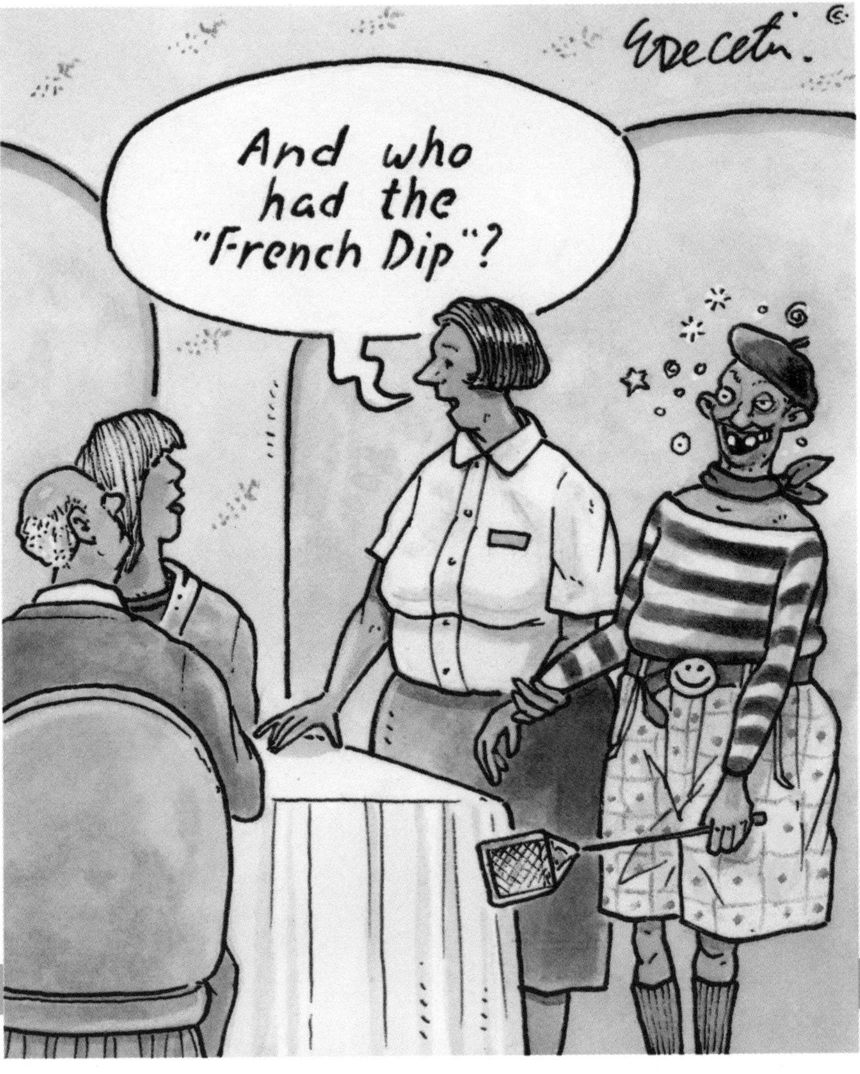
And who had the "French Dip"?

Ass [as]:
a fool; an idiot.

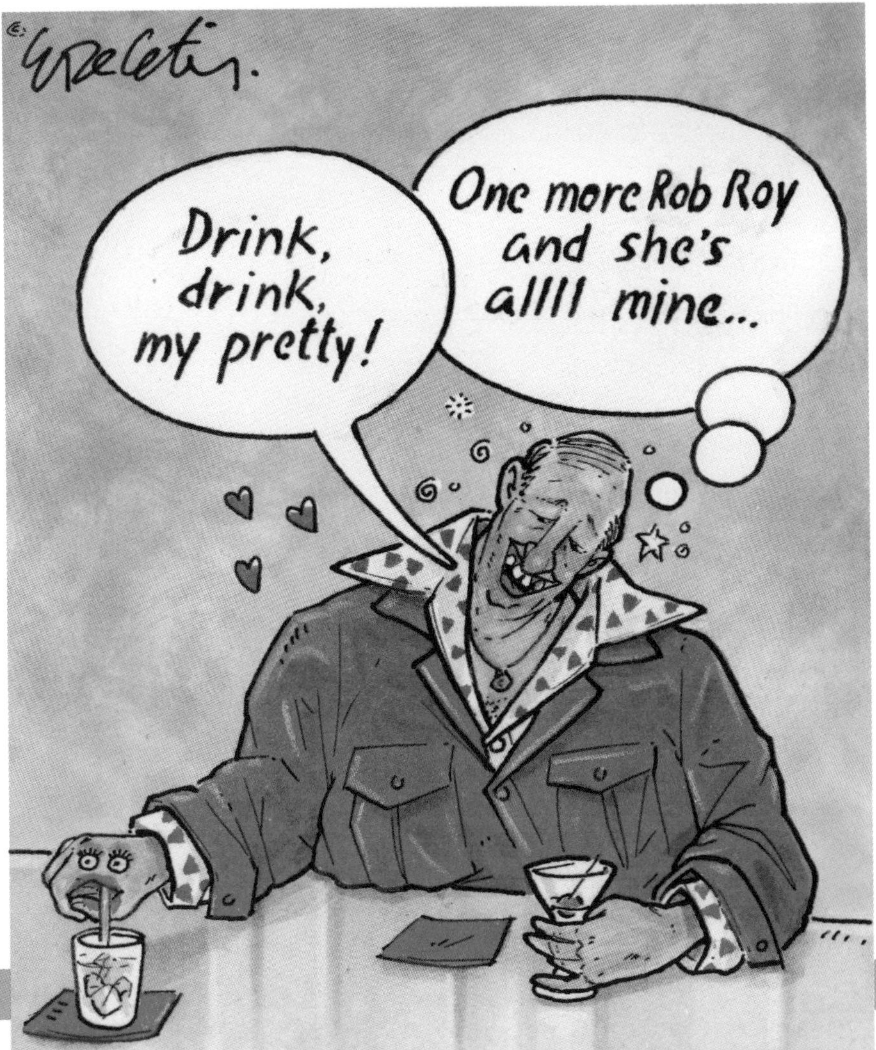
Drink,
drink,
my pretty!
One more Rob Roy
and she's
allll mine...

Hulgus [Et]:
bum; not always the buttocks region.

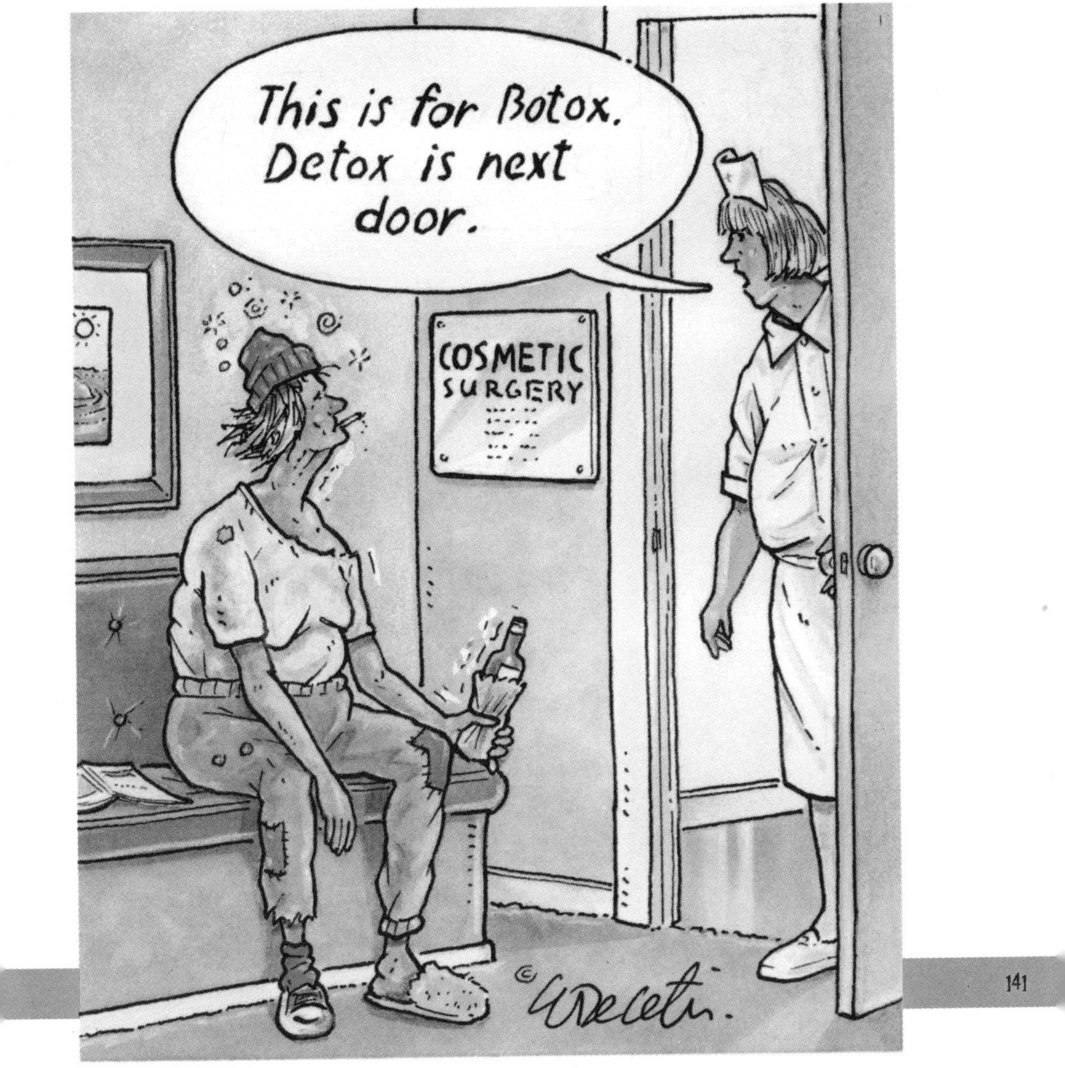
This is for Botox. Detox is next door.
COSMETIC SURGERY

Crack [krâk]:
attempt; try but not always succeed with intended look.

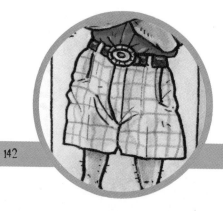

Cowboy boots and Bermuda shorts:
Sartorial suicide for the unsuspecting Nathan.

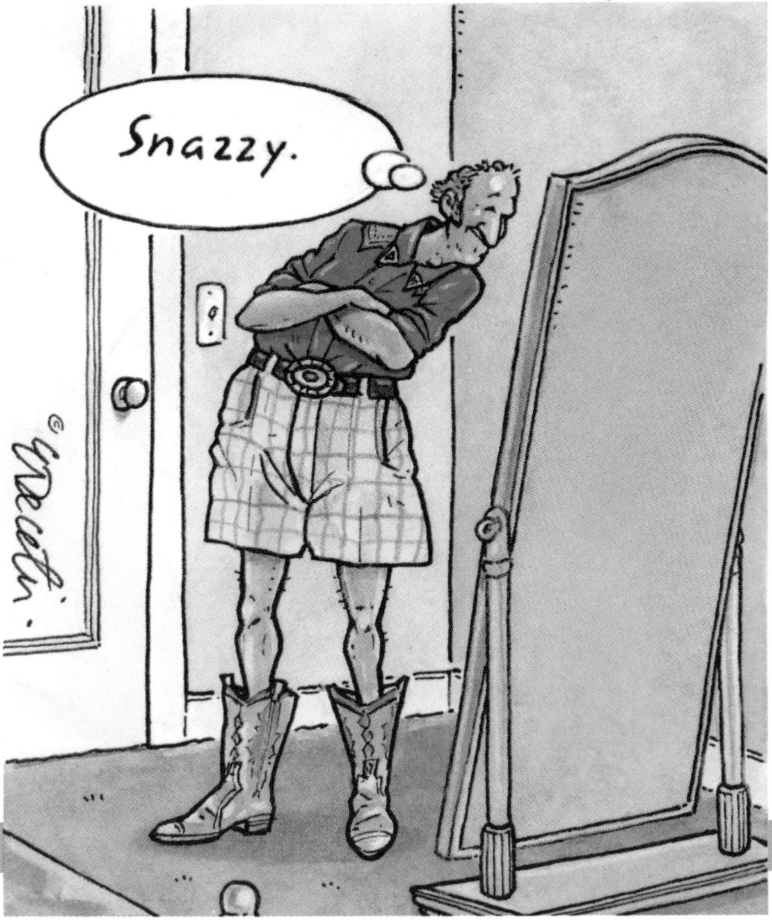
Snazzy.
© Vecchi.

Back side [bak-sahyd]:
the rear or back part or view of an object, person, scene, etc.

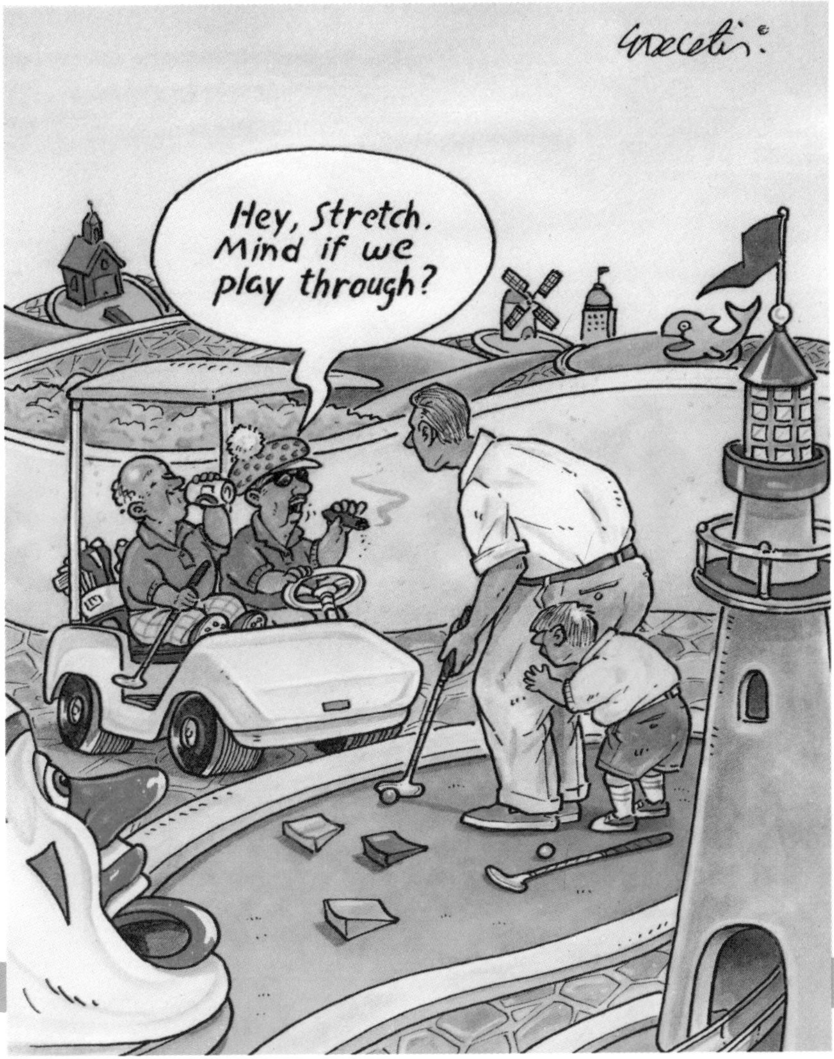
Hey, Stretch. Mind if we play through?

Crackpot [krâkpot]:
an eccentric or unconventional person.

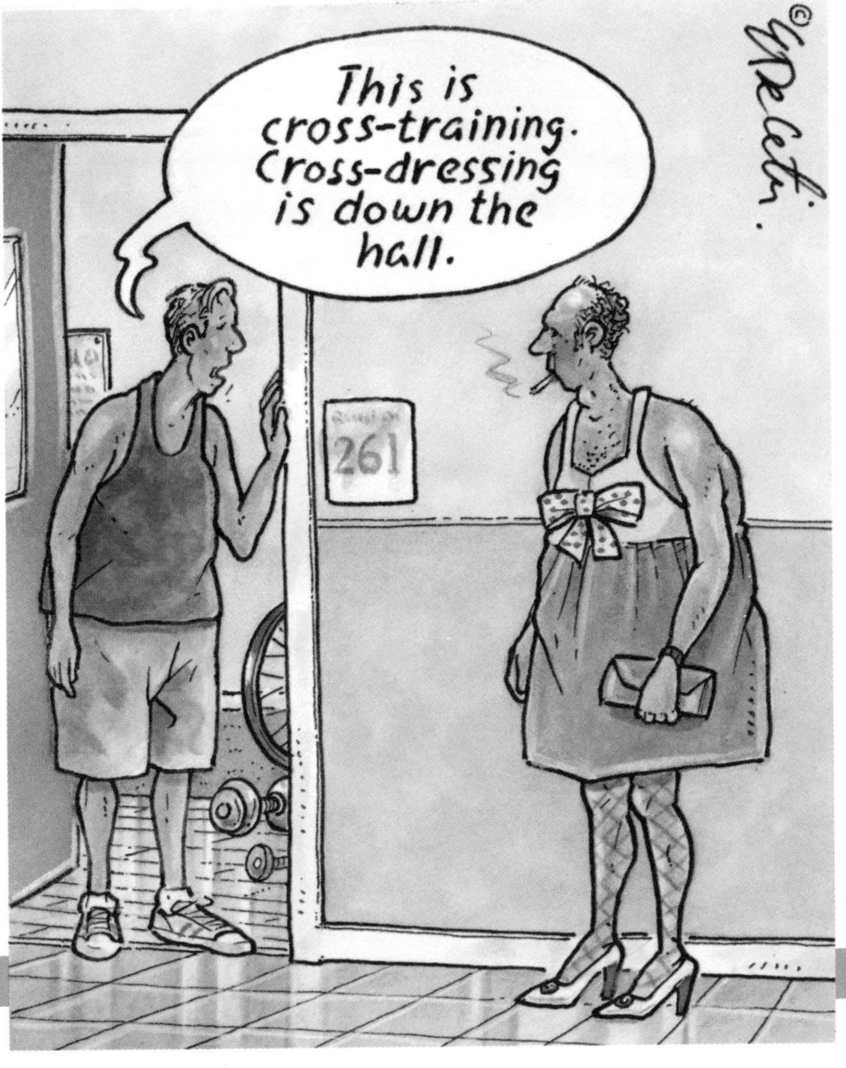
This is cross-training. Cross-dressing is down the hall.
261

Cracked [krâked]:
broken in tone, as the voice; marred by an error in judgment.

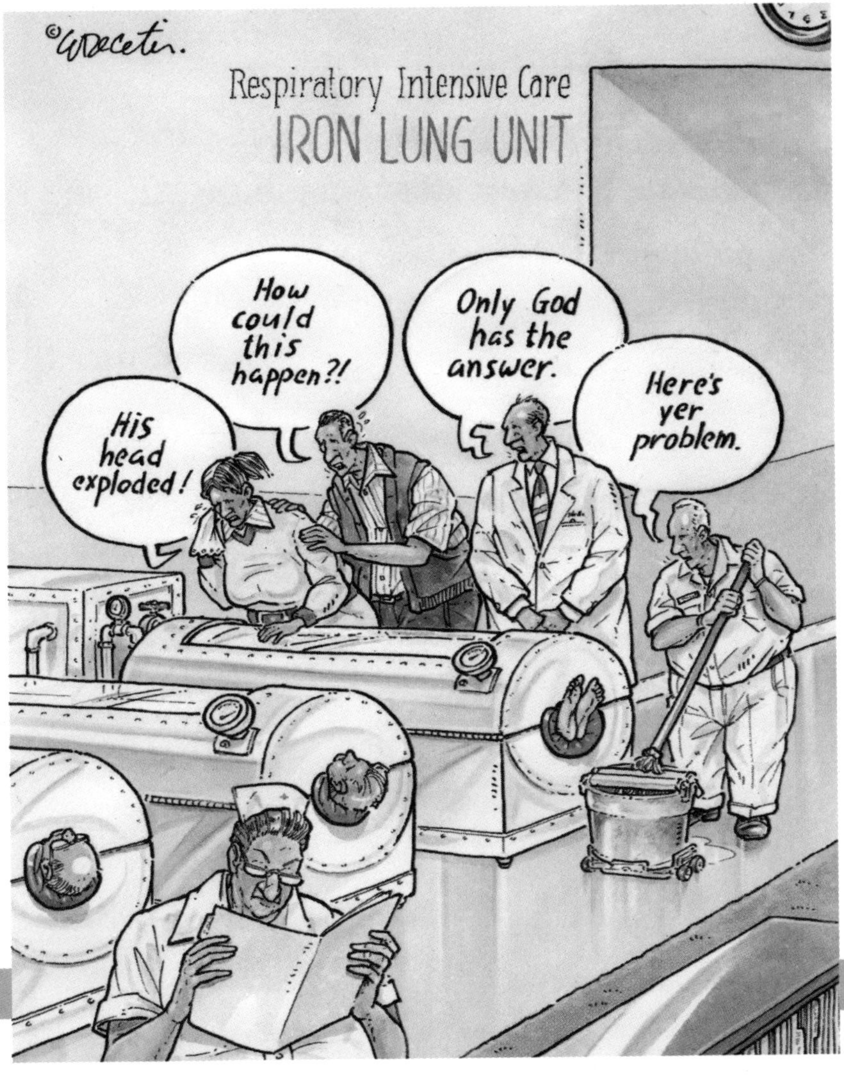
©Vodecetin.
Respiratory Intensive Care
IRON LUNG UNIT
His head exploded!
How could this happen?!
Only God has the answer.
Here's yer problem.

Gebraten dummkopf [G]:
fried ass.

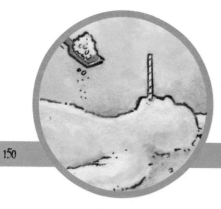

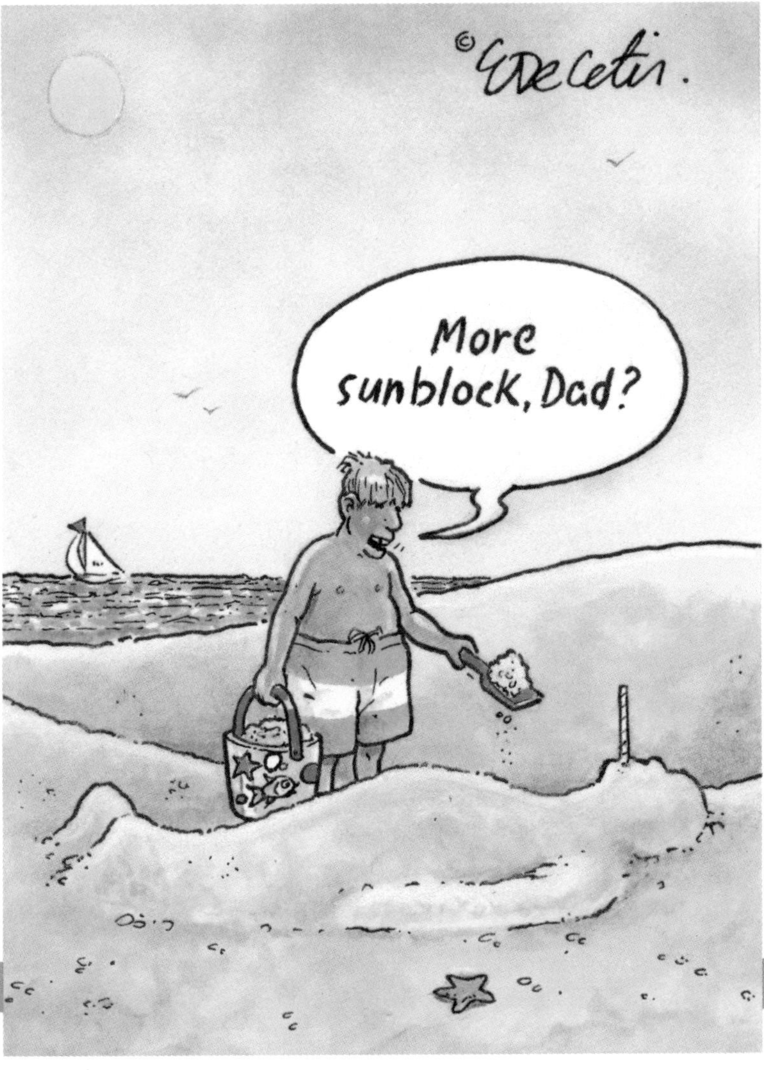
©EDeCetir.
More sunblock, Dad?

Analogien problemen [Sw]:
anal problems (enough said).

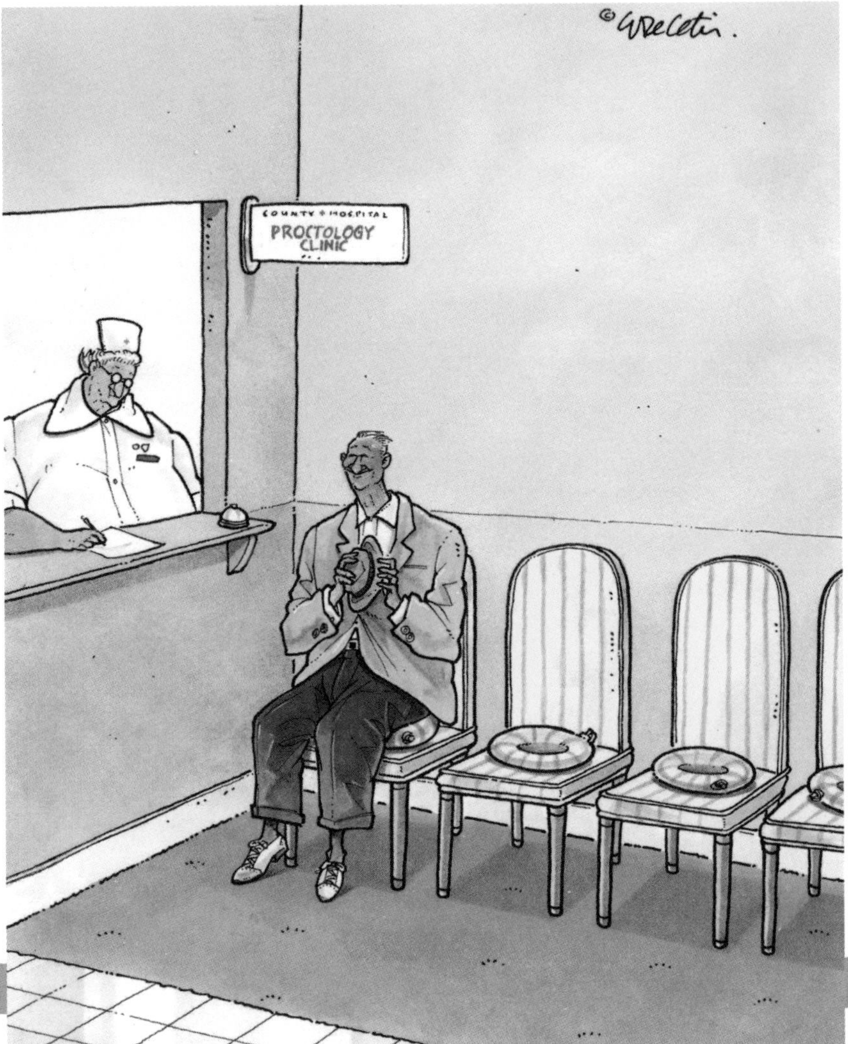
©GWeCetin.
COUNTY HOSPITAL
PROCTOLOGY
CLINIC

Crack [krâk]:

to tell, to joke; to pull pranks.

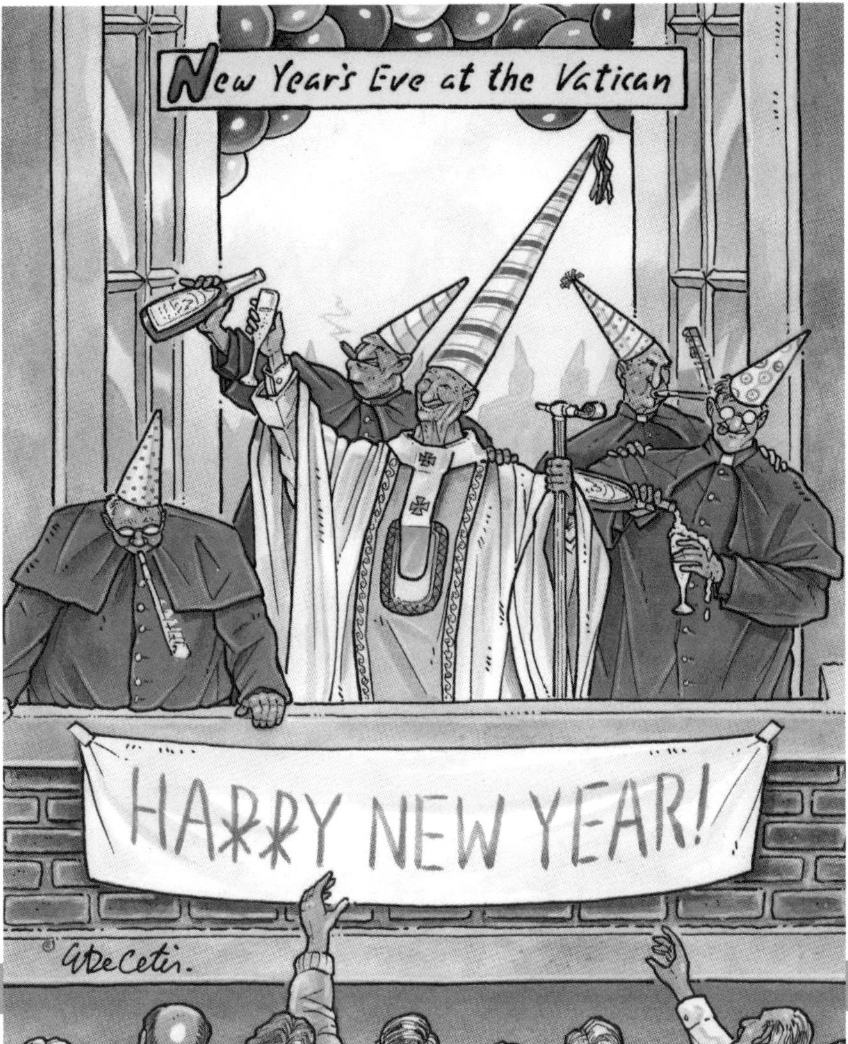
New Year's Eve at the Vatican
HA**Y NEW YEAR!
deCeti.

Crack [krâk]:
a breakdown; a change, esp. in health.

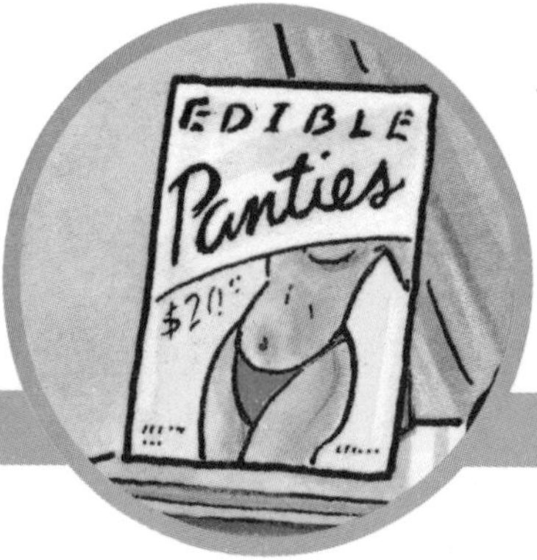
EDIBLE
Panties
$20

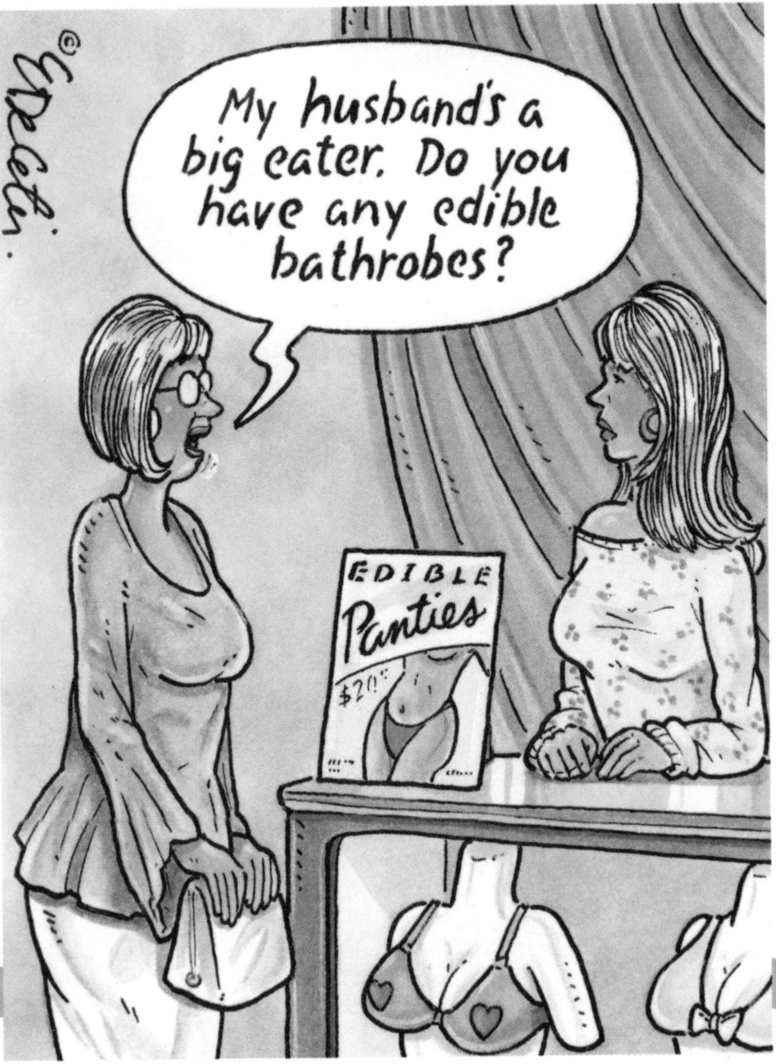
My husband's a big eater. Do you have any edible bathrobes?
EDIBLE
Panties
$20

Analog gnagsår [Norw]:
the buttocks; a place where chafing is common.

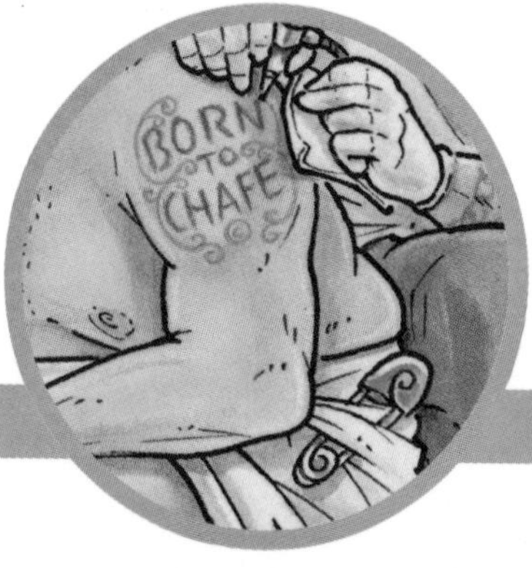
BORN
TO
CHAFE

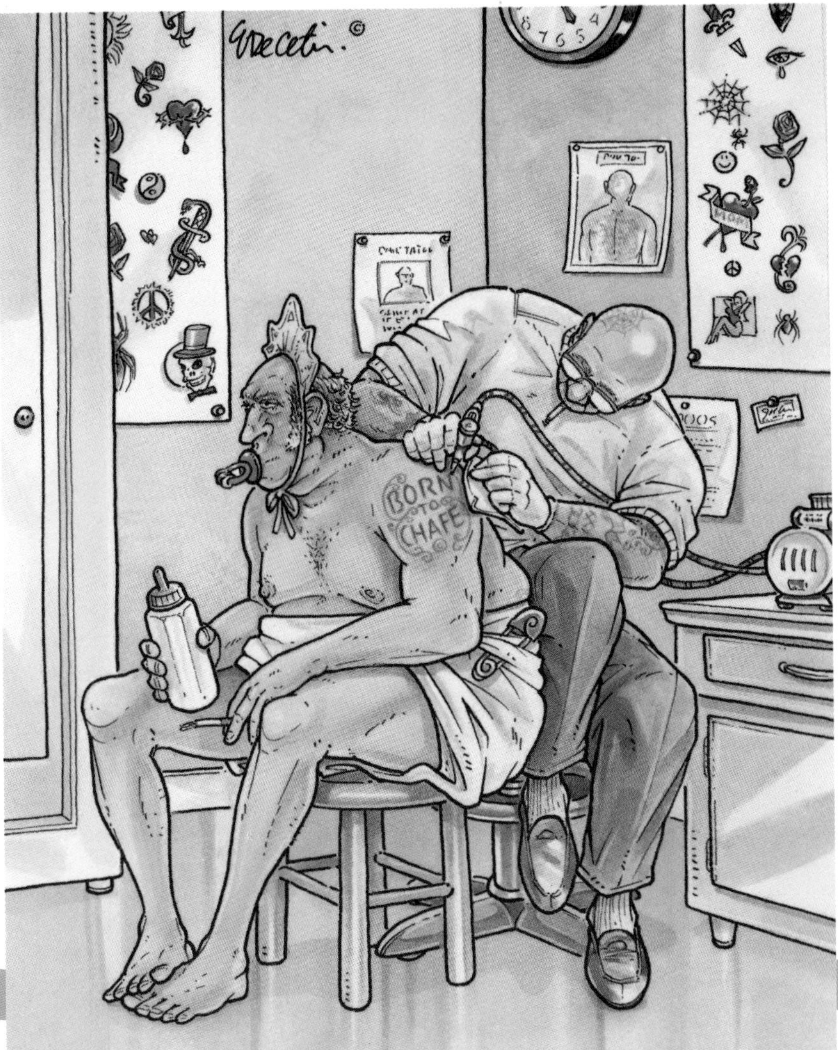
BORN TO CHAFE

Crack [krâk]:
attempt at something; that which is not always successful.

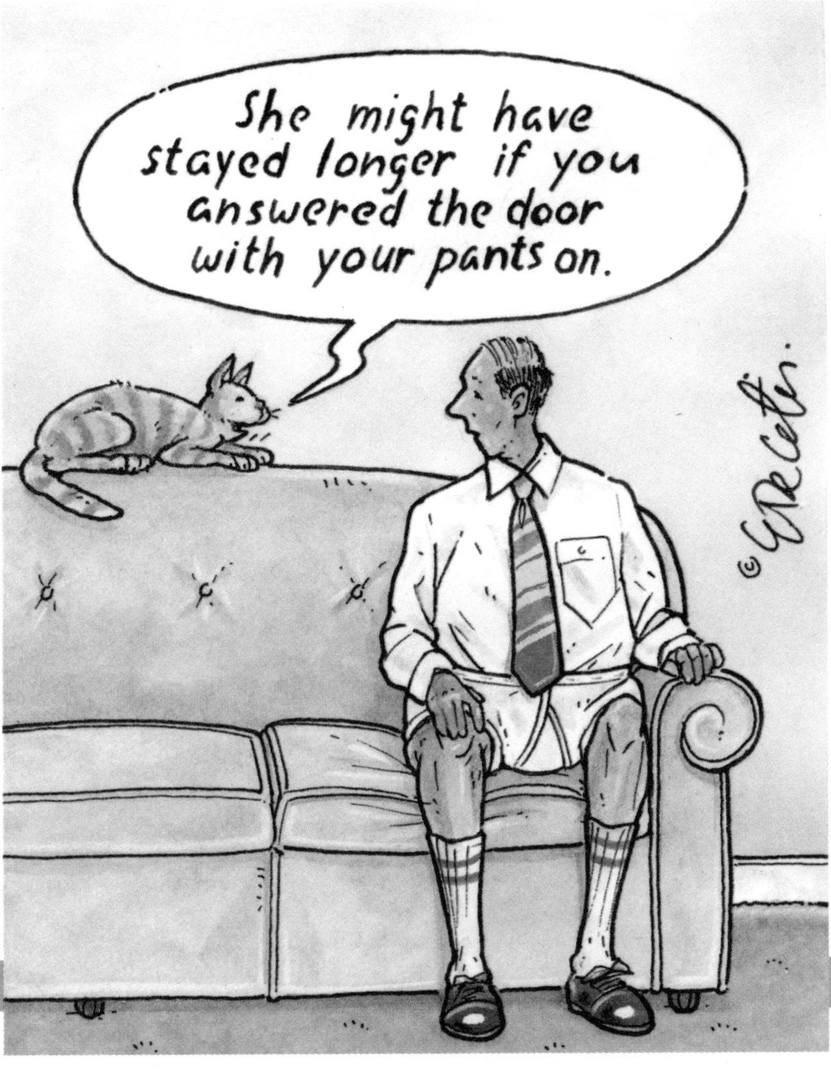
She might have stayed longer if you answered the door with your pants on.

Crack [krâk]:
a flaw or defect.

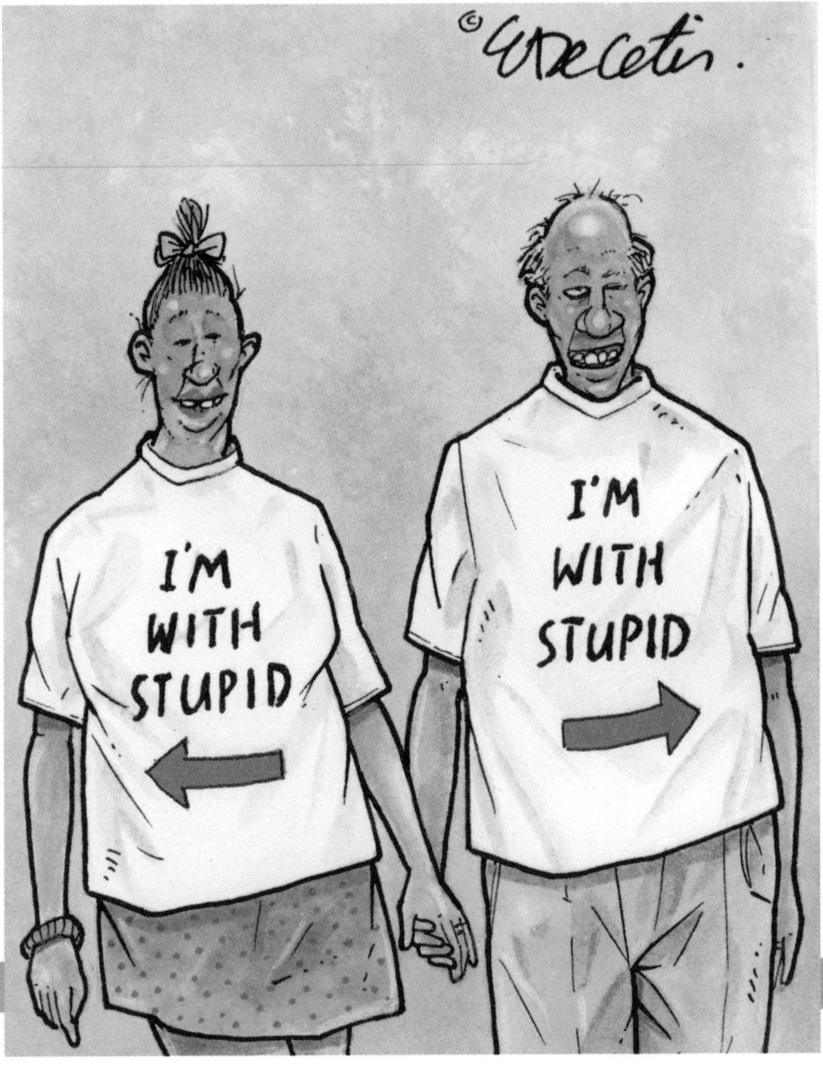
©Ed. de Cetis.
I'M WITH STUPID
I'M WITH STUPID

Crack [krâk]:

to hit; to make an attempt at something, to swing.

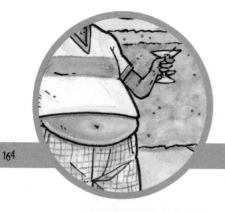

This would be Andy's first and last day as golf instructor at Sunset Oaks Country Club.

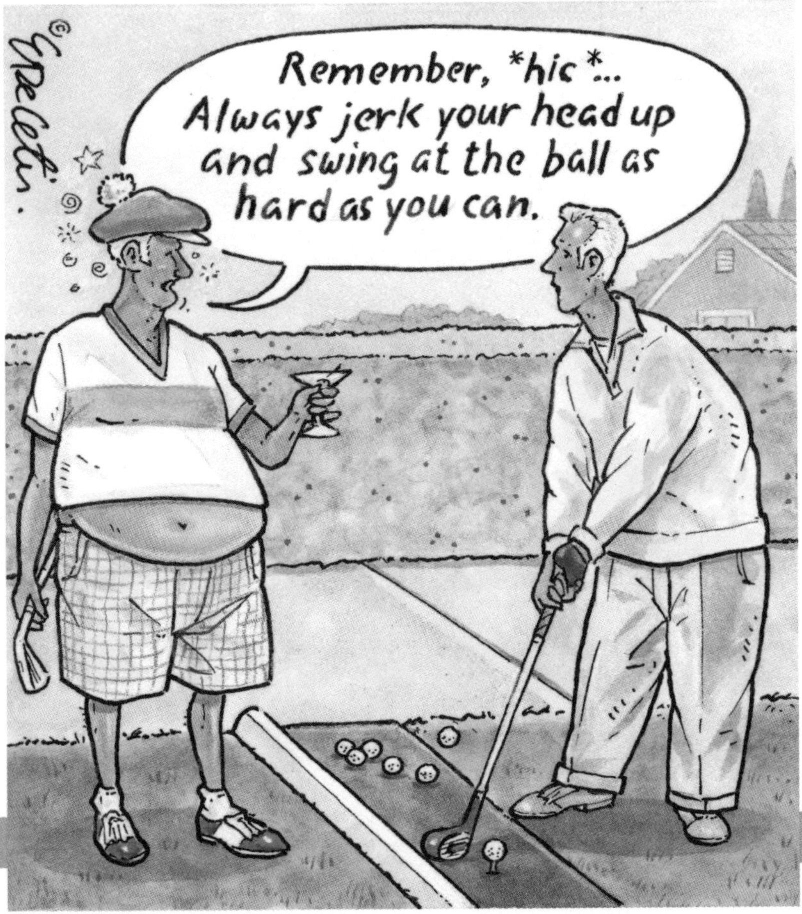
Remember, *hic*... Always jerk your head up and swing at the ball as hard as you can.

Can [kan]:

the buttocks; an exposure not always suited for public events.

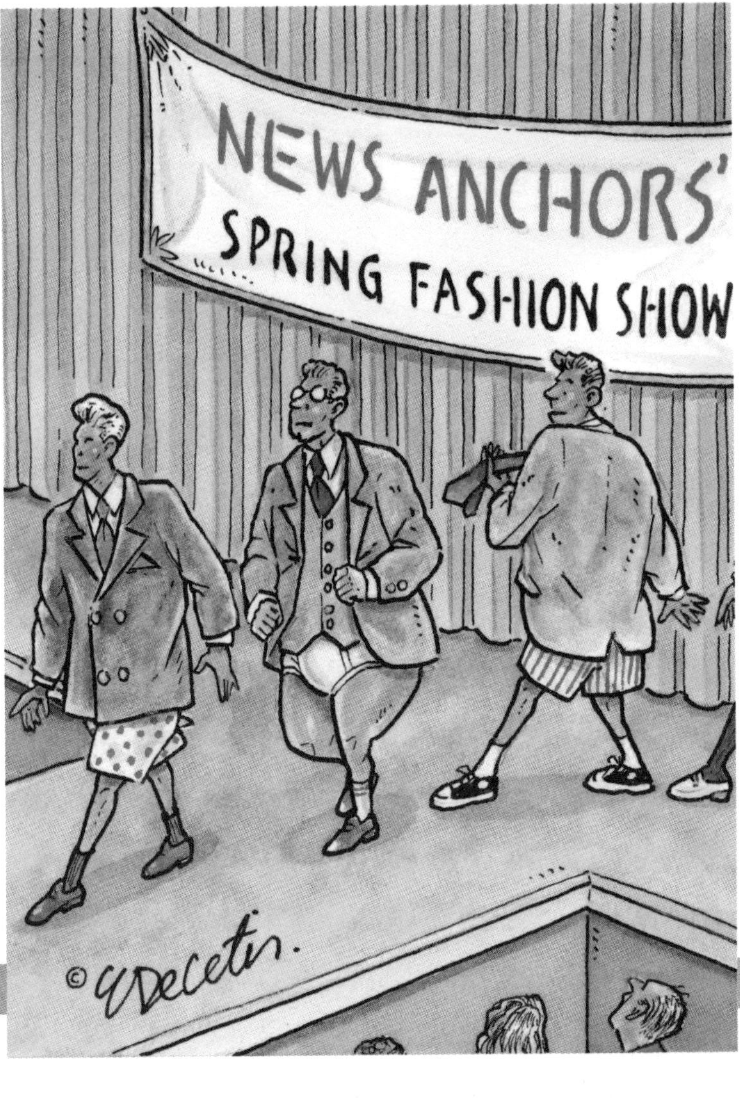
NEWS ANCHORS'
SPRING FASHION SHOW
© E. Decetis.

Crack [krâk]:
to tell (a joke); to take a witty action.

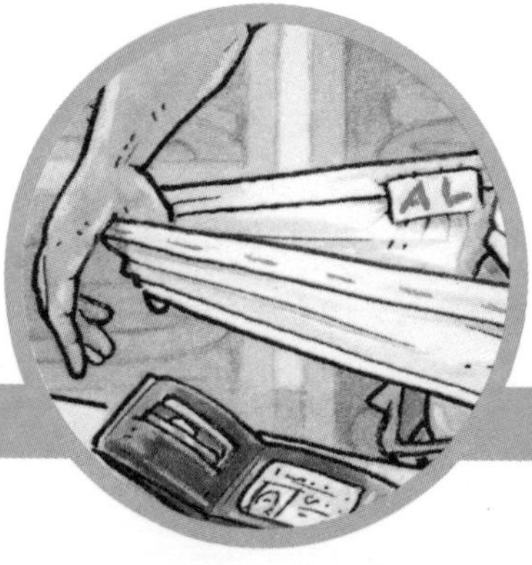
AL

Al was happy to provide the clerk with a second form of ID.

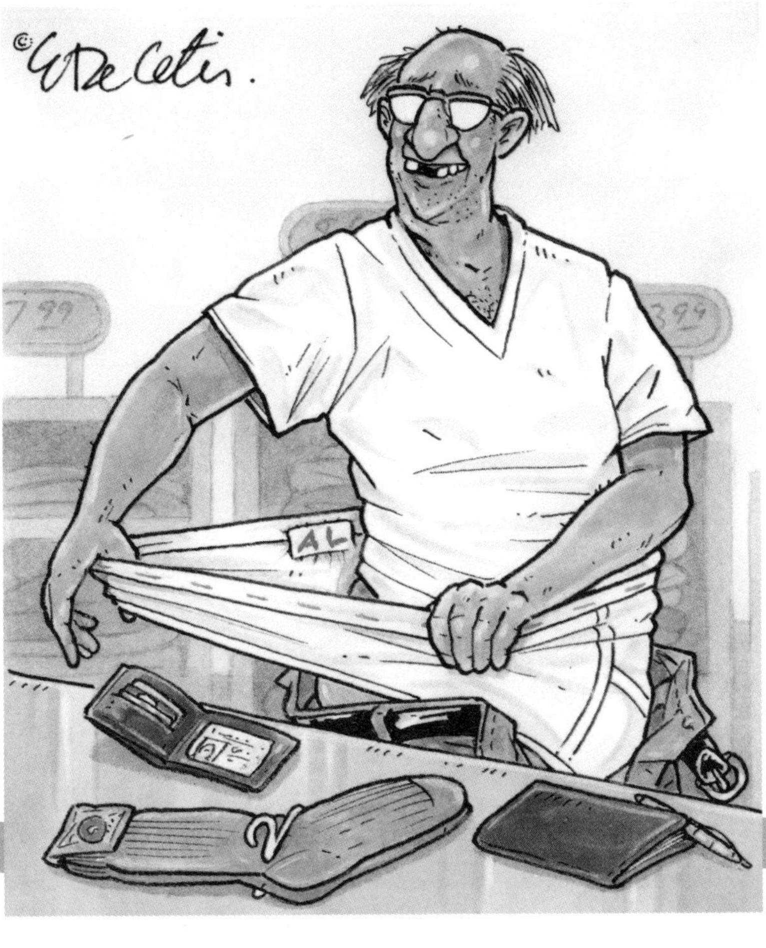
AL

Hátsó hajítás [Hung]:
the buttocks or rear; the ass and what comes out of it.

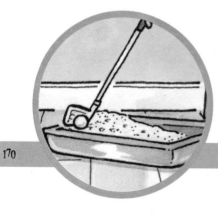

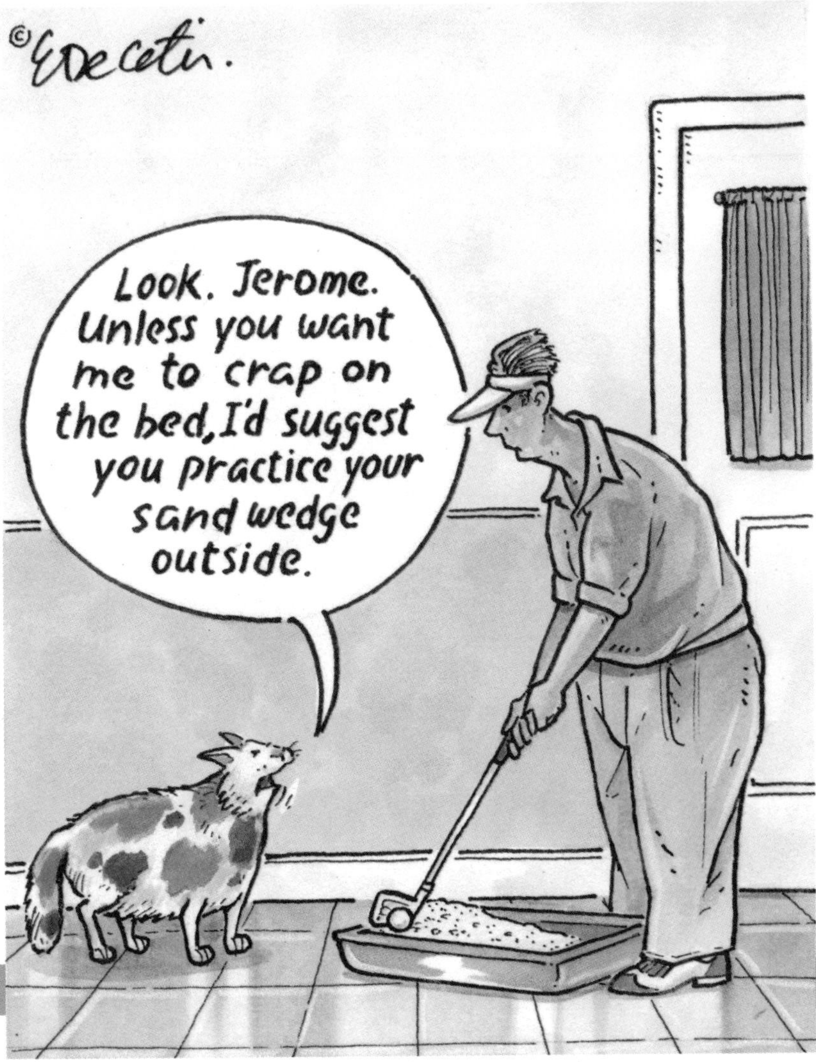
©EDeCetin.
Look. Jerome. Unless you want me to crap on the bed, I'd suggest you practice your sand wedge outside.

Crack [krâk]:

in chemistry, to decompose as a result of being subjected to heat.

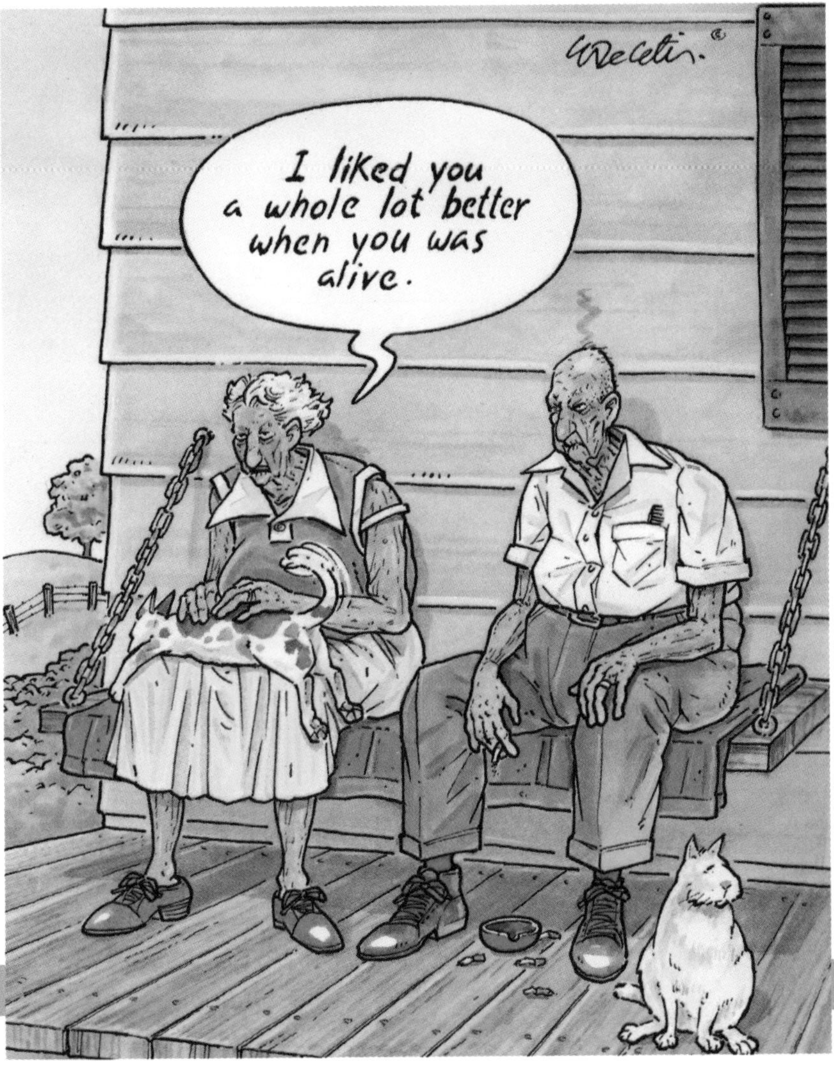
I liked you a whole lot better when you was alive.

Ass [as]:
the fleshy part of the human body that one sits on.

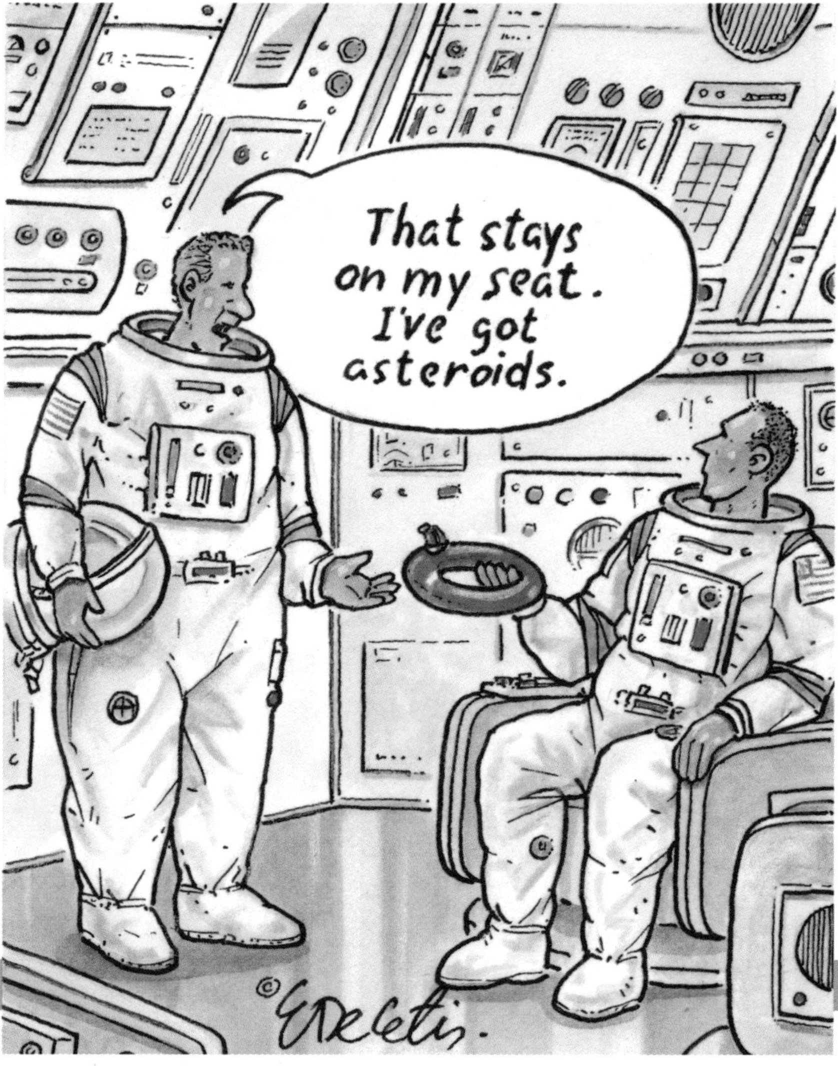
That stays on my seat. I've got asteroids.

Delik [Turk]:
the ass hole; a hole, vent, or opening;
often a place not meant for insertion.

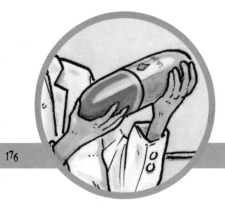

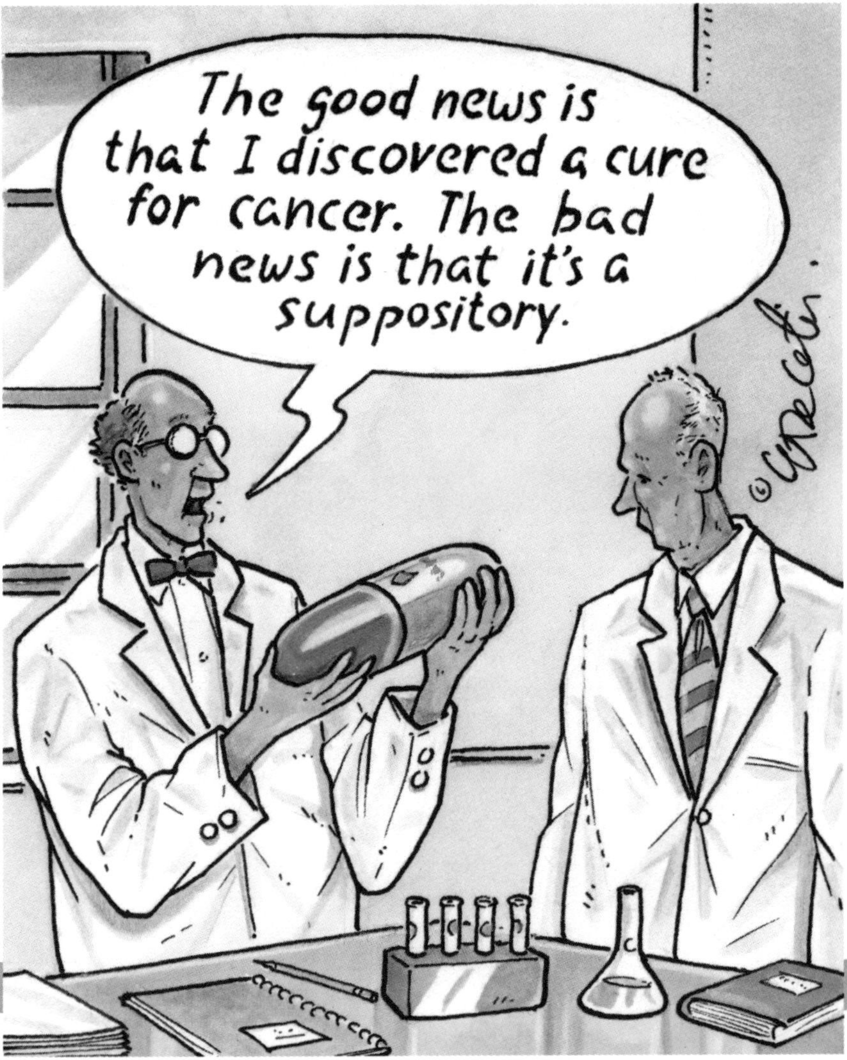
The good news is that I discovered a cure for cancer. The bad news is that it's a suppository.
©Cotham

Chapter Four:
By the Light of the Moon

Måne [Dan]:
the buttocks; the act of flashing a moon (ass).

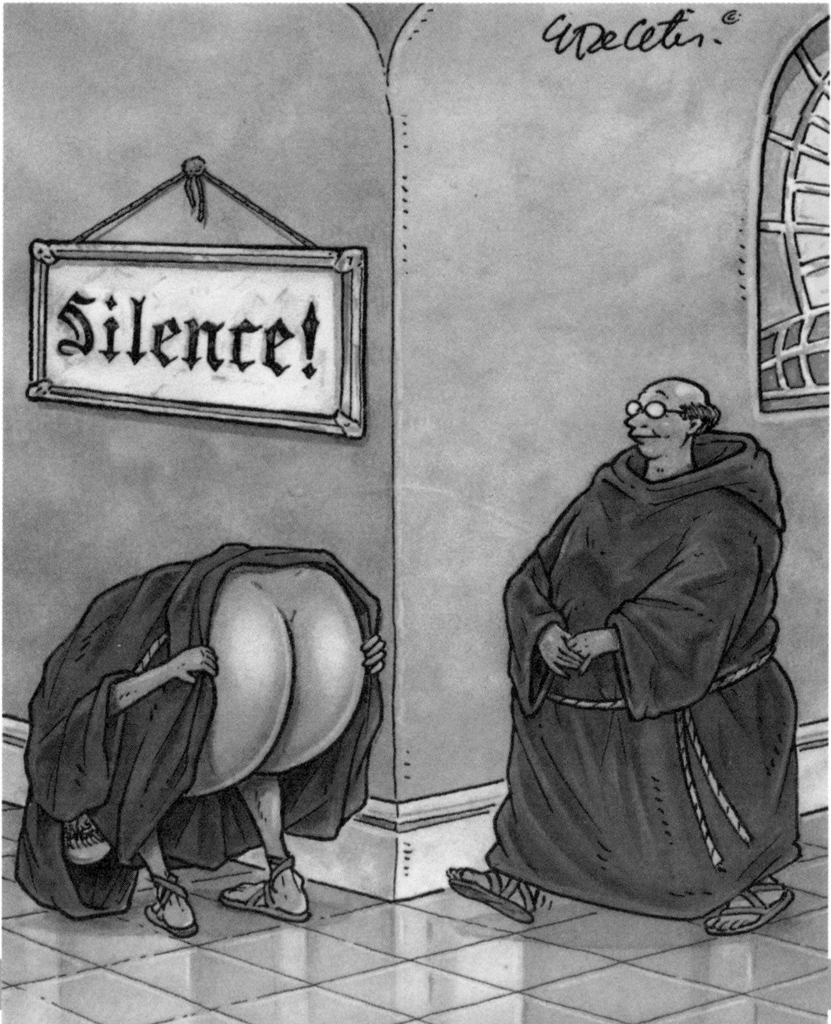
Silence!

Crack [krâk]:
to amuse, joke; to crack a joke.

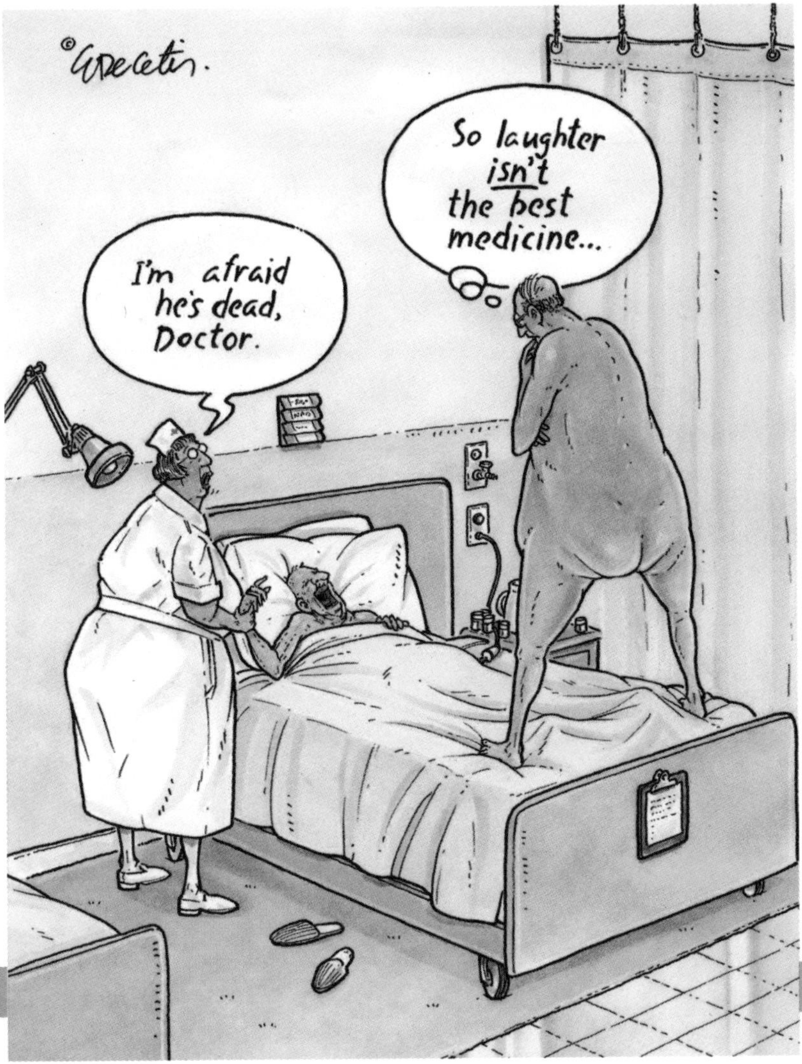
©Wrecetin.
I'm afraid he's dead, Doctor.
So laughter isn't the best medicine...

Crackle [krâkəl]:
to make short, sharp noises.

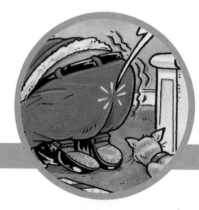

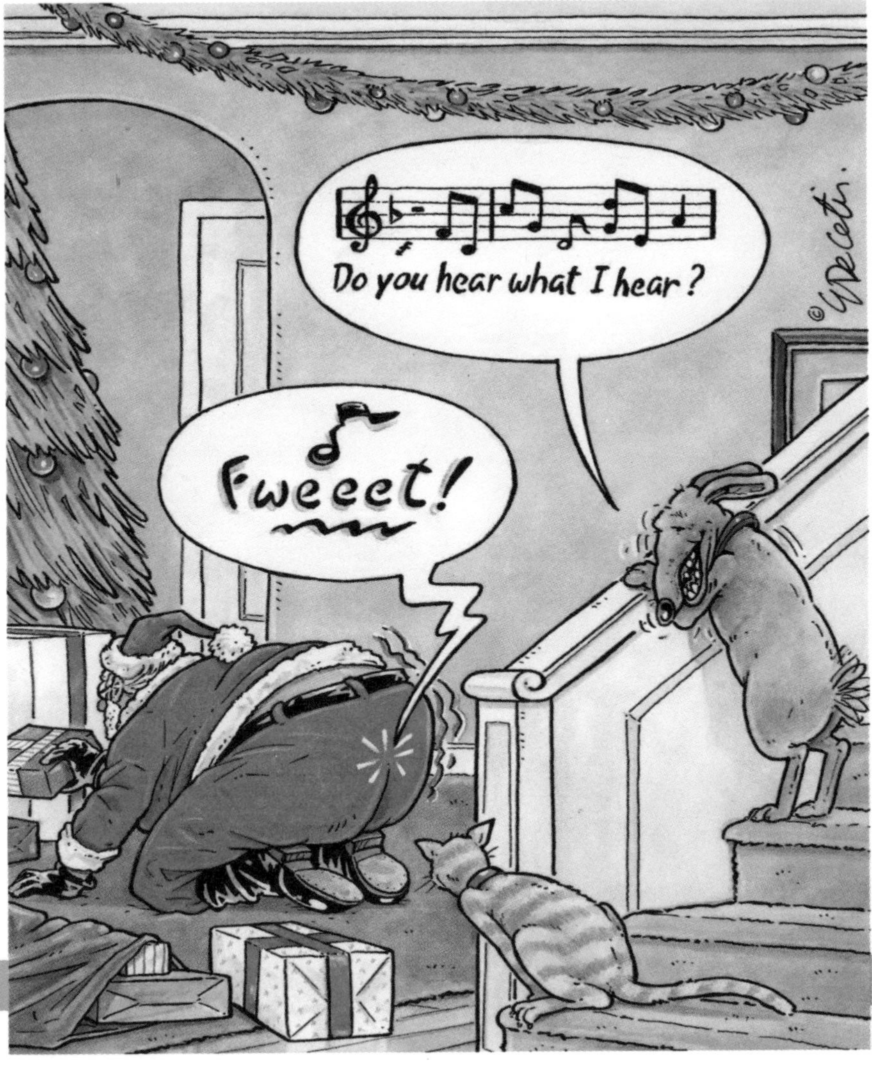
Do you hear what I hear?
Fweeet!
©GDeceti

A il posteriore di [It]:
at the rear of something; where one can decorate.

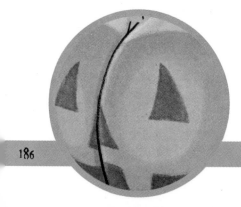

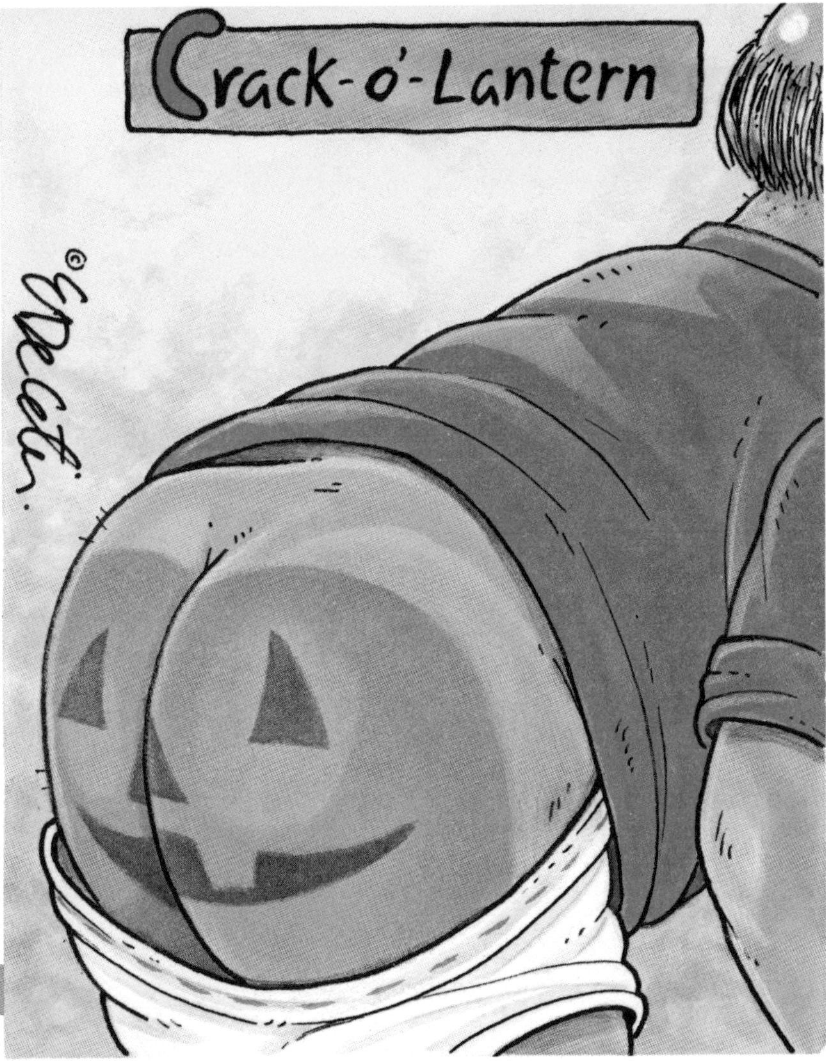
Crack-o'-Lantern
© EDeCeta.

À revers [Fr]:
at the rear or where something protrudes from the rear.

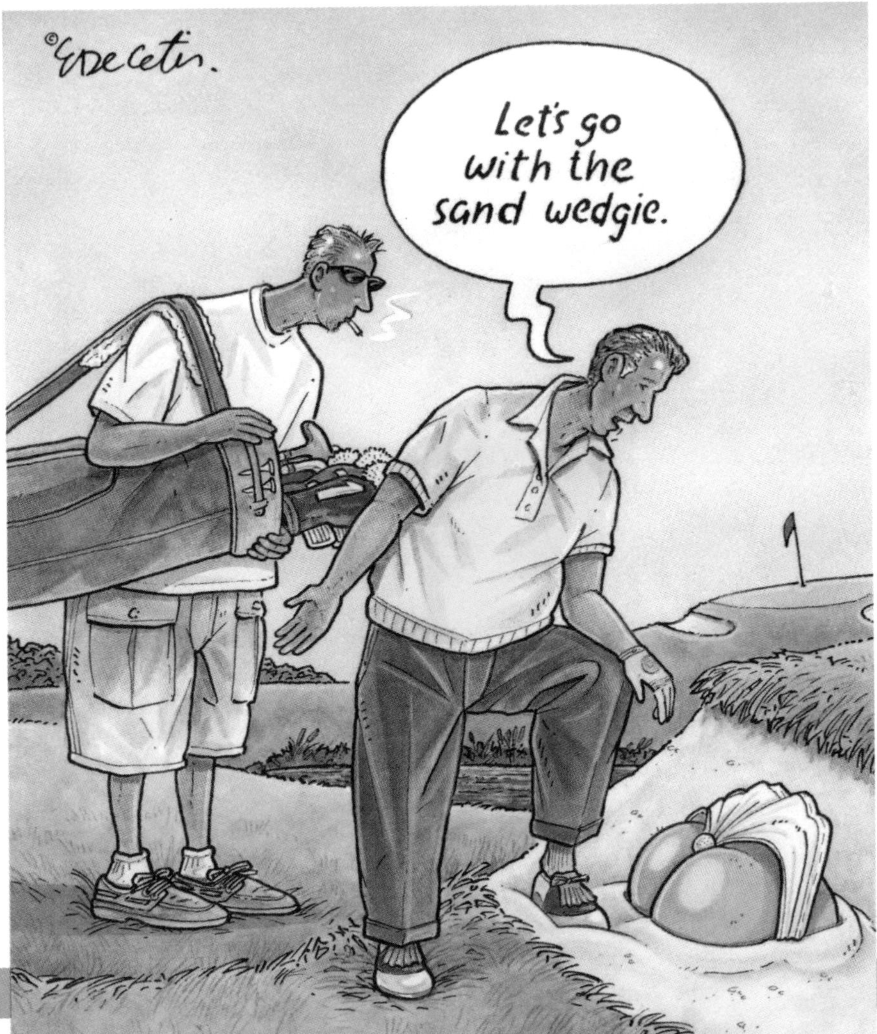
Let's go
with the
sand wedgie.

Fanny [fan-ee]:
the buttocks; a region that always looks better in pictures.

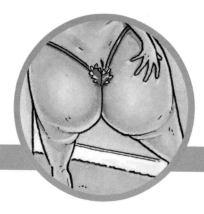

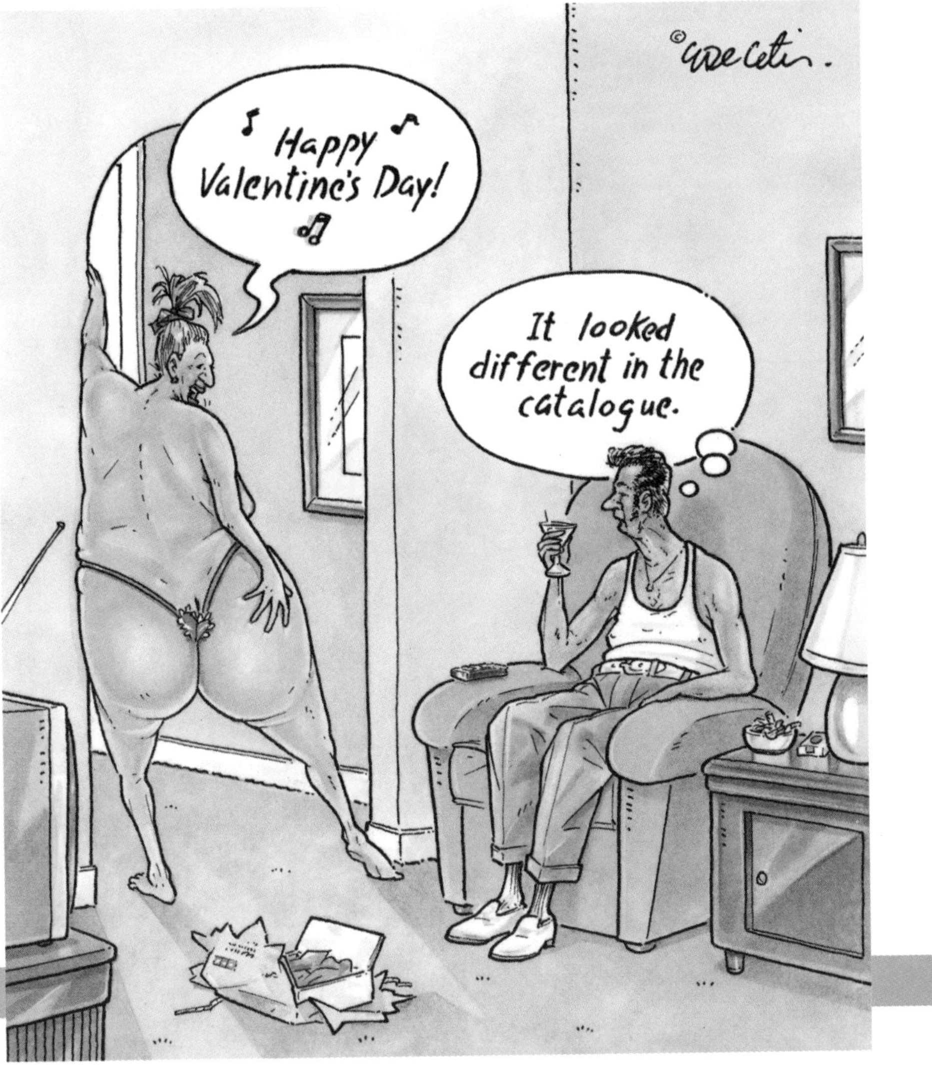
©Lyle Cetin.
Happy Valentine's Day!
It looked different in the catalogue.

Rump [ruhmp]:
the rear part of the body; area generally not displayed in public.

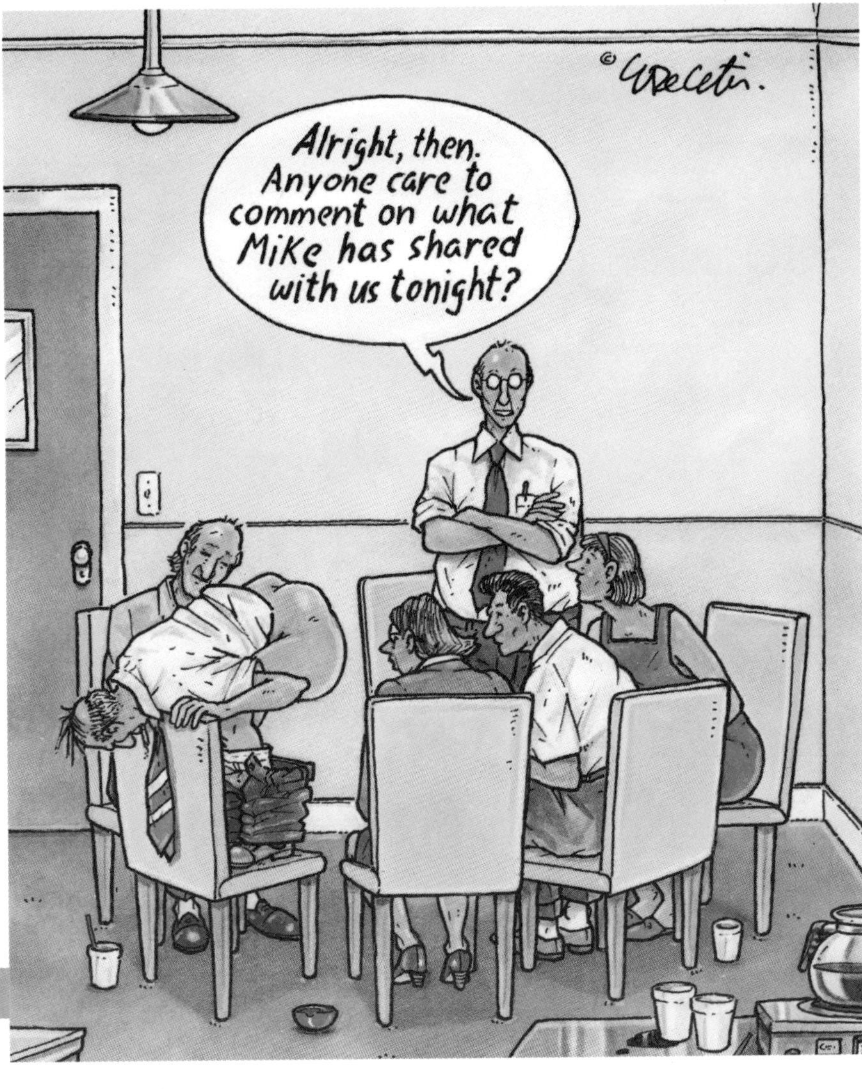
©Gregoretti.
Alright, then. Anyone care to comment on what Mike has shared with us tonight?

Altáj [Hung]:
rear end or the exposure of private parts.

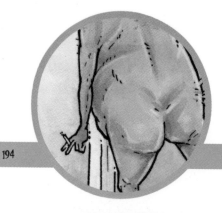

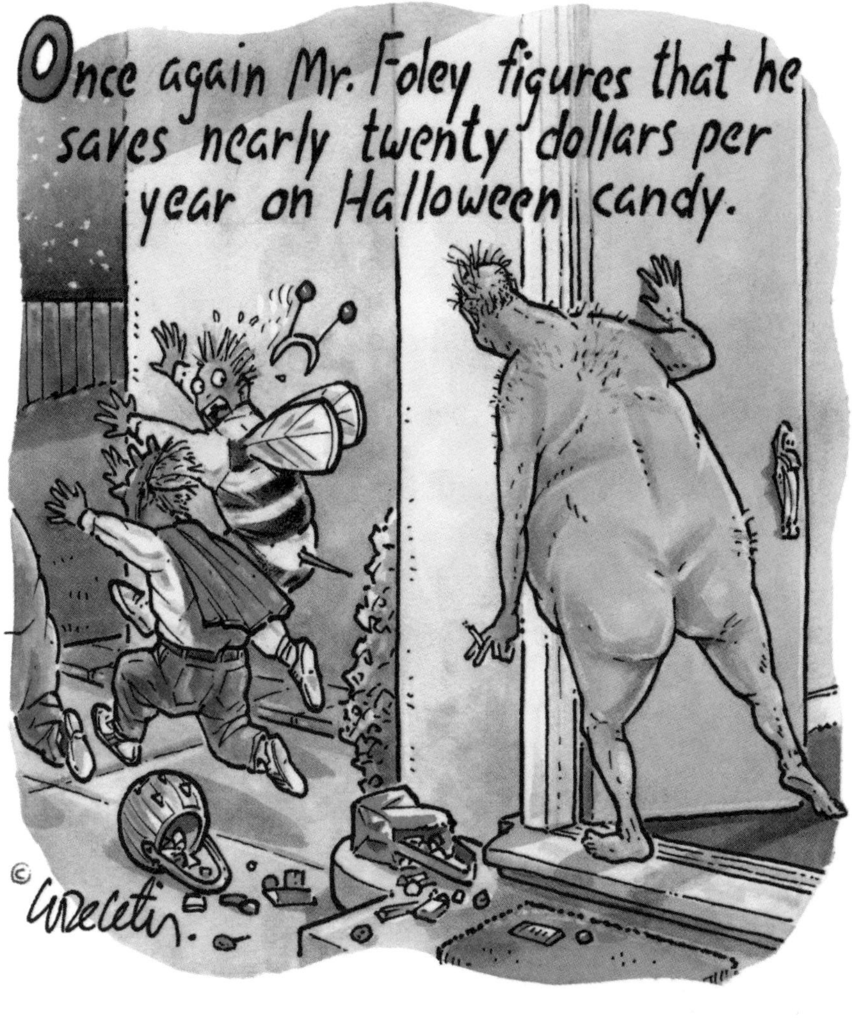
Once again Mr. Foley figures that he saves nearly twenty dollars per year on Halloween candy.

Crack [krâk]:
a break or fissure, common in fruits and vegetables.

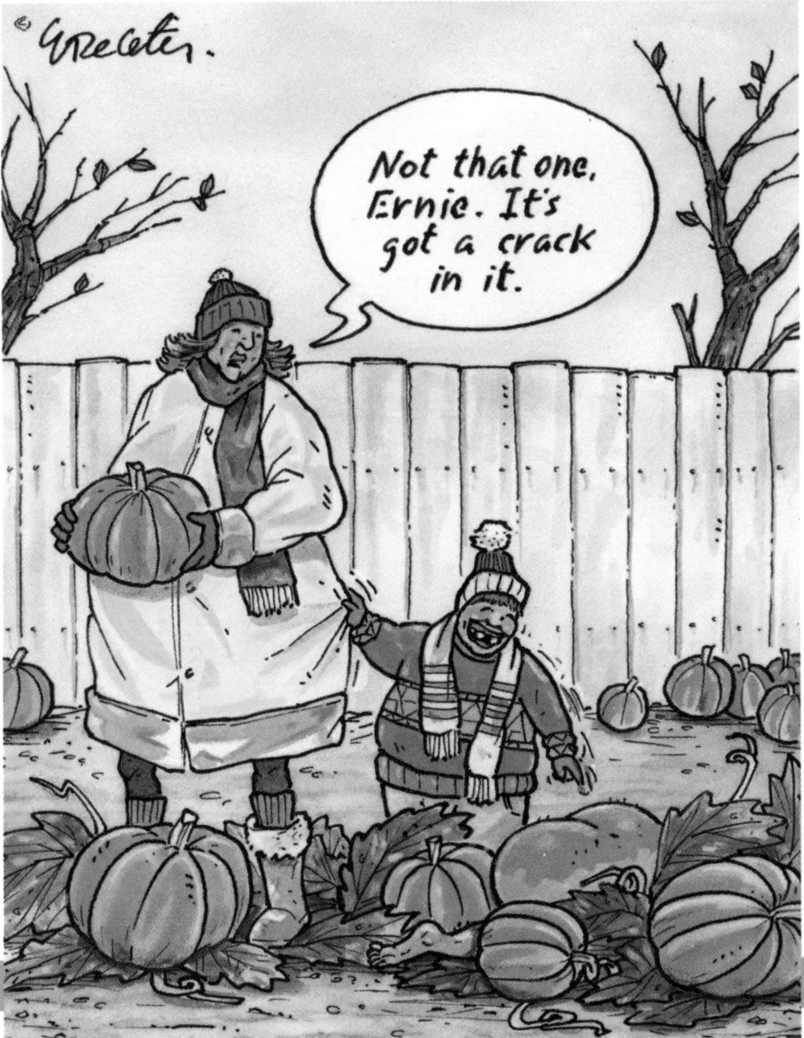
Not that one, Ernie. It's got a crack in it.

Crack [krâk]:

a separation between two fleshy protrusions; an act that affects one deeply.

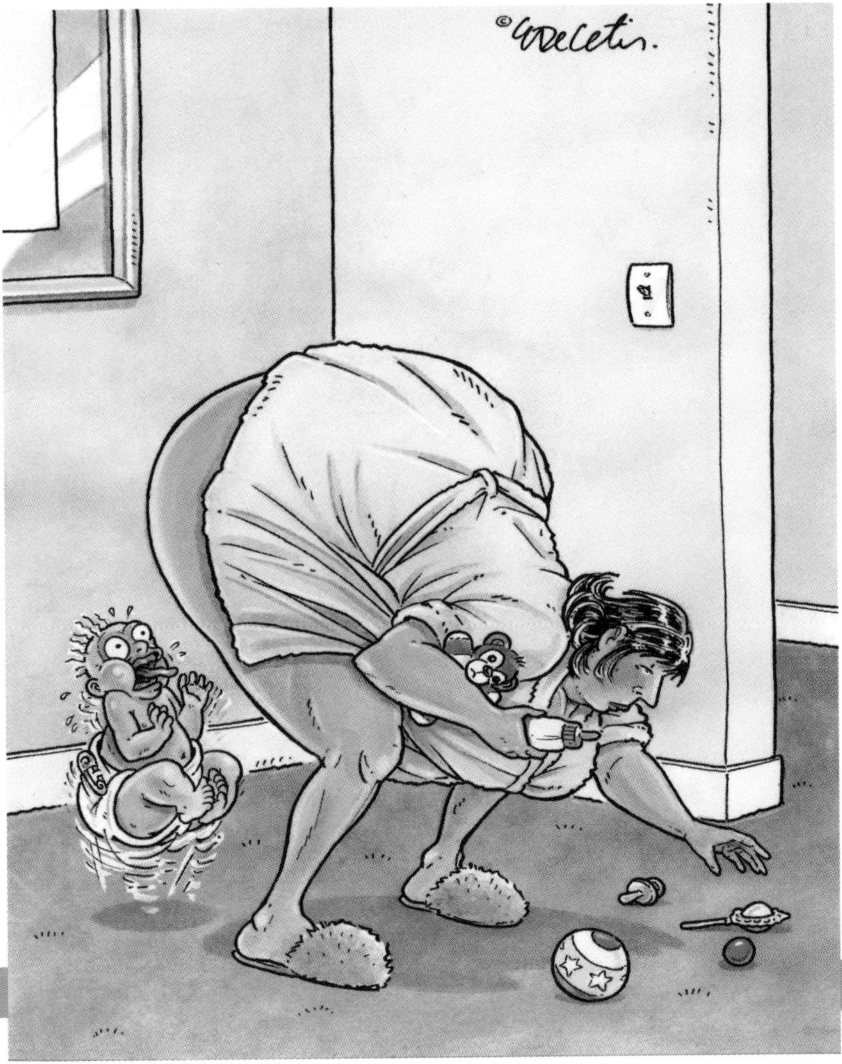

Gat [Afrik]:
a hole or vent in the rear; ass hole, anus.

A recurring crisis at the Farkinski farm

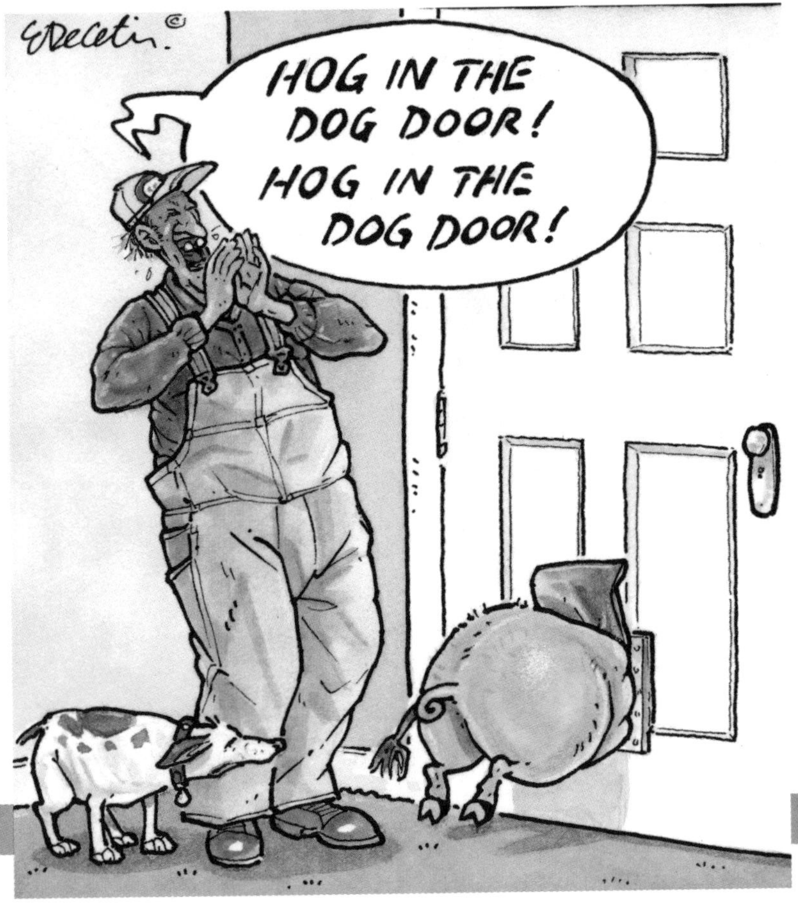
HOG IN THE DOG DOOR! HOG IN THE DOG DOOR!

Vista traseira [Pg]:
a rear view; what's behind, often derogatory.

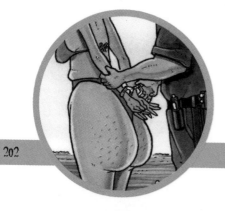

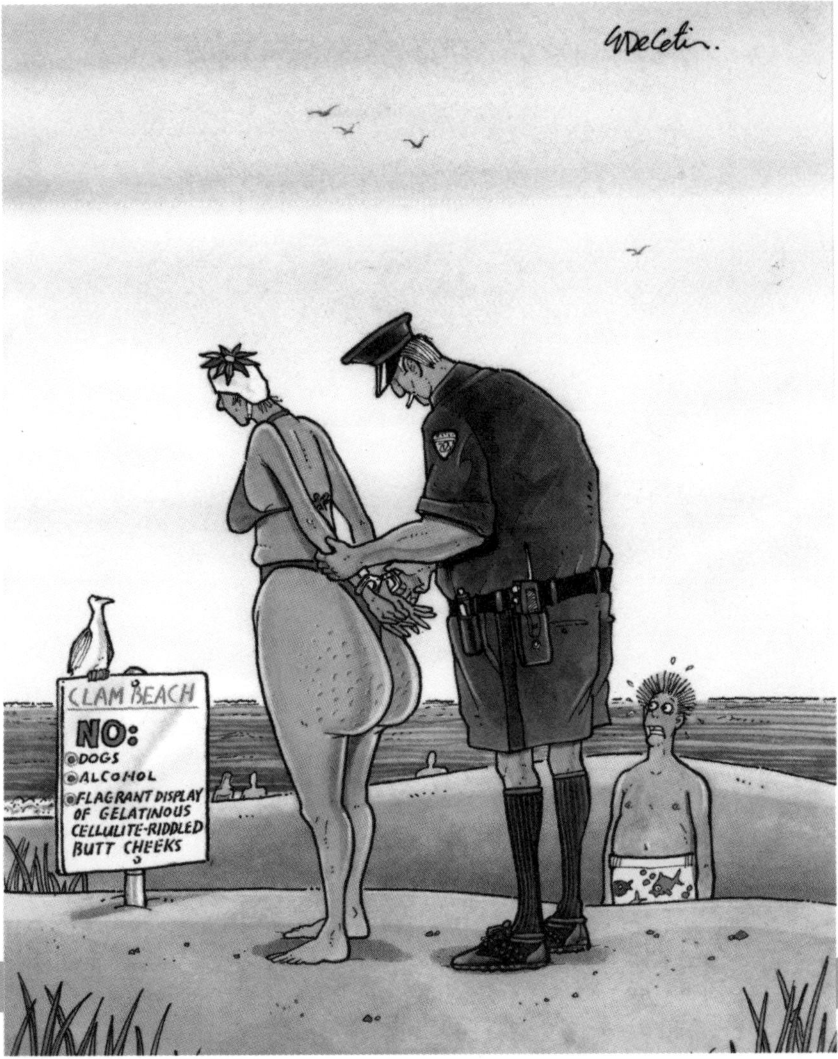
CLAM BEACH
NO:
DOGS
ALCOHOL
FLAGRANT DISPLAY OF GELATINOUS CELLULITE-RIDDLED BUTT CHEEKS

Crack [krâk]:
to hit or press against something.

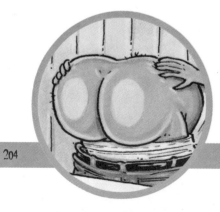

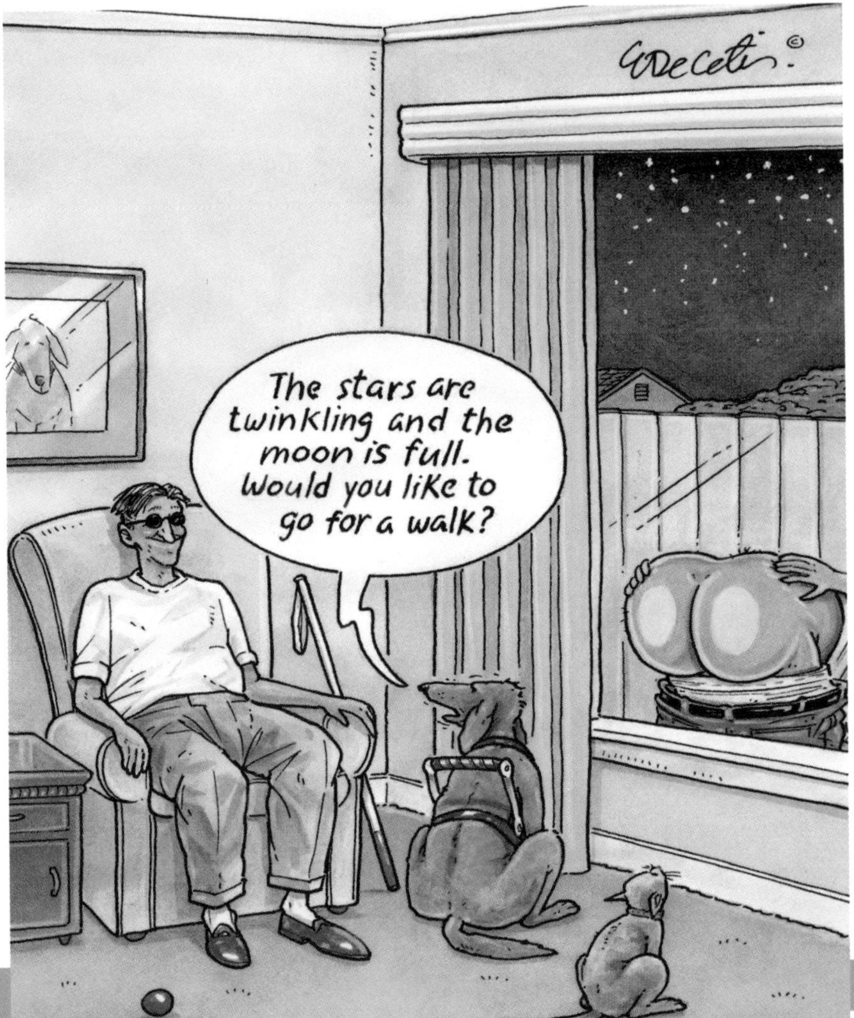
The stars are twinkling and the moon is full. Would you like to go for a walk?

Buns [bnz]:
a set or pair of rolls, often sweet.

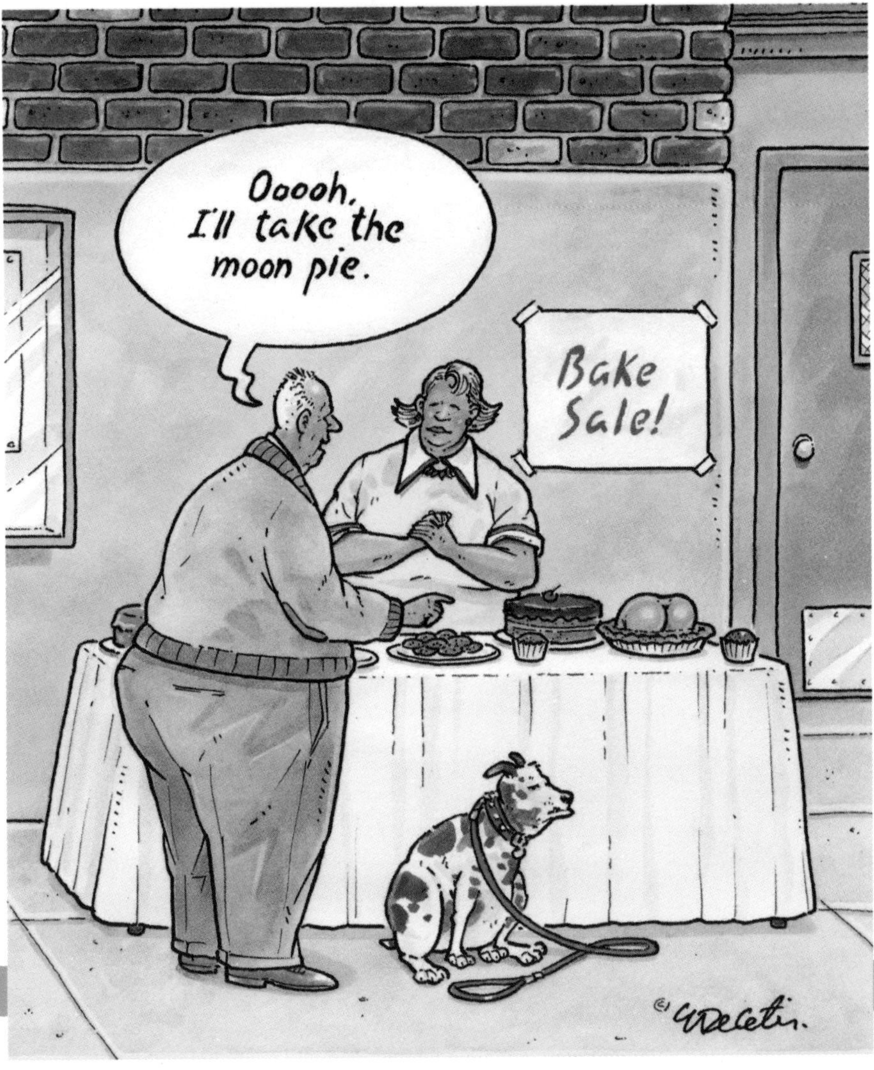
Ooooh. I'll take the moon pie.
Bake Sale!
© GDeCeta.

Achterste [Du]:
the behind; the rear; a place to avoid.

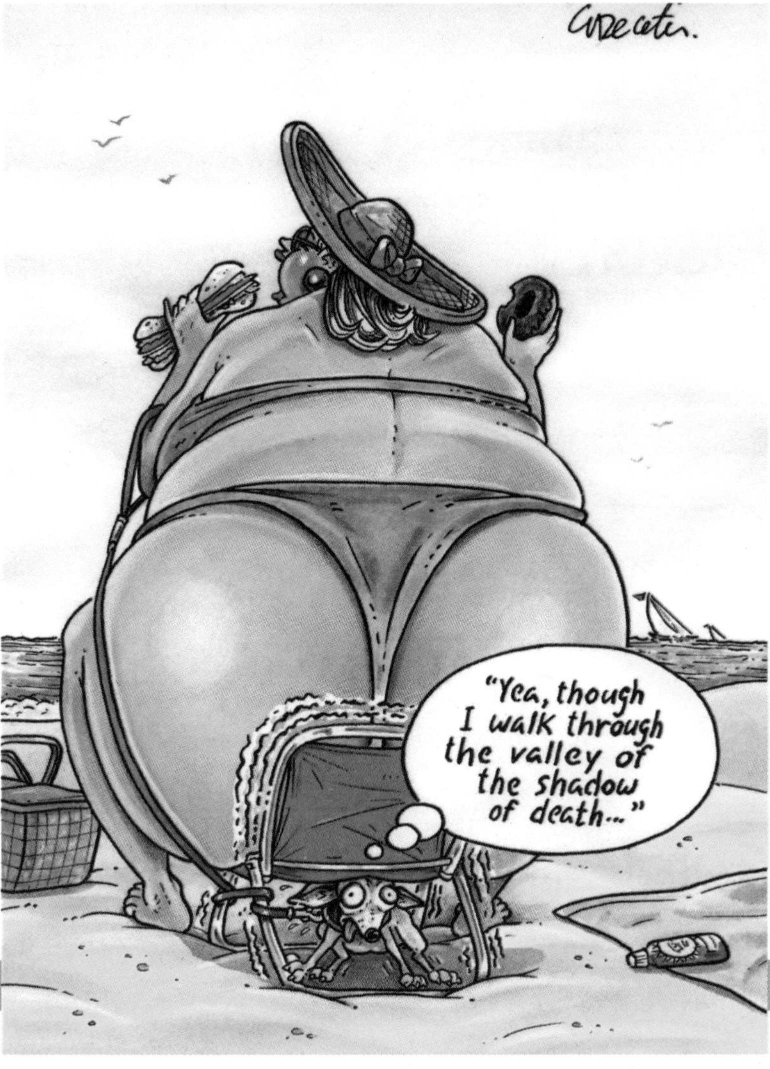
"Yea, though I walk through the valley of the shadow of death..."

Moon [mün]:
the planetary satellite; exposure of one's buttocks.

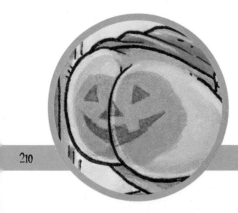

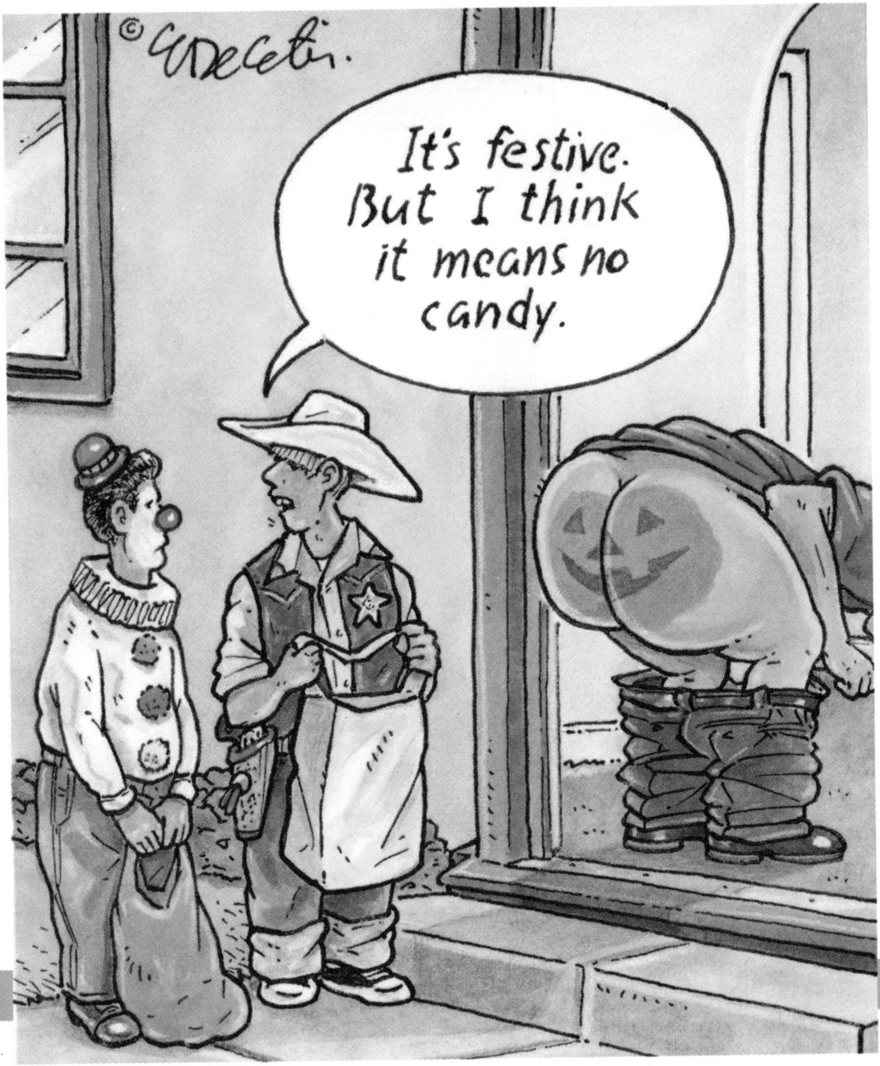
©EDeCebi.
It's festive. But I think it means no candy.

Train arrière [Fr]:
caboose, the rear end; a great finishing touch.

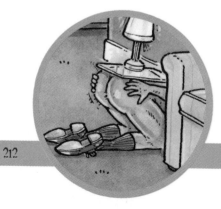

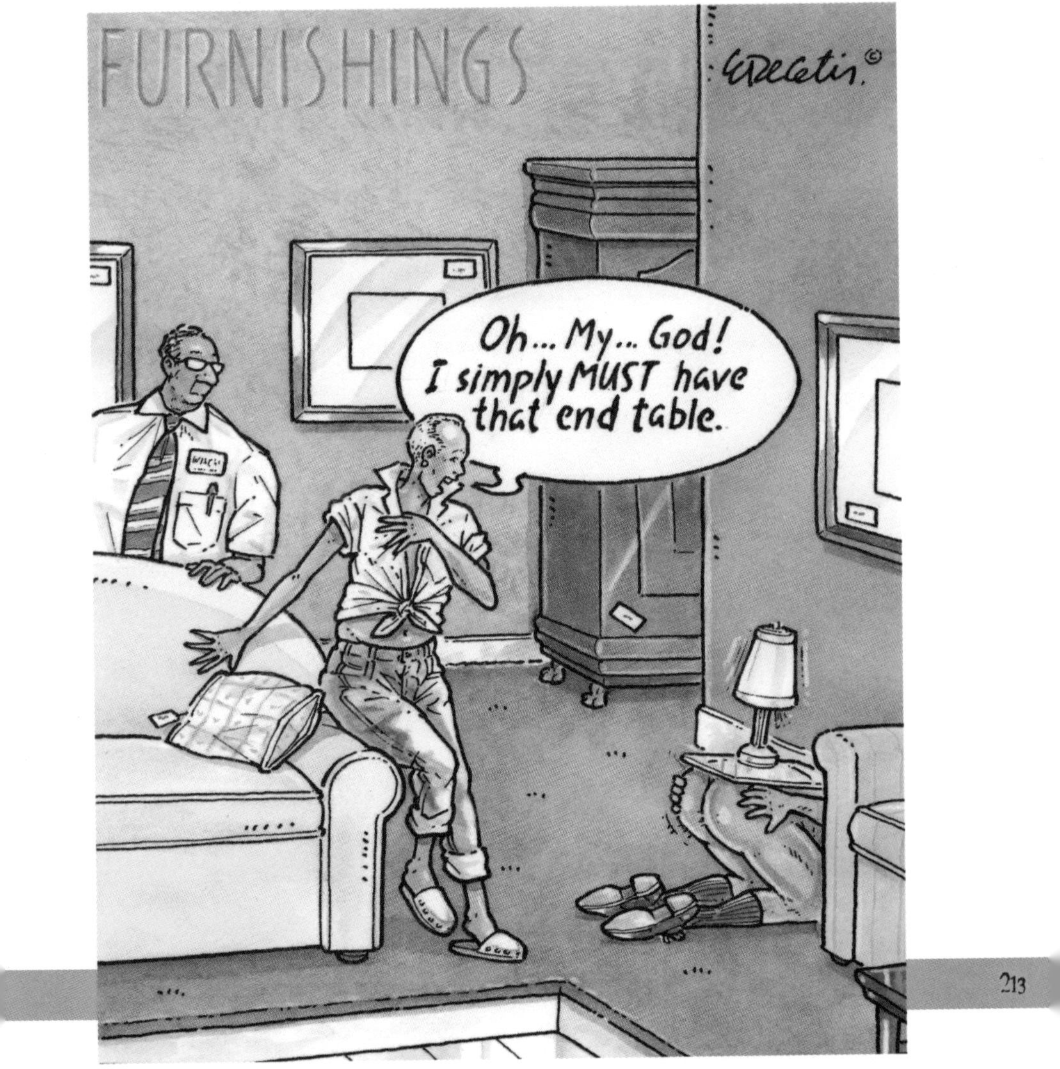
FURNISHINGS
Oh... My... God! I simply MUST have that end table.

Crack [krâk]:
a crevasse, a deep open crack,
esp. one in a glacier or snow.

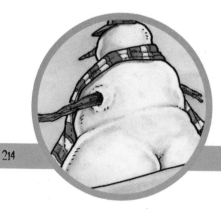

Frosty the Repairman

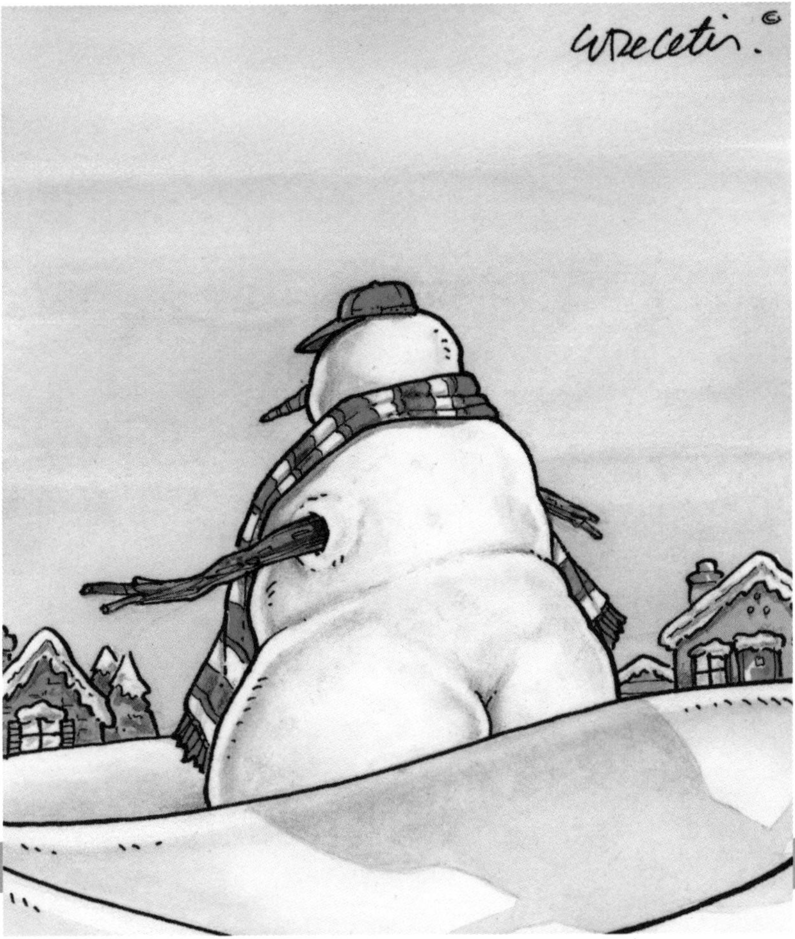

Crackdown [krâkdoun]:
the applying of punishment when rules are broken; enforcement.

Santa pauses at a "Naughty List" house.

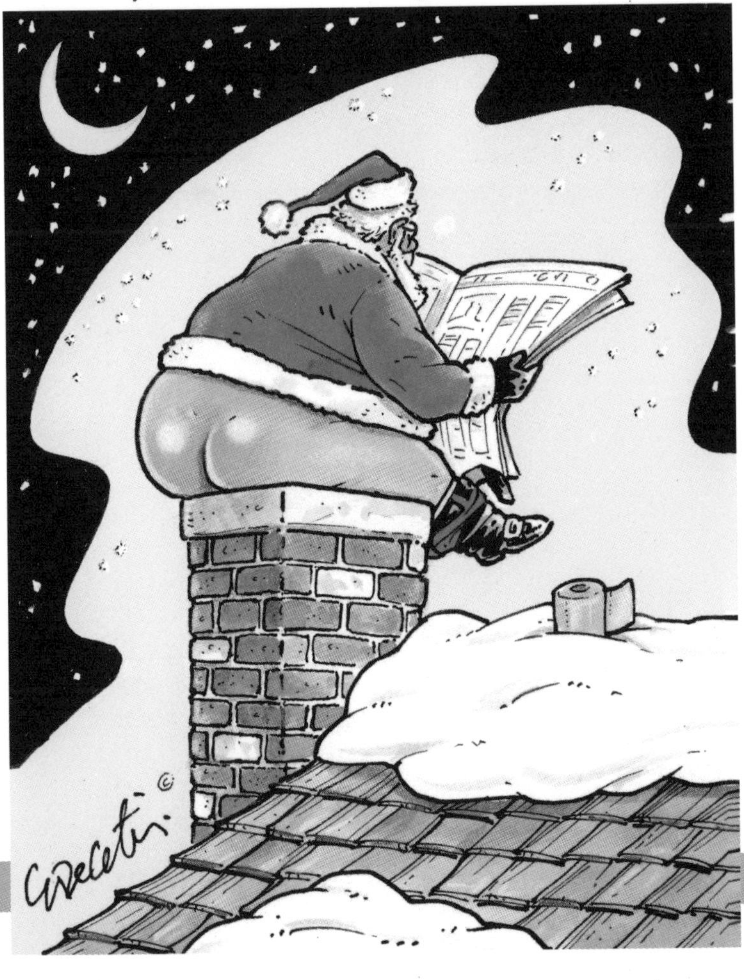

Crack [krâk]:
to solve; to make a discovery.

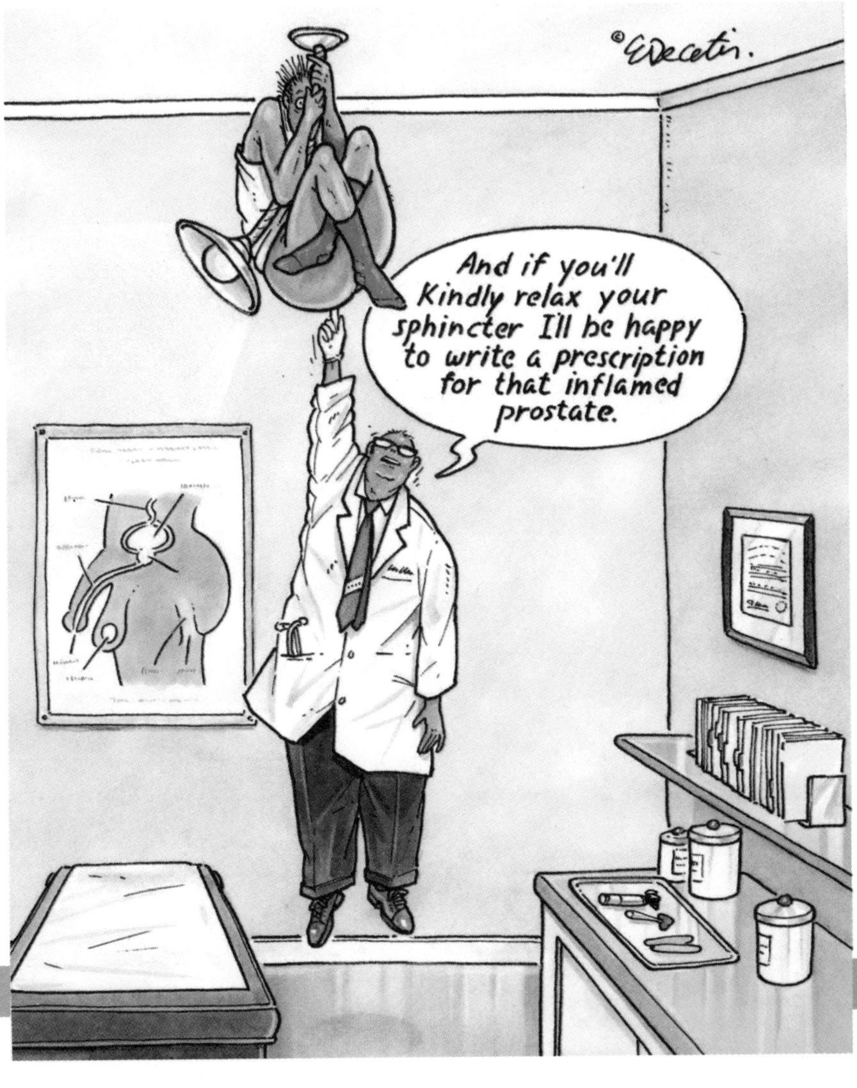
©EDecetis.
And if you'll Kindly relax your sphincter I'll be happy to write a prescription for that inflamed prostate.

Posteriore proiezione [It]:
the rear and what projects from it; rear projection.

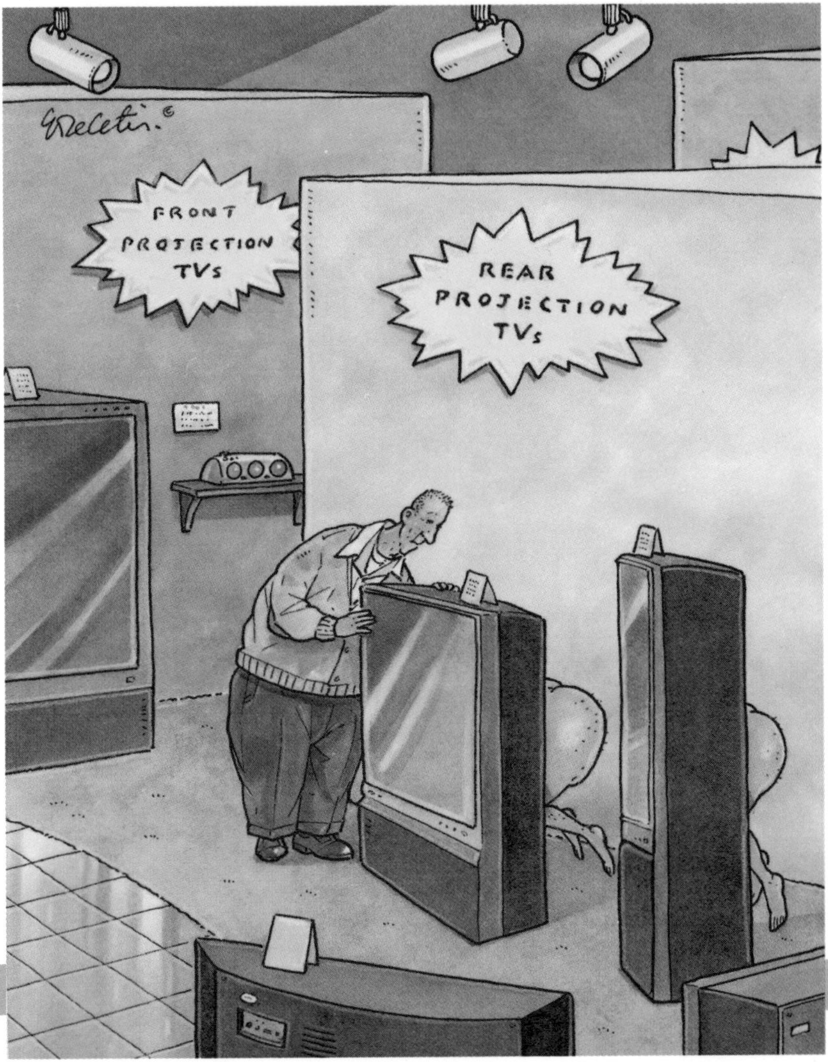
FRONT PROJECTION TVs
REAR PROJECTION TVs

Crack [krâk]:
an attempt to solve a problem; an opportunity.

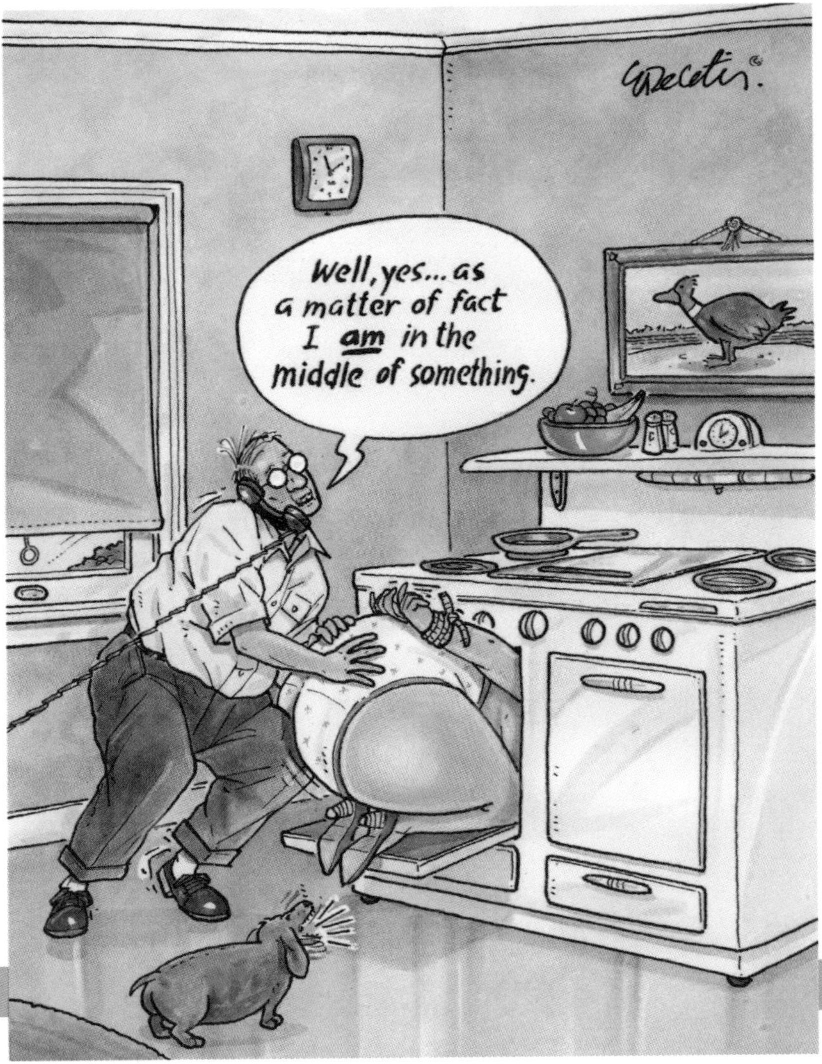
Well, yes... as a matter of fact I am in the middle of something.

Crack [krâk]:

fracture, fissure; a surface break, a collision.

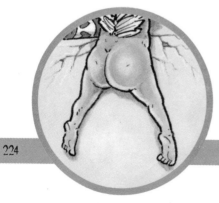

Stupid Cupid

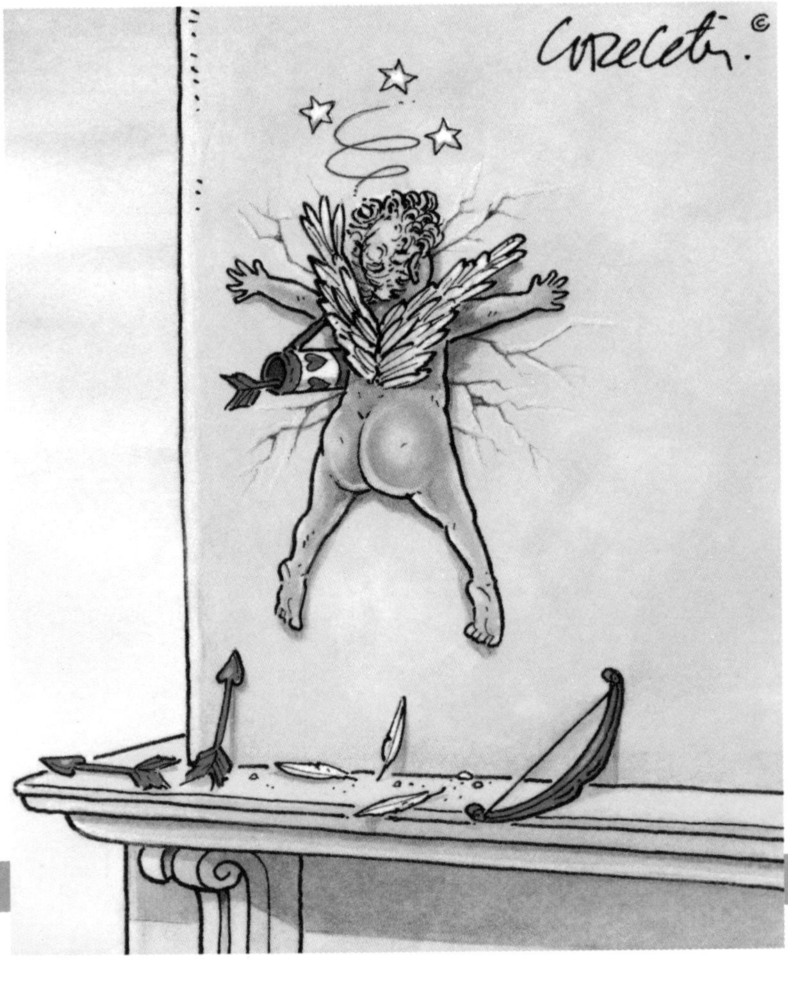
Corzelcetin ©

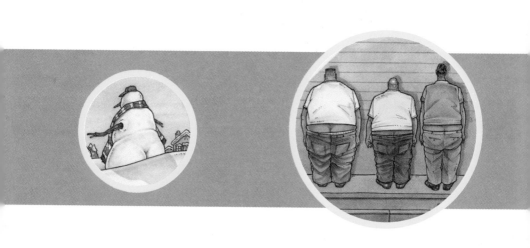

Chapter Five:
You Animal!

Iza [Hr]:
the rear or behind; that which may be exposed.

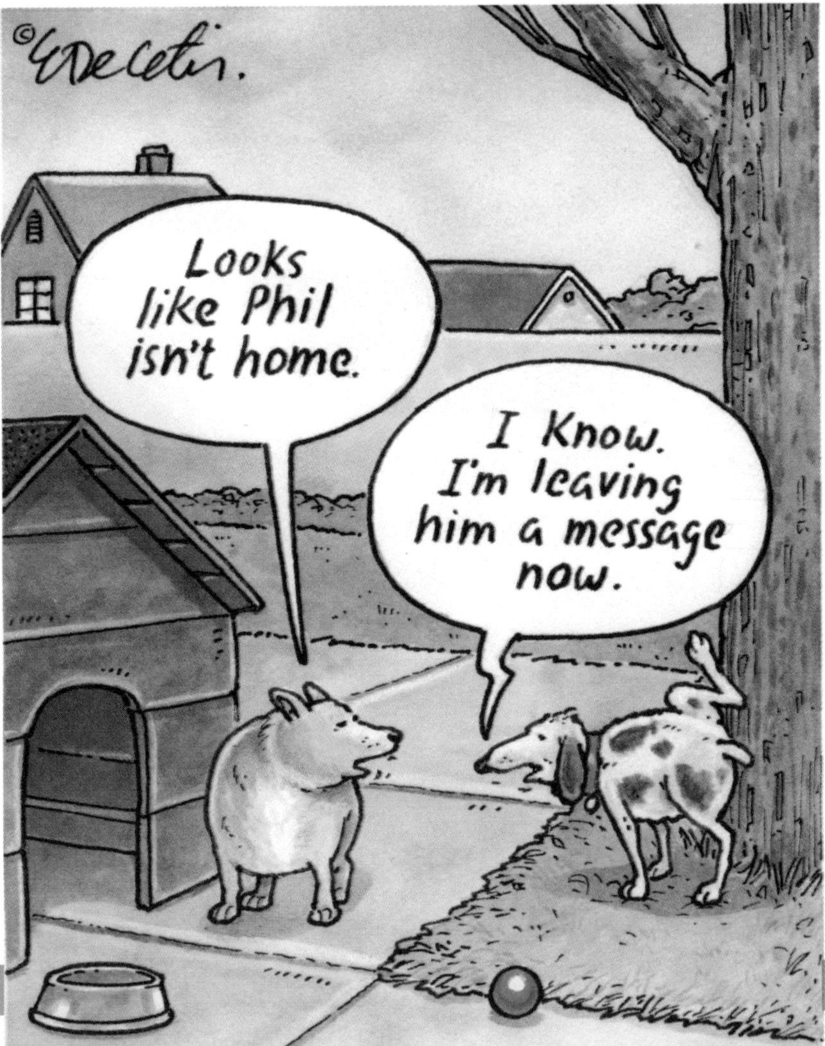
©EDeCetis.
Looks like Phil isn't home.
I Know. I'm leaving him a message now.

Ass [as]:
Any of several hoofed mammals of the genus Equus,
resembling and closely related to horses but having
a smaller build and longer ears, and including the
domesticated donkey.

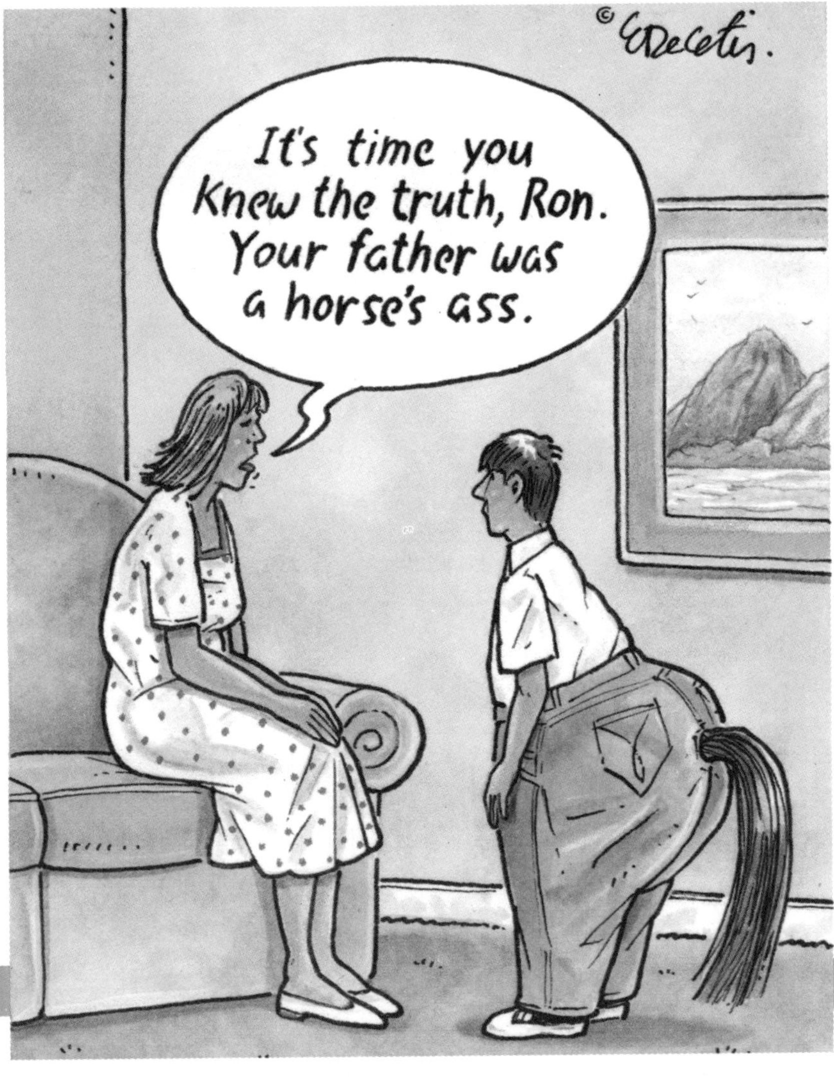

It's time you Knew the truth, Ron. Your father was a horse's ass.

Espalda [Sp]:
the rear or backside; an underplace that requires no wrapping.

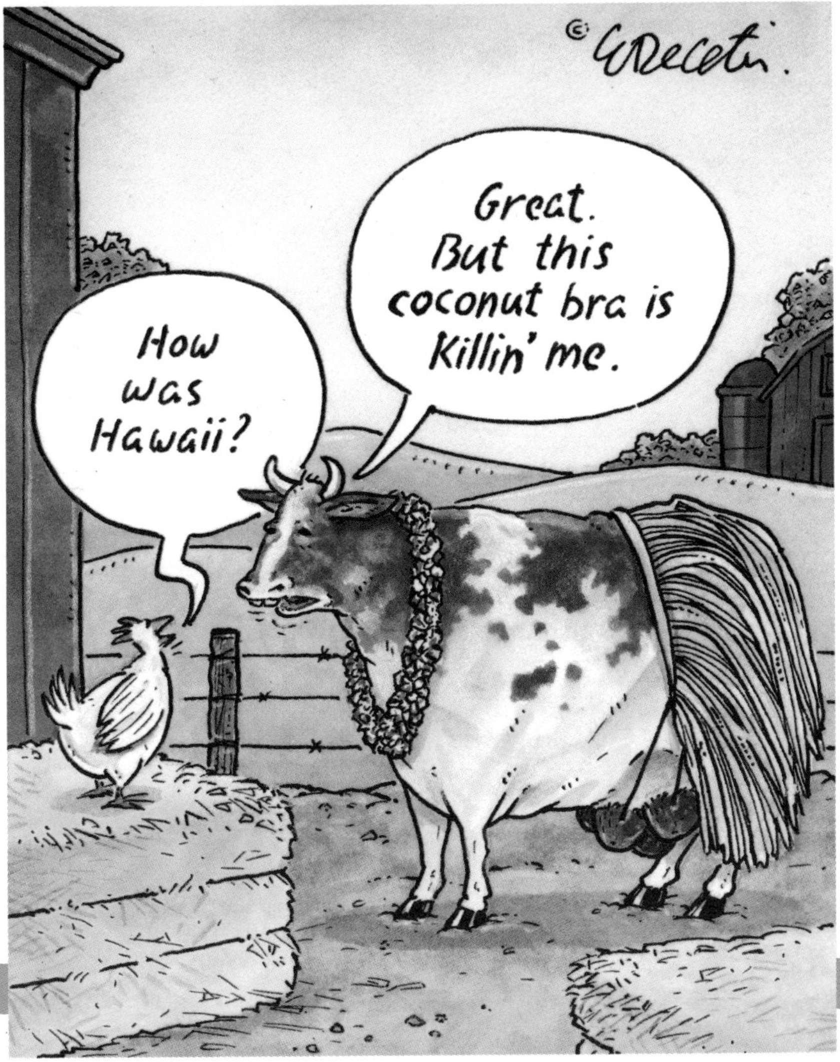
How was Hawaii?
Great. But this coconut bra is Killin' me.

Posterior [po-steer-ee-er]:
situated behind or at the rear of.

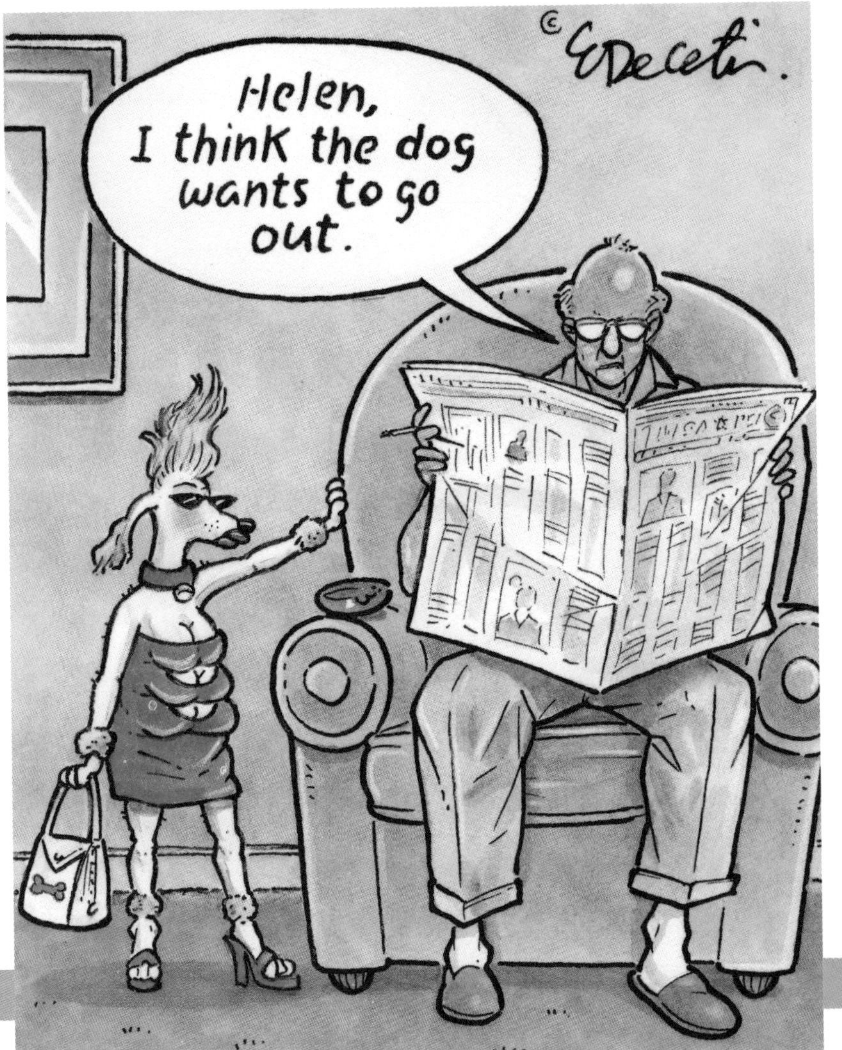
Helen,
I think the dog
wants to go
out.
© EDecetis.

Crack [krâk]:
to pass through (a barrier), pertaining to various things.

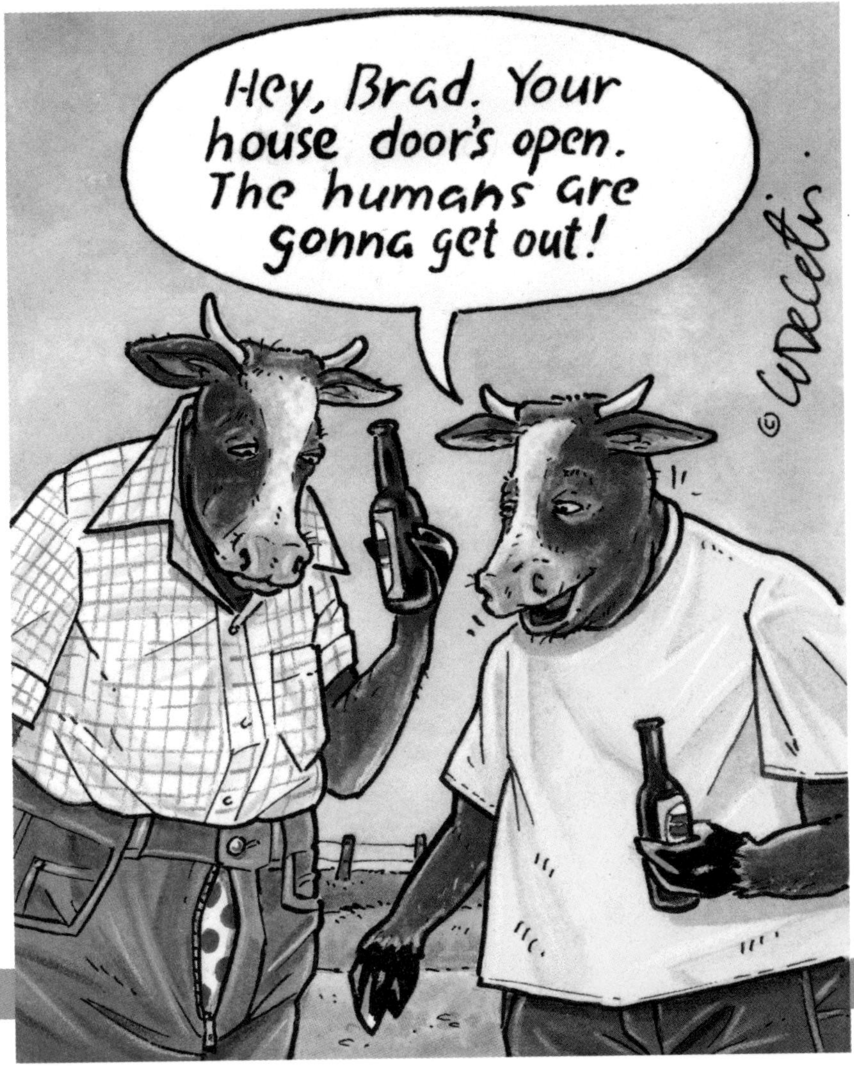
Hey, Brad. Your house door's open. The humans are gonna get out!

Bas [Fr]:
bottom; having to do with the lower part of things.

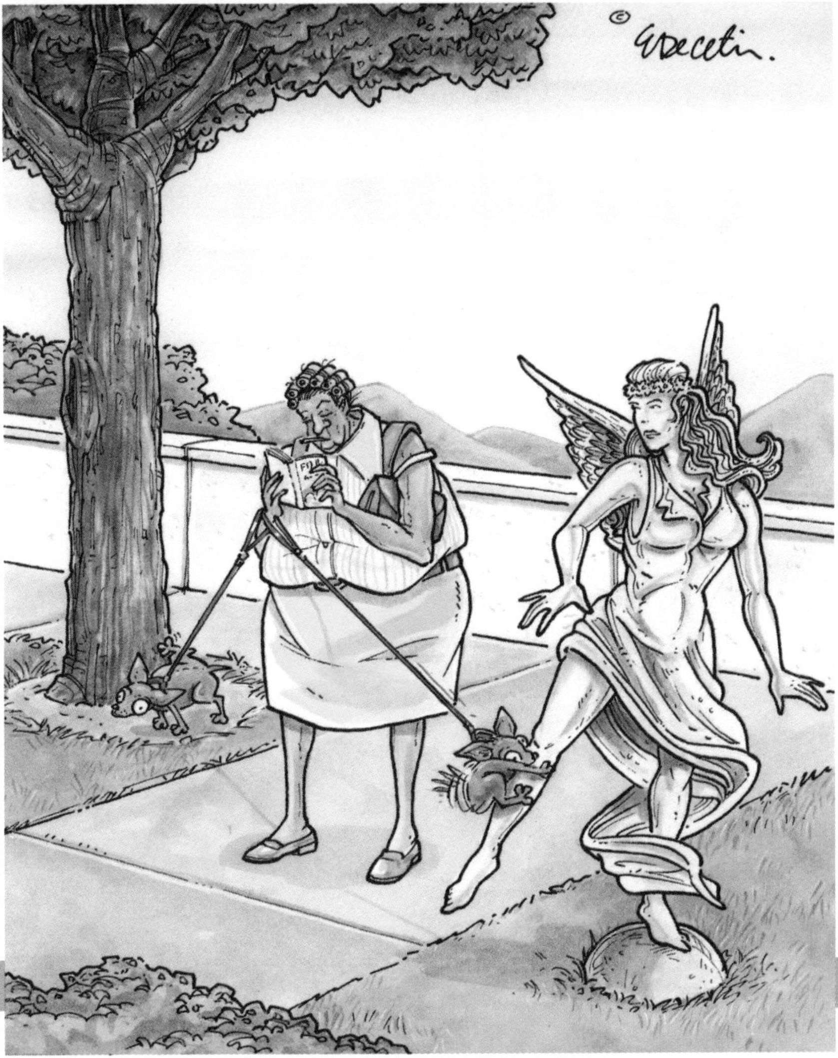

Parte posteriore [It]:
the rear; an area that can lead to lower self-esteem.

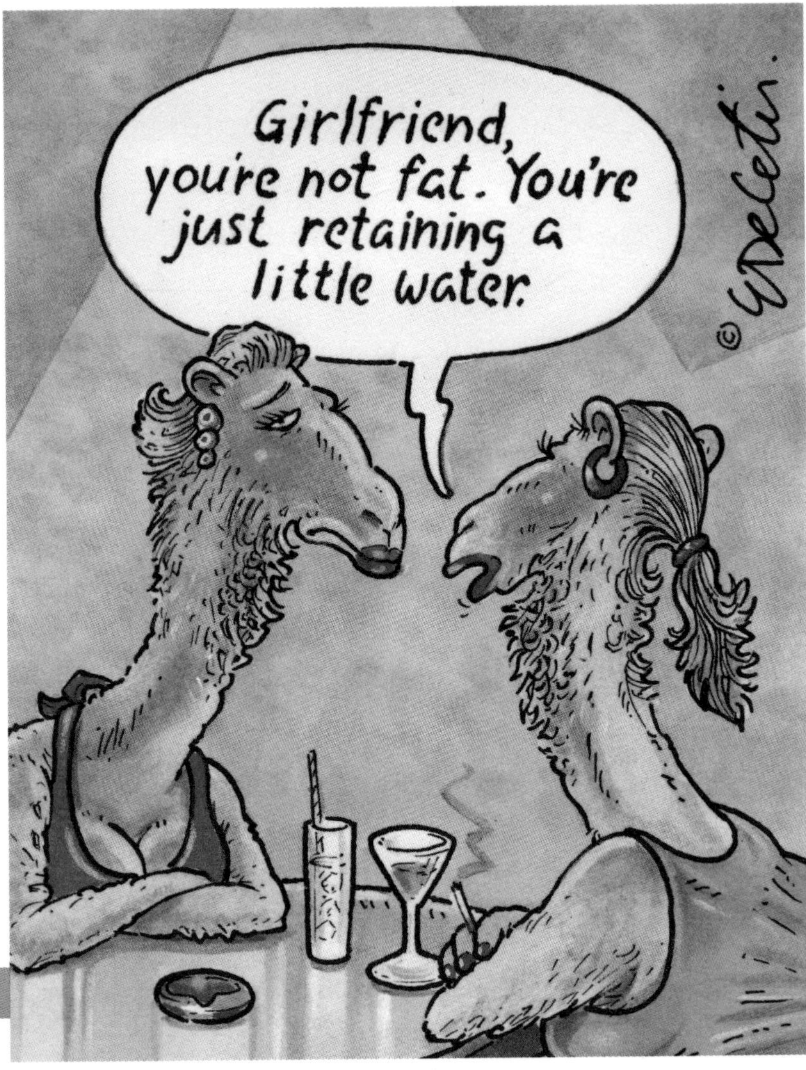
Girlfriend, you're not fat. You're just retaining a little water.
© G.DeCoteau

Posto [poss-to] [Sp]:
seat; something for a person to sit on.

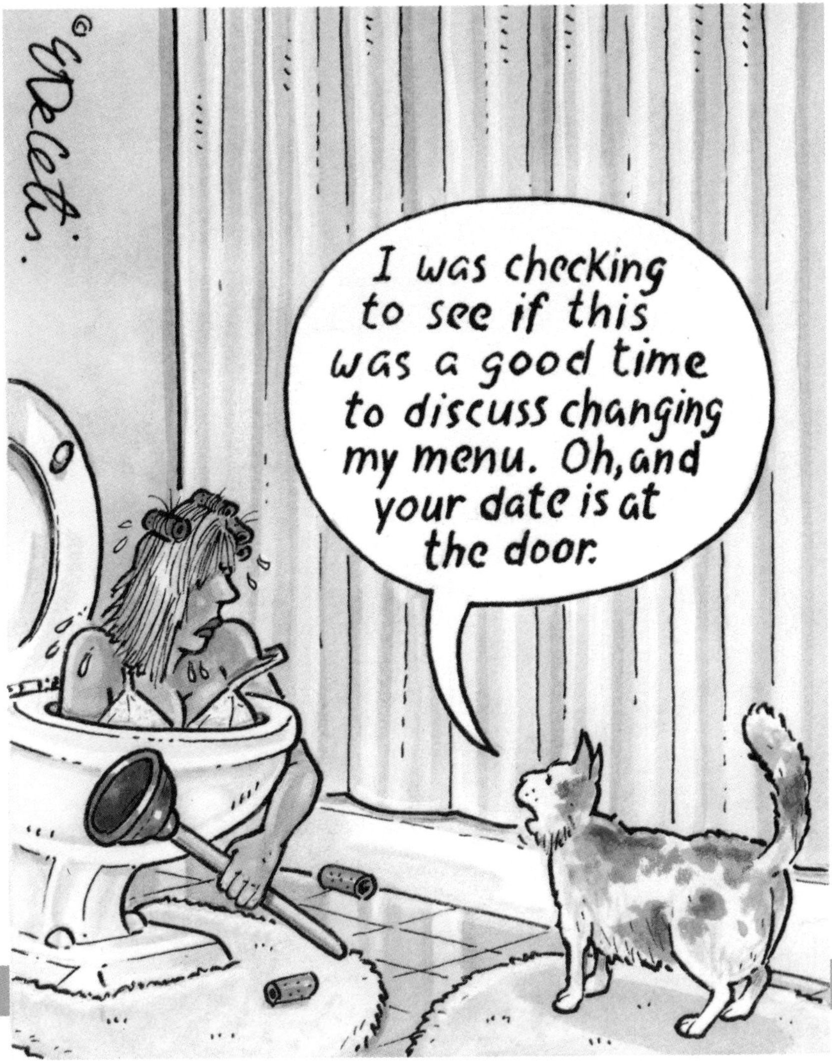
I was checking to see if this was a good time to discuss changing my menu. Oh, and your date is at the door.

Ass [as]:

a pompous fool who often makes obvious remarks.

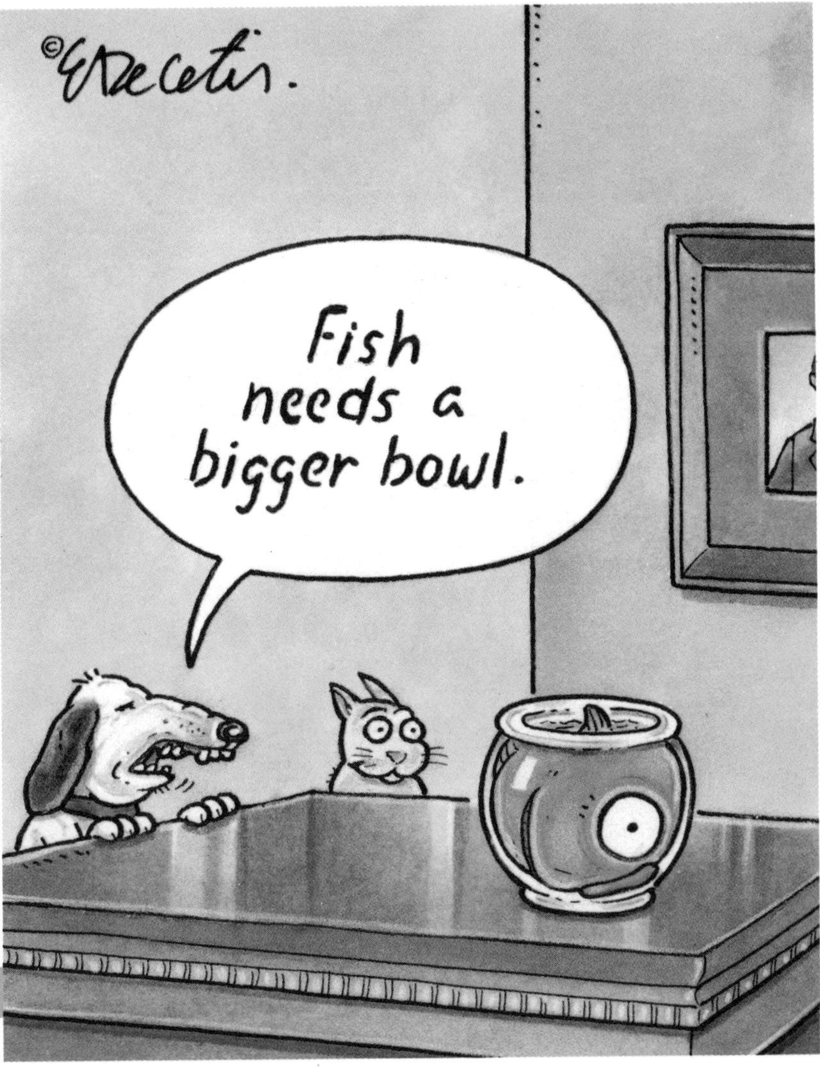
©Erdecotis.
Fish needs a bigger bowl.

Fesse [fayss] [Fr]:
(n.) slang: cheek, buttock, fanny; (vb.) to deliver, kick butt.

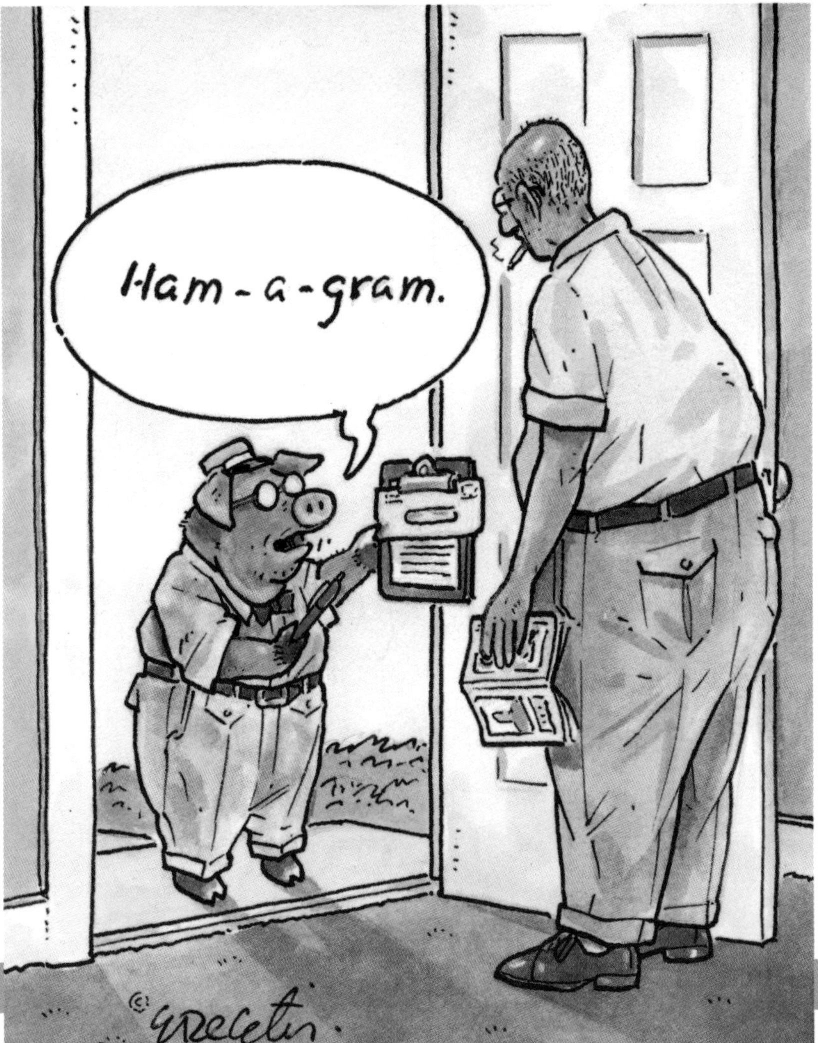
Ham-a-gram.
©Grzelak.

Crack [krâk]:
separation caused by sudden impact.

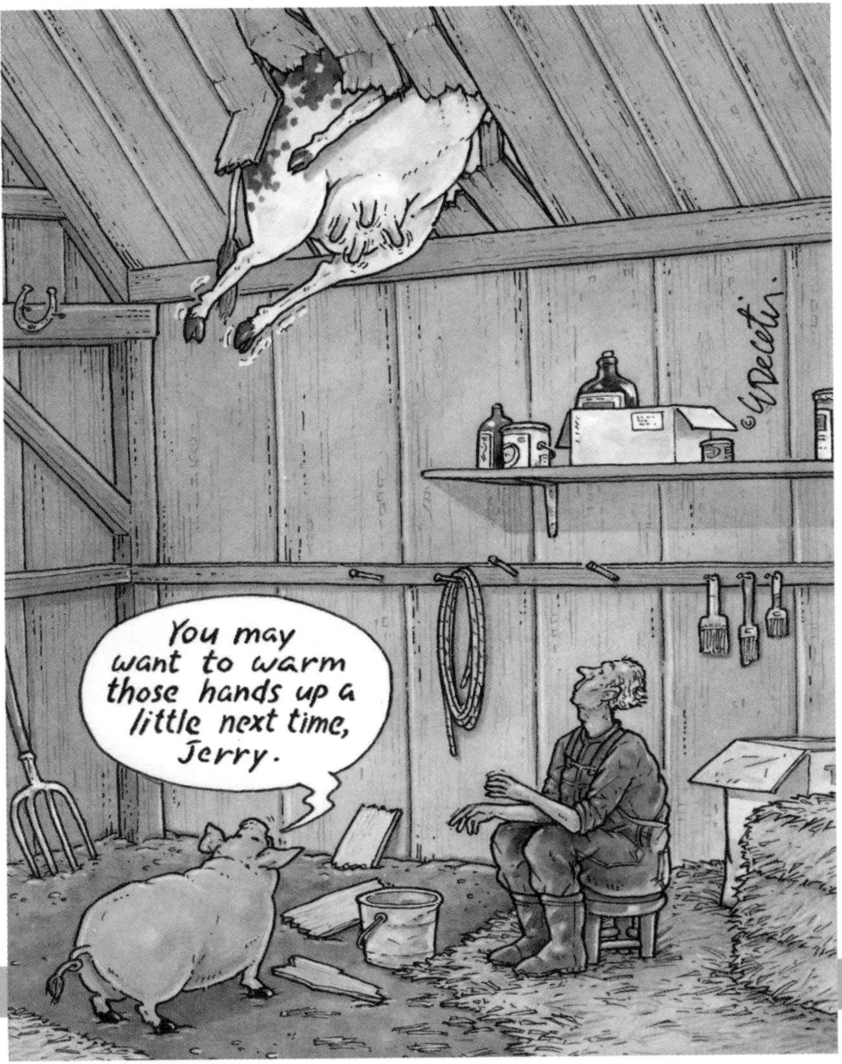
You may want to warm those hands up a little next time, Jerry.
©Decetis

Crack [krâk]:
to tell, as in crack a joke; to wisecrack.

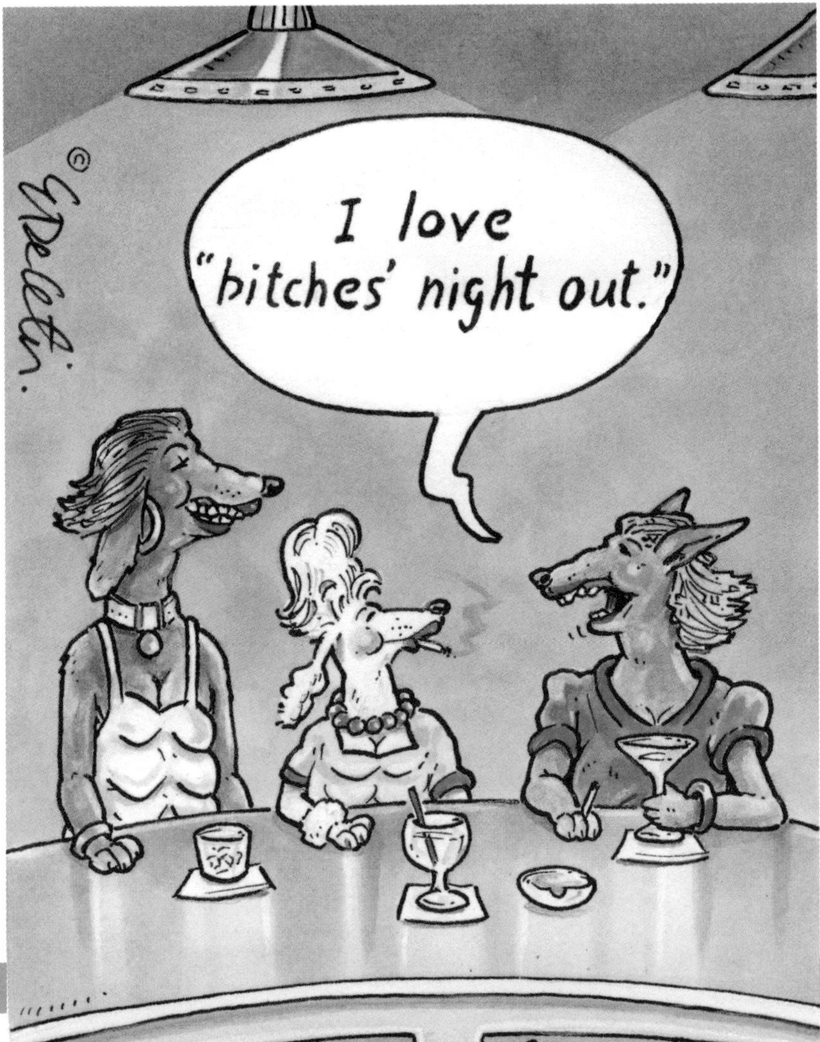
I love "bitches' night out."

Crack [krâk]:
a split or snag; an opening made by forcibly pulling apart.

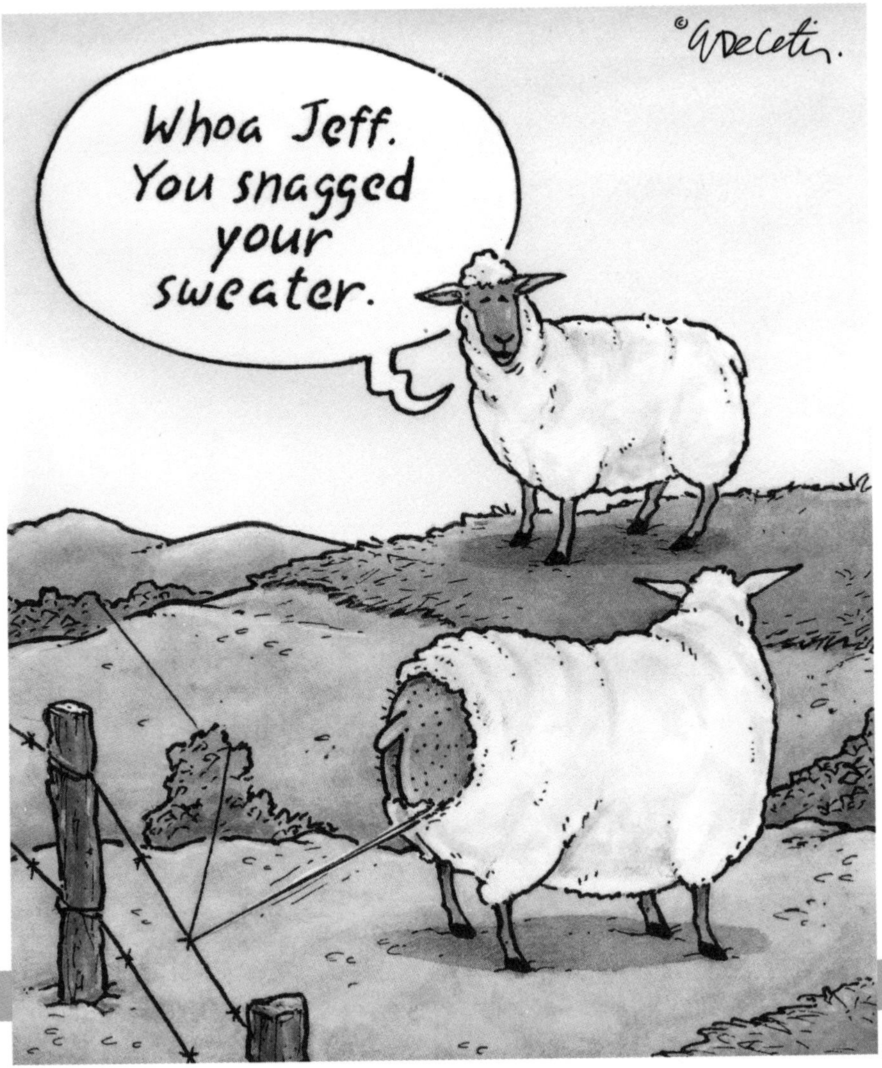
Whoa Jeff. You snagged your sweater.

Crack [krâk]:

a blemish resulting from a break; a state of complete separation t
could be unhealthy for the heart.

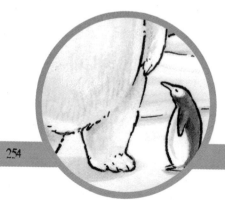

Bipolar Bears

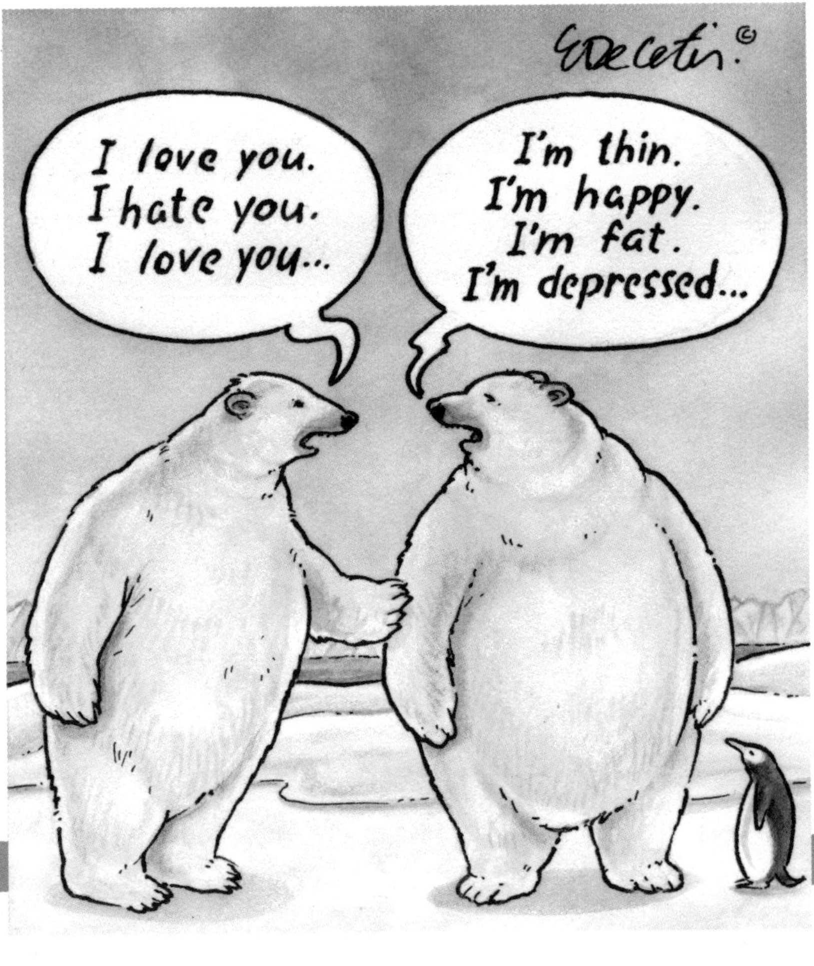

I love you.
I hate you.
I love you...
I'm thin.
I'm happy.
I'm fat.
I'm depressed...

Taga [Et.]
the buttocks, behind; area with often foul odors.

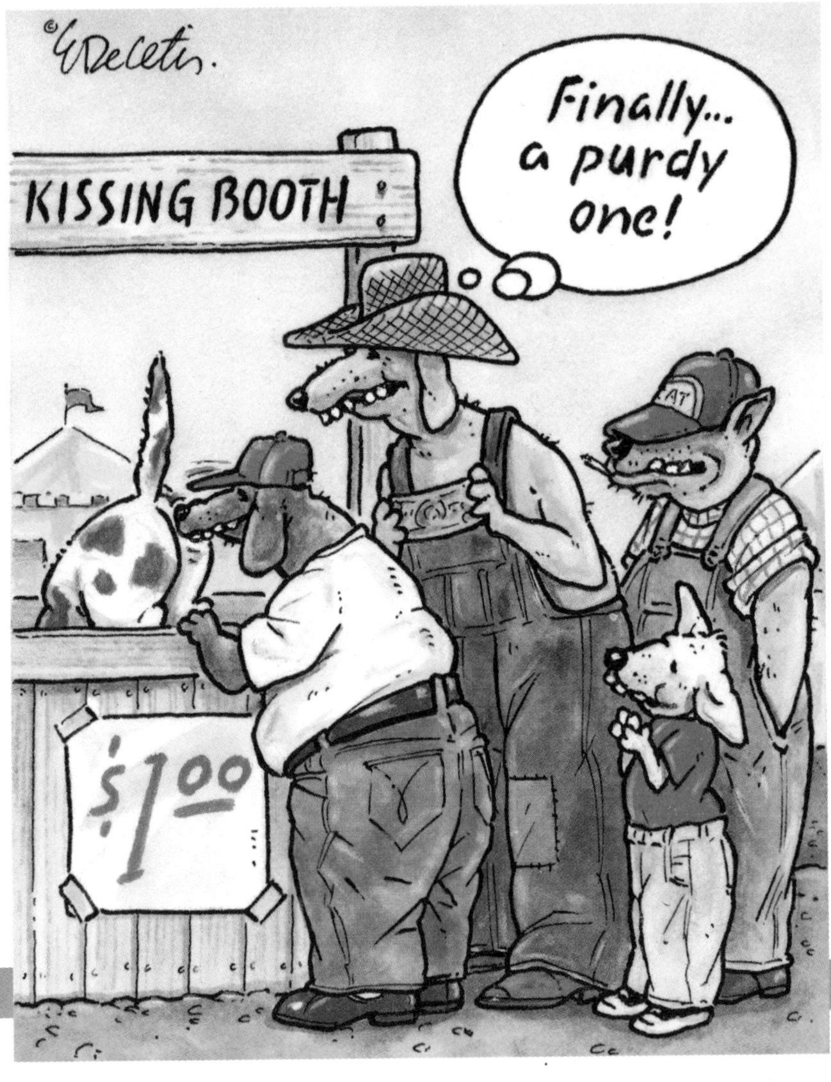
KISSING BOOTH
Finally... a purdy one!
$1.00
CAT

Crack [krâk]:
to tell; to spill the beans.

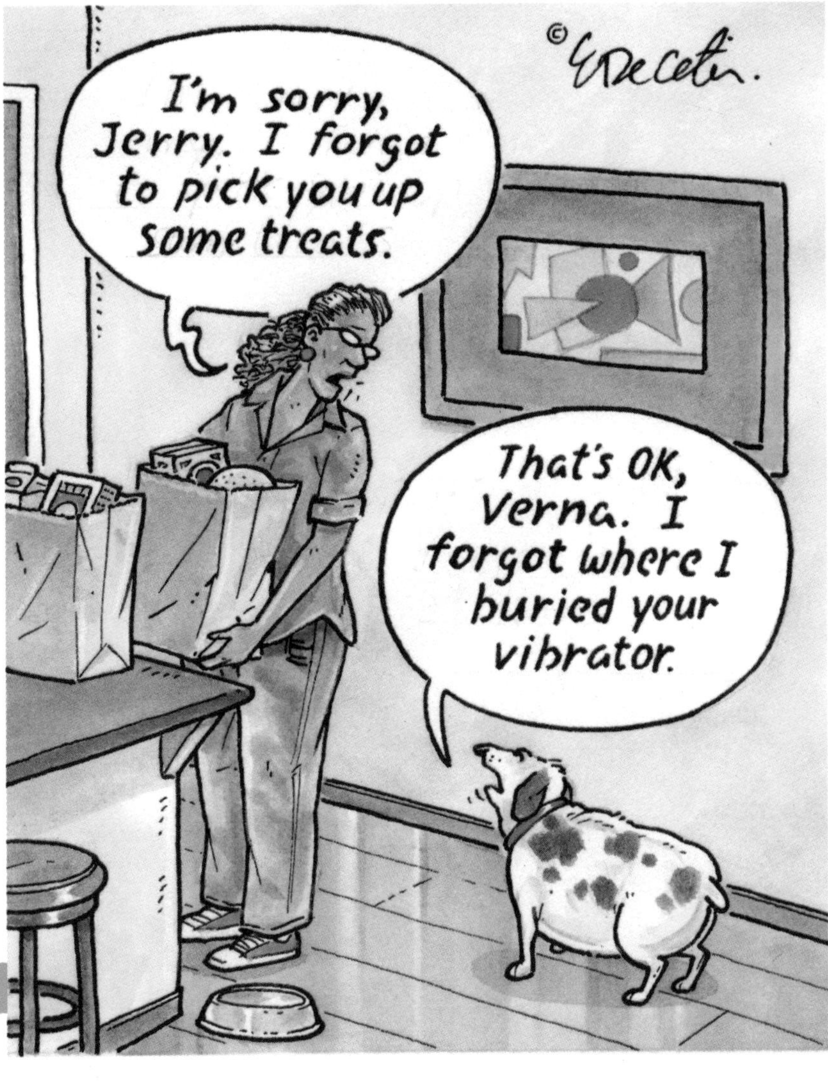
©Erdecelin.
I'm sorry, Jerry. I forgot to pick you up some treats.
That's OK, Verna. I forgot where I buried your vibrator.

Crack [krâk]:
to utter or tell with humor: to crack a smile.

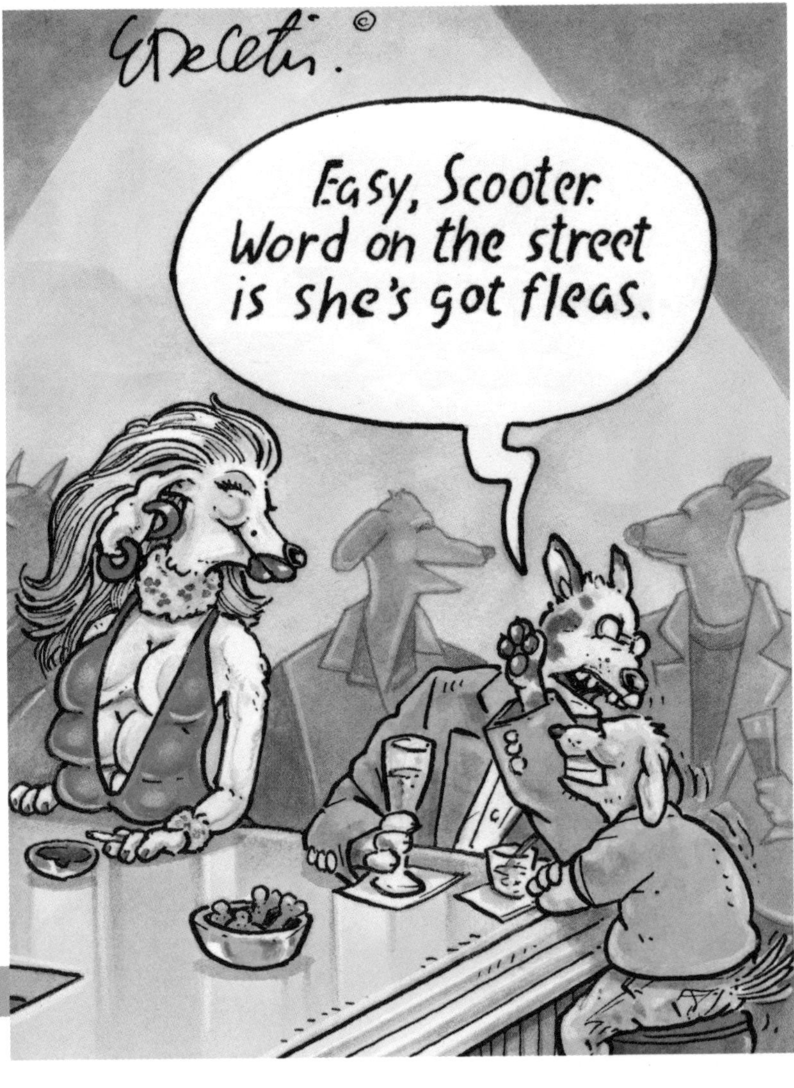
Easy, Scooter. Word on the street is she's got fleas.

Ass [as]:
one deficient in judgment and common sense.

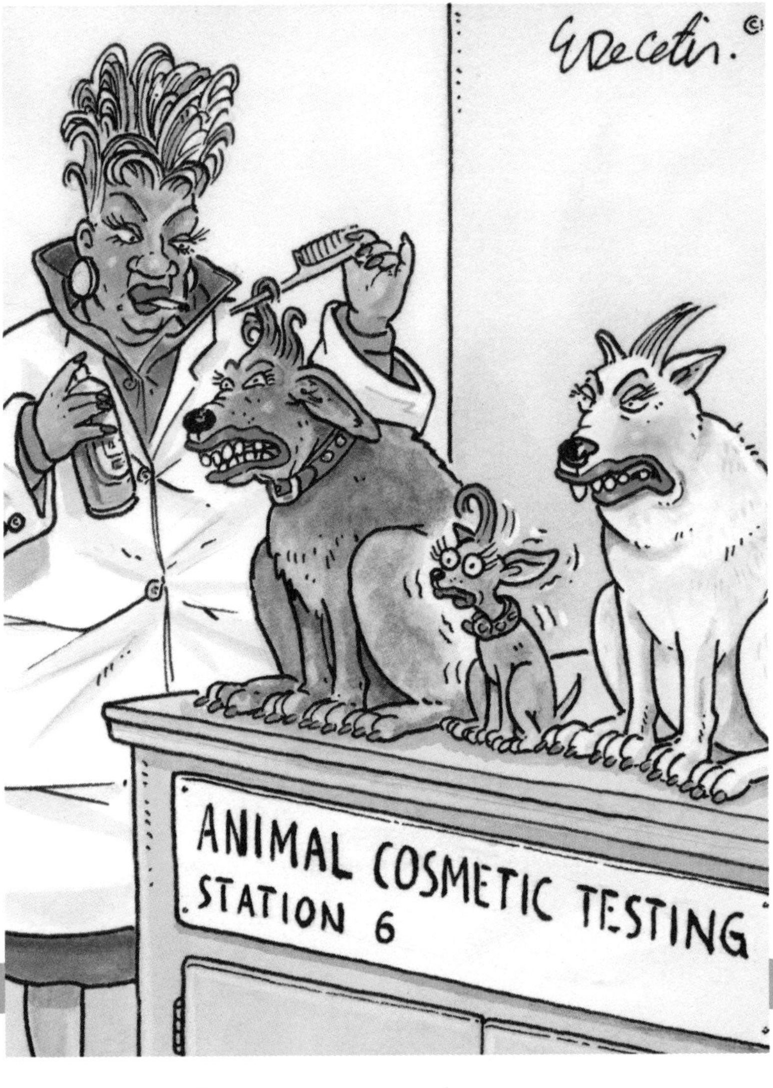
EDecetin.©
ANIMAL COSMETIC TESTING
STATION 6

Crack [krâk]:
a chance, an opportunity to try something new.

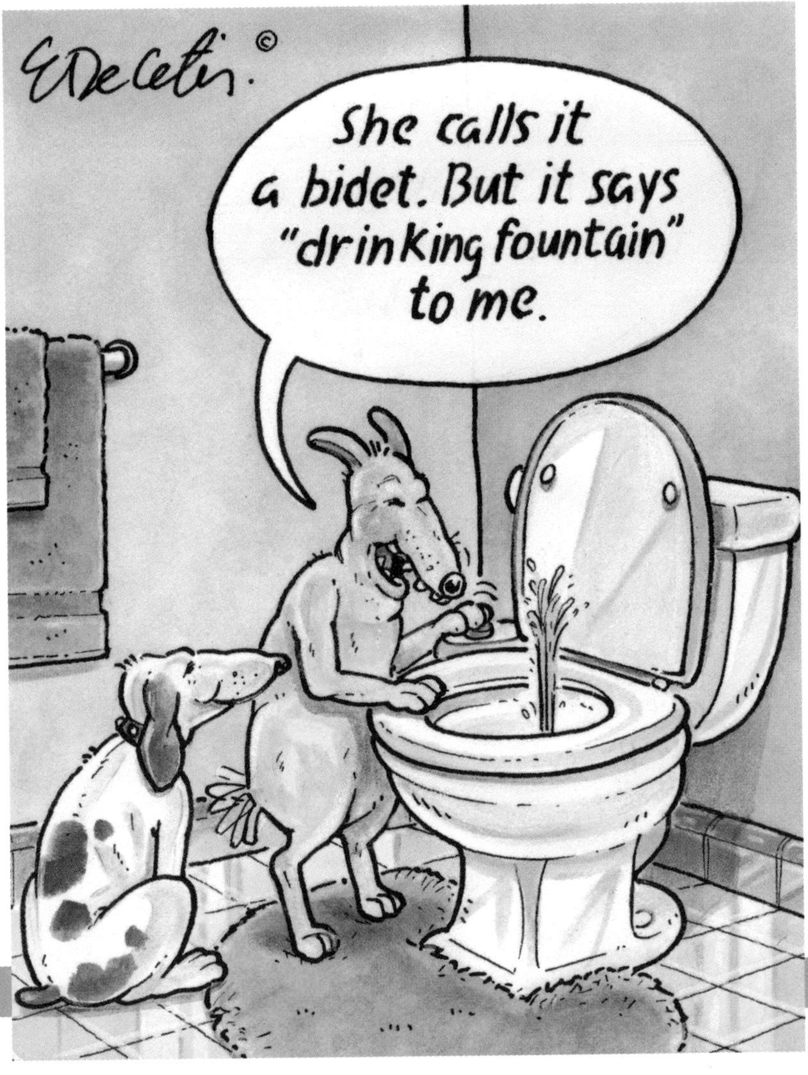
EDeCelis ©
She calls it a bidet. But it says "drinking fountain" to me.

Rückwärtig Ausgang [G]:
at the rear, rear end; can be the cause of embarrassment.

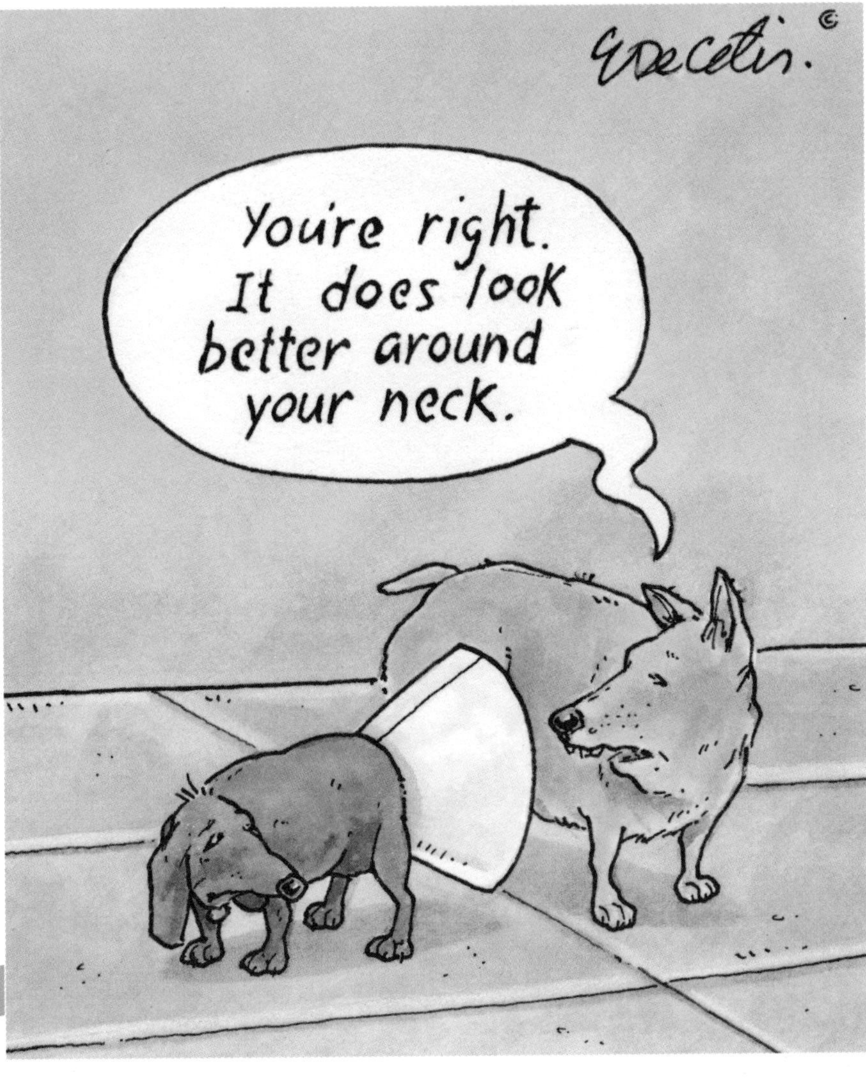
You're right. It does look better around your neck.

Crack [krâk]:
a moment, an instant; an opportunity.

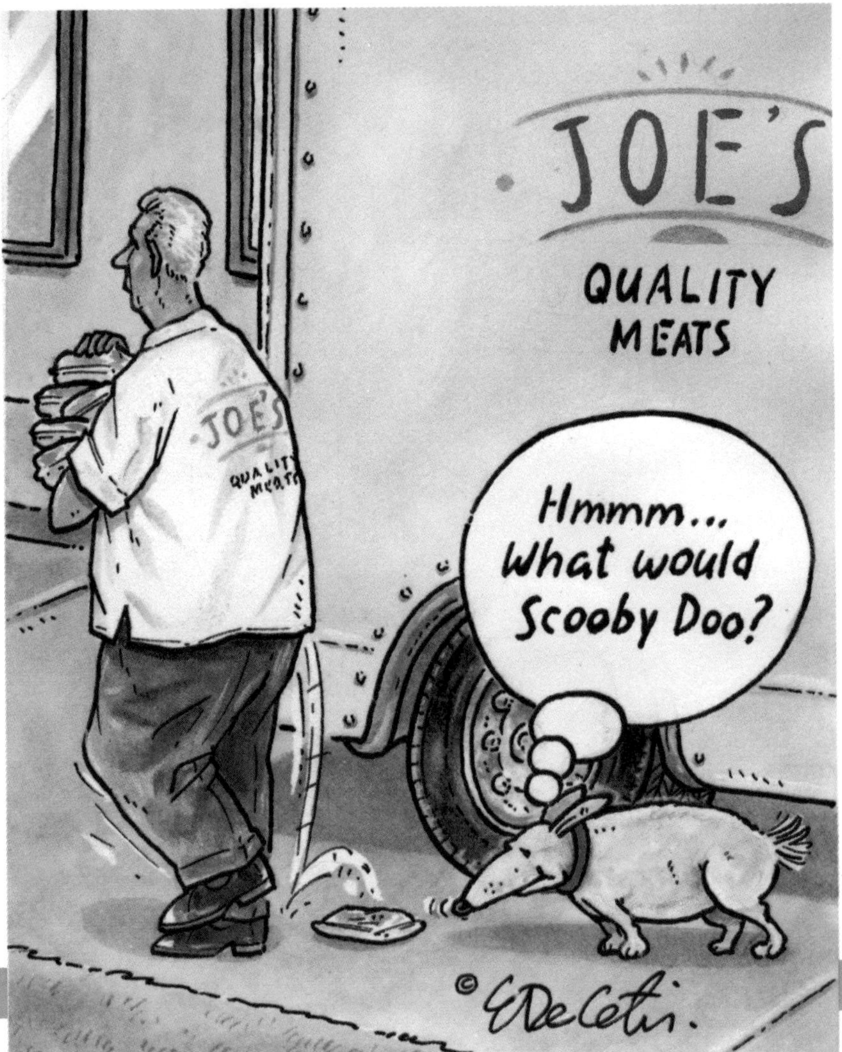
JOE'S
QUALITY MEATS
JOE'S
QUALITY MEATS
Hmmm... What would Scooby Doo?
© EDeCeti.

Crack [krâk]:

to break, split, or snap apart; as in the friendly atmosphere began to crack.

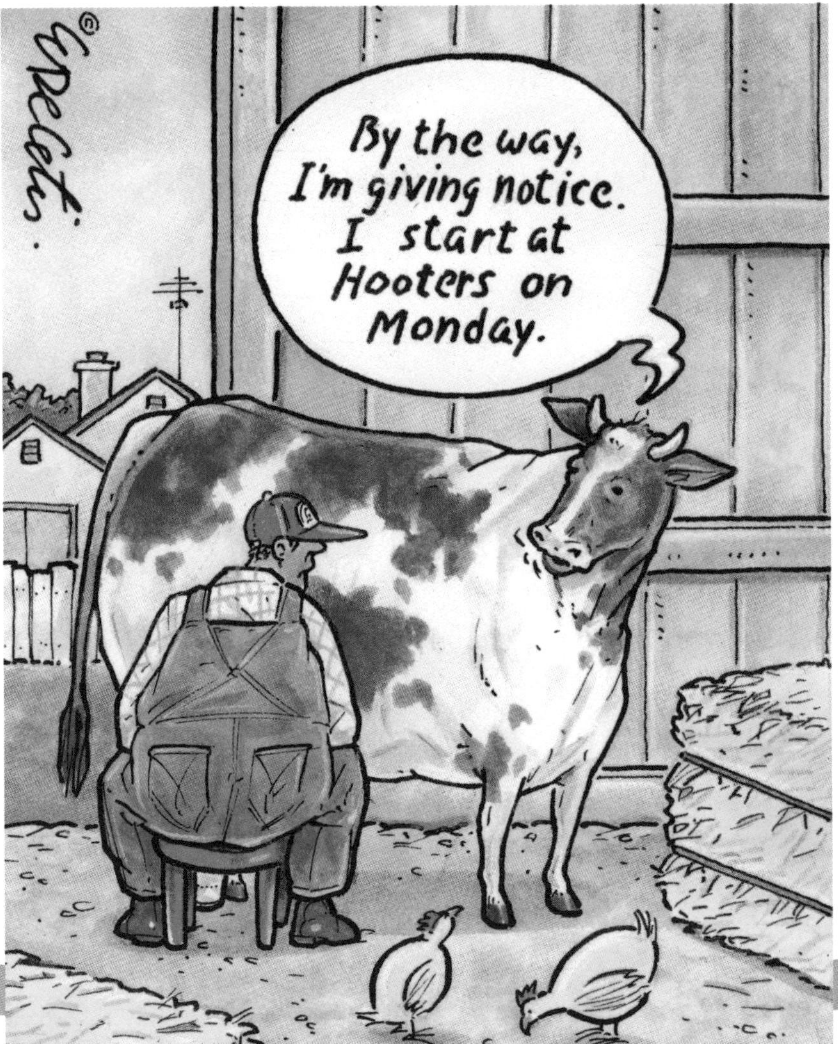
By the way, I'm giving notice. I start at Hooters on Monday.

Butt [bʌt]:
the larger or thicker end of something.

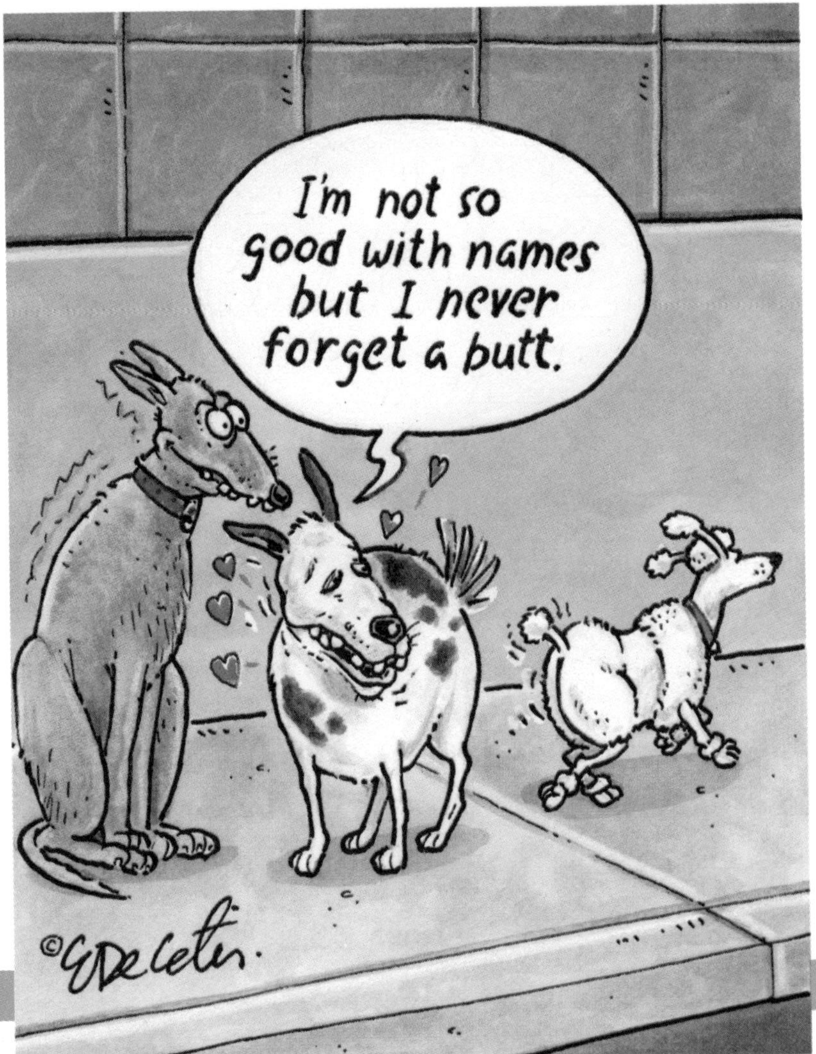
I'm not so good with names but I never forget a butt.
©EDeCeles.

Arsch [G]:
ass; a foolish person; a loser.

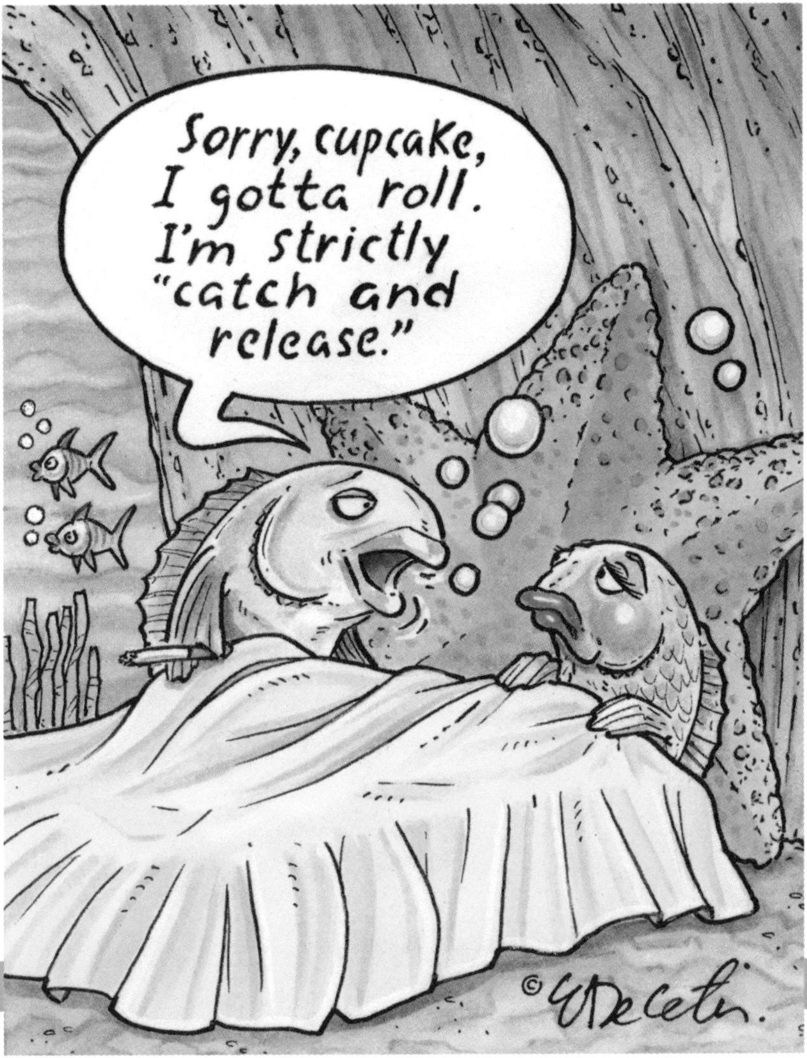
Sorry, cupcake, I gotta roll. I'm strictly "catch and release."
©EDecels

Crackpot [krâk pot]:
one given to eccentric or lunatic notions.

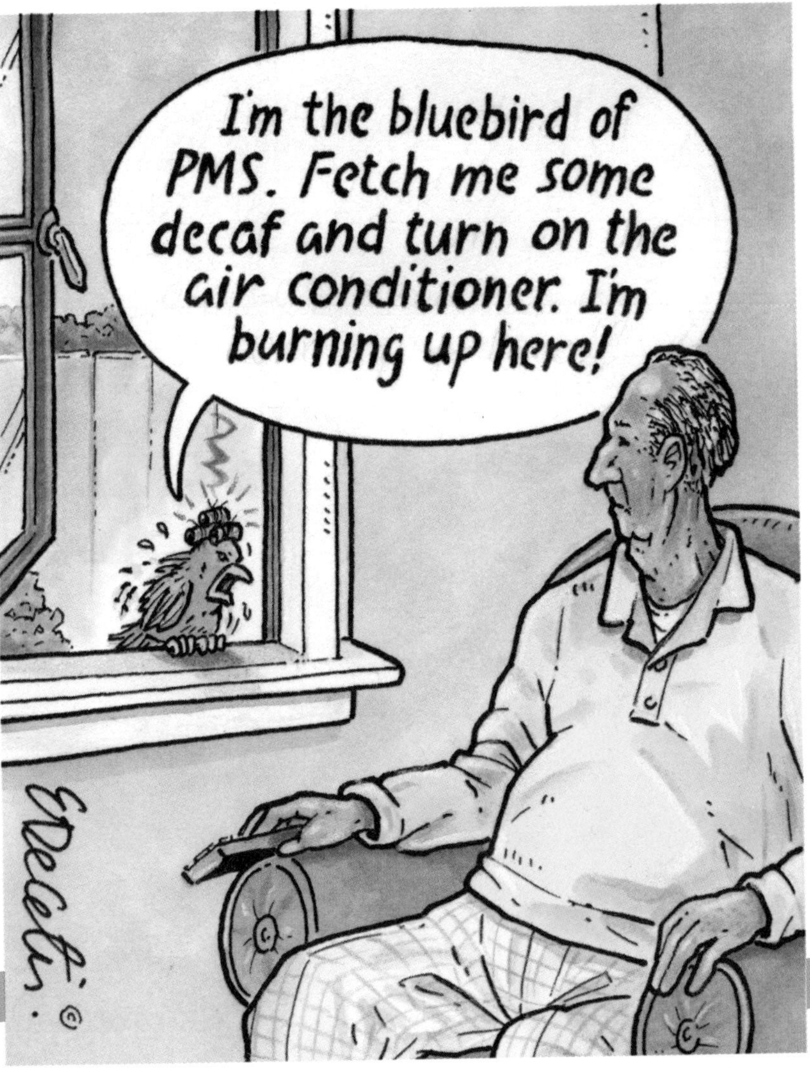
I'm the bluebird of PMS. Fetch me some decaf and turn on the air conditioner. I'm burning up here!

Crack [krâk]:
a weakness or flaw caused by a deficiency; low self-esteem.

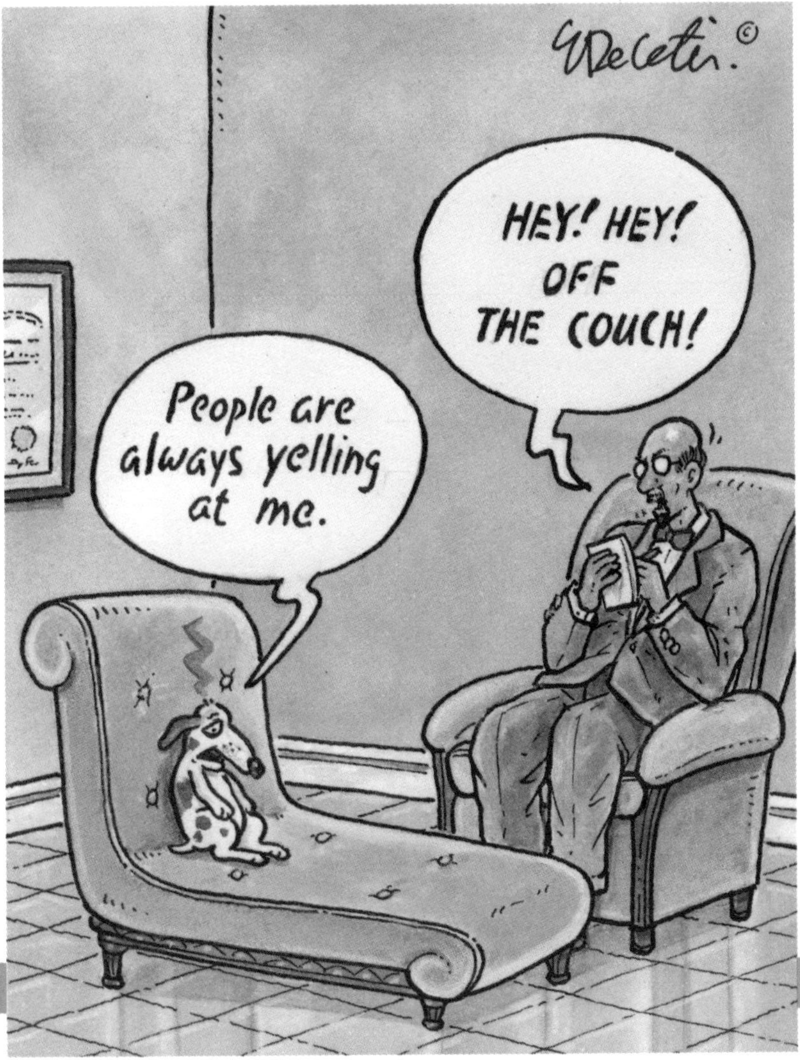

People are always yelling at me.
HEY! HEY! OFF THE COUCH!